THE NEW MARKETING

Sara Miller McCune founded SAGE Publishing in 1965 to support the dissemination of usable knowledge and educate a global community. SAGE publishes more than 1000 journals and over 800 new books each year, spanning a wide range of subject areas. Our growing selection of library products includes archives, data, case studies and video. SAGE remains majority owned by our founder and after her lifetime will become owned by a charitable trust that secures the company's continued independence.

Los Angeles | London | New Delhi | Singapore | Washington DC | Melbourne

Cheryl Burgess & Mark Burgess

THE NEW MARKETING

How to Win in the Digital Age

Los Angeles | London | New Delhi
Singapore | Washington DC | Melbourne

Los Angeles | London | New Delhi
Singapore | Washington DC | Melbourne

SAGE Publications Ltd
1 Oliver's Yard
55 City Road
London EC1Y 1SP

SAGE Publications Inc.
2455 Teller Road
Thousand Oaks, California 91320

SAGE Publications India Pvt Ltd
B 1/I 1 Mohan Cooperative Industrial Area
Mathura Road
New Delhi 110 044

SAGE Publications Asia-Pacific Pte Ltd
3 Church Street
#10-04 Samsung Hub
Singapore 049483

Editor: Matthew Waters
Assistant editor: Jasleen Kaur
Assistant editor: digital: Sunita Patel
Production editor: Tanya Szwarnowska
Copyeditor: Jane Fricker
Proofreader: William Baginsky
Indexer: Adam Pozner
Marketing manager: Abigail Sparks
Cover design: Francis Kenney
Typeset by: C&M Digitals (P) Ltd, Chennai, India

Library of Congress Control Number: 2020933403

British Library Cataloguing in Publication data

A catalogue record for this book is available from the British Library

ISBN 978-1-5264-9011-7
ISBN 978-1-5264-9010-0 (pbk)

CONTENTS

To Kent, Sarah, and Norma, who support and inspire us every day.

Photo: Joanie Schwarz

Cheryl Burgess is co-founder and CEO of Blue Focus Marketing®, a consulting firm that delivers future-ready marketing and training solutions to customer-centric organizations. She is the co-author of the pioneering and bestselling book *The Social Employee*, which features in-depth success stories from IBM, AT&T, Cisco, Dell, Adobe, Southwest and Domo.

Cheryl is a global speaker and has been named a Top 12 Business Speaker by *HuffPost*. She is a LinkedIn Learning course author for *Social Employees: The New Marketing Channel*. Cheryl's ideas have appeared in *MIT Sloan Management Review*, *HBR Italia*, *Fast Company* and *Forbes*; she is a former special advisory board member to *The Economist* and *The Economist Intelligence Unit*. Other projects include the Wharton Future of Advertising 2020 program and the popular Wharton Business Radio 'Marketing Matters' series on XM Radio. As an IBM VIP influencer and futurist, Cheryl has spoken at numerous IBM events and contributed to leading initiatives such as The Future of Work.

Cheryl is an advisory board member to Omnicom's sparks & honey, a technology-led cultural consultancy that is disrupting the consulting, research and agency worlds.

She is a frequently invited guest speaker for Rutgers University graduate programs and has earned a BA in Journalism from the University of Pittsburgh. Twitter: @ckburgess

To Kent, Sarah, and Norma, who support and inspire us every day.

Photo: Joanie Schwarz

Cheryl Burgess is co-founder and CEO of Blue Focus Marketing®, a consulting firm that delivers future-ready marketing and training solutions to customer-centric organizations. She is the co-author of the pioneering and bestselling book *The Social Employee*, which features in-depth success stories from IBM, AT&T, Cisco, Dell, Adobe, Southwest and Domo.

Cheryl is a global speaker and has been named a Top 12 Business Speaker by *HuffPost*. She is a LinkedIn Learning course author for *Social Employees: The New Marketing Channel*. Cheryl's ideas have appeared in *MIT Sloan Management Review, HBR Italia, Fast Company* and *Forbes*; she is a former special advisory board member to *The Economist* and *The Economist Intelligence Unit*. Other projects include the Wharton Future of Advertising 2020 program and the popular Wharton Business Radio 'Marketing Matters' series on XM Radio. As an IBM VIP influencer and futurist, Cheryl has spoken at numerous IBM events and contributed to leading initiatives such as The Future of Work.

Cheryl is an advisory board member to Omnicom's sparks & honey, a technology-led cultural consultancy that is disrupting the consulting, research and agency worlds.

She is a frequently invited guest speaker for Rutgers University graduate programs and has earned a BA in Journalism from the University of Pittsburgh. Twitter: @ckburgess

Mark Burgess is co-founder and president of Blue Focus Marketing®, a brand consultancy that builds brands from the inside out. He is co-author of the revolutionary bestseller *The Social Employee*. Mark is a renowned global speaker and delivered a TEDx Talk on '*The Rise of the Social Employee*'.

Mark is an adjunct marketing professor at the Rutgers University Master of Business & Science degree program. And he teaches MBA and executive education courses at Rutgers Business School. Mark was published in the inaugural edition of *Rutgers Business Review: 'Shaping the Future: The New Social Ecosystem'*. He teaches online marketing courses at eCornell and UCLA and has designed online marketing and digital certificate programs for leading universities.

Mark began his career as an adman on Madison Avenue at McCann. He has held senior roles in marketing and digital strategy at AT&T and PwC. Mark was a recipient of two Effie Awards for global marketing effectiveness.

Mark is a two-time course author for LinkedIn Learning, including Integrated Marketing Strategies that is generating thousands of course completions. He was a contributor to the Wharton Future of Advertising 2020 project.

As an expert trainer for the American Marketing Association, Mark delivered industry-leading content marketing and integrated marketing workshops to hundreds of marketers.

Mark earned an Executive MBA from Fairleigh Dickinson University, and a BA from the University of Pittsburgh. He completed marketing certificates at Dartmouth College and Duke University. Twitter: @mnburgess

ACKNOWLEDGMENTS

When a movie ends and the credits start to roll, we often fail to notice the myriad contributors or even where the movie was shot. While we couldn't afford to write this book on location in China, France, Denmark, Norway, the UK, Singapore, Australia, New Zealand and Morocco, we conversed with people around the world by Skype or phone, though in some cases we interviewed them in New York City near our home. Essentially, we scoured the globe for experts, and we found them.

We are immensely grateful to all the extraordinary people who shared this journey with us. This book has been an incredibly challenging and inspiring journey that led us to the realization that the future is coming faster than we think. Experts from around the world echoed this and cheered us on – telling us that this is a much-needed book for students, professors, marketers and business leaders alike.

Most importantly, our heartfelt thanks to Cheryl's mother, Norma Keith, and our son Kent Burgess and Sarah Walton for their love and support. Thank you for your patience while our deadlines were looming larger every day, leaving little time to share the joys of life. Without your support, we couldn't have written this book.

A very special thank you to our Foreword author Jonah Berger, who took time out while writing his new book, *The Catalyst*, and supporting us writing in his Foreword that 'the timing couldn't be better'.

We want to thank our Afterword author, *New York Times* contributor Kevin Randall, for his inspiration, ideas and invaluable resources. And his tenacity in landing interviews with some of the most difficult to reach people on the planet. We are grateful for his encore; he was the Afterword author for our first book as well – *The Social Employee*.

Our book is expressly written for business/marketing students who want to be future-ready and for marketing practitioners and business leaders who want to navigate the evolving digital landscape in our hyper-connected, AI-driven world. *The New Marketing* is the result of our collective insights from many years of leading innovative marketing strategy teams and Mark's work in academia, developing training, designing and teaching online and classroom MBA and graduate courses at leading universities. We have tapped the minds of over 50 global luminaries in their respective fields bridging knowledge from practitioners and academia to focus on challenges marketers face today and will face in the future.

We are grateful to the brilliant minds who helped fuel our vision of *The New Marketing* and their assistants for coordinating our interviews and permission approvals. Here are the superstars that we interviewed by first name alphabetical order:

Ashwani Monga, Blake Buisson, Brendan Murray, Brian Solis, Chris Detert, Chuck Martin, Daniel Binns, David Armano, David Edelman, Deborah Silver, Dennis Boyle, Dorie Clark, Fred Han, Geoffrey Colon, Howard Belk, Jane Cheung, Jay Baer, Jay Milliken, Jean-Marc Dompietrini, Jennifer Aaker, Jodie Sangster, Joe Willke, Jon Dick, Jon Ferrara, Jon Iwata, Julie Kehoe, Kathleen Hall, Katrina Troughton, Kevin Randall, Kevin Troyanos, Kyle Nel, Loren Angelo, Martin Lindstrom, Naomi Bagdonas, Nis Frome, Parry Malm, Paul Roetzer, Peter Hartzbech, Peter Skillman, Pini Yakuel, Randy Frisch, Ravi Dhar, Rishad Tobaccowala, Russ Klein, Scott Brinker, Stacy Smolin Schwartz, Susan Credle, Terry Young, Thomas Zoega Ramsoy, Tim Calkins, Tom Peters, Warren Quach, William Arruda, William Putsis, Zain Raj.

We are eternally grateful to our publisher, SAGE Publishing, for their vision and enthusiastic support to write this exciting book. And we are also honored to be selected by SAGE to write our book, shortly before they officially announced that they partnered with the American Marketing Association (AMA) to publish the portfolio of AMA journals. We want to thank Matthew Waters, the commissioning editor at SAGE. He was our book's champion and kept the wind in our sails. It has been a pleasure working with assistant editor, Jasleen Kaur, who was phenomenal at every touchpoint along our journey. And a special thank you to our book's production editor, Tanya Szwarnowska, who was truly amazing and helpful, and to our book's cover designer, Francis Kenney, for his out-of-the-box creativity.

Special thanks to an outstanding group of reviewers, which included educators, MBA and graduate business students, and marketing professionals, listed by first name alphabetical order:

Anthony Yacullo, Brendan Murray, Brian Ducey, Burcak Ertimur, Courtney Harris, Craig Moran, Cynthia Newman, Deborah Silver, Deirdre Christofalo, Fay Alwattari, Jeremi Bauer, Judy Bellem, Marco Aguilera, Monica Liming-Hu, Nis Frome, Zain Raj.

We would also like to thank the countless others who have been instrumental in helping us with our project. Thank you to our research assistant, Chas Hoppe, for your orchestration of Big Data and Sam Kennedy for your outstanding web development work. Annalie Killian who helped bring magical 'sparks' and 'superpowers' to our book. And to Daryl Pereira for his insights and generous time. A special thank you to Tom Peters for your years of wisdom and inspiration.

Thank you to Tracy Tuten for your friendship and precious time while writing your new book, *Principles of Marketing for a Digital Age* (also SAGE Publishing), and offering advice and counsel on being an author for SAGE.

Finally, thanks to all the other members of our communities, both online and offline, who have enriched our lives and made a difference in this book.

FOREWORD

What does marketing mean to you?

If you ask most people what they think marketing is, they'll give you an old-school, outdated definition. Marketing is sales. Marketing is advertising. Marketing is convincing people to buy things by talking about how great or valuable that they are.

That definition doesn't work anymore.

Today's brands have to be laser-focused on creating relationships with their audience. They must be willing to meet customers where they are, understand their needs, and communicate value from the *customer's* standpoint, not from the brand's. This means dropping the company-centric, product-centric, or service-centric approach and focusing more on who their customer is and what their customer wants – from designing products and services to communicating to the customer.

In other words, marketers must understand how to humanize their brands.

Why? Because people don't trust ads anymore. They are far more likely to trust recommendations from their friends and family. Their purchasing decisions are driven by these kinds of relationships, and they expect the brands they buy from to understand that. The brands that can engage their customers with warmth and personality, that can partner with their customers to help them reach their goals, will spark a deep, lasting connection with their audience.

Those connections have real value in the marketplace. Once a person has connected with a brand, they want to share that connection with others – with friends, with family, and with peers. In so doing, they generate brand value through word of mouth.

As consumers, we've known about the value of word of mouth all along. We rely on trusted networks when considering what books to read, what movies to watch, or even what B2B service providers to work with. We rely on our peers because we trust them and believe what they have to say.

However, it wasn't until social media came along that we as marketers could see the volume of these word-of-mouth conversations, measure them, and begin to generate insights on what people are saying, at what scale, and over how long. Once we did, we immediately sought ways to tap into that word of mouth's raw power to influence these conversations and create value for our brands however we could.

But how? After all, while the value of word of mouth is clear, generating it isn't a cut-and-dried process. While buying ads, for instance, is a clear and relatively uncomplicated process that scales easily, generating word of mouth and building influence are not.

This poses a great challenge – and an even greater opportunity – for the next generation of marketers: How can they crack the word-of-mouth code? How can they acquire or generate word of mouth at scale in a way that is useful, repeatable and results-driven?

The answer begins with data. While traditionally marketing has been all about creativity – the most interesting idea, the cleverest pitch, the most exciting campaign – today analytics is at the core of almost every aspect of marketing. Consumer data has allowed marketers to study their buyers more carefully and implement ideas much better than ever before. They impact the way we design campaigns, the way we communicate, the platforms on which we share content, the pricing that we choose, and even the way that we display products in stores.

Powering these data-driven efforts is the rise of artificial intelligence (AI). As of this writing, marketers' understanding of AI is still in its infancy. However, it has already proven quite useful at pulling behavioral insights from text-based data – it will eventually be able to do the same for video- and image-based data as well. Deploy an AI program to monitor and mine open-ended responses from online reviews, blogs and social media content, and you will end up with valuable insight in a relatively short amount of time. This is a game-changer for marketers, allowing them to predict outcomes and make brand-based decisions better than they ever could before.

However, while data and AI will certainly play a valuable role in the future, they are certainly not the be-all, end-all of modern marketing. While these advanced tools help drive insights, they still require a human touch to be deployed effectively.

Today's marketers have more channels and platforms on which to share their message than ever before. This is great news when it comes to giving your audience opportunities to interact with your brand. However, many organizations suffer from siloed marketing efforts. Different channels are managed by different parts of the organization. One group manages the Twitter feed, while another manages the CEO's blog, and so on. This makes it hard to share a consistent, cohesive message. If the folks that are doing your customer service are different than the folks that are thinking about your advertising, the messages aren't necessarily going to be the same.

Customers don't care about who in the organization manages what channel. All they care about is a consistent brand experience. Integrated marketing allows brands to keep their message consistent across channels. Unfortunately, many brands find it hard to pull off. The brand of the future must become better at designing more cohesive and effective organizations that interact consistently with their customers.

Again, this comes back to humanizing the brand and creating authentic experiences. In this regard, storytelling is an invaluable tool in the modern marketer's arsenal. The best stories are sticky and memorable, burrowing themselves in our minds and forging lasting emotional bonds. Marketers can use stories as vehicles to convey important brand messages, but they must do so in a way that's authentic. Consumers are smart; they can spot an inauthentic play on emotion every time – and when they do, they're less likely to trust the brand going forward.

With all these factors conspiring to change marketing as we know it – data, AI, integrated marketing and storying, just to name a few – marketers need a comprehensive, unified vision of what this new world looks like and how marketers can thrive within it. In *The New Marketing*, authors Cheryl Burgess and Mark Burgess have done exactly that. It's easy for marketers to feel like they're being pulled in a thousand directions at once. In this book, Cheryl and Mark draw upon their decades of marketing experience to examine the latest trends in marketing, analyze what it means, and offer a unified path forward.

In many ways, the future of marketing is vast and unknown. On the one hand, it's driven by data and the need to scale insights in a way that is valuable to a large company. On the other hand, it's driven by a need to tell stories, humanize your brand, and connect with customers on a one-to-one basis. Marketing must be led by a scientific, data-driven approach to consumer behavior, but that approach must be augmented by creativity and deep, human understanding of customer needs.

This book presents both facets in equal measure, offering marketers the building blocks they need to function while laying out a clear path to the future. In so doing, Cheryl and Mark are doing a great service to their field, and the timing couldn't be any better. I'm excited to see these considerable insights shared with the next generation of marketing scholars – and even more excited to see what that next generation creates with them.

Jonah Berger, PhD Professor at the Wharton School at the
University of Pennsylvania and author of *Contagious*,
Invisible Influence and *The Catalyst*

'Seismic shifts and accelerating technological change are reshaping marketing. This book arms MBA students and marketers with the knowledge they need to dive confidently into the future.'

David Aaker, Vice Chairman of Prophet, author, recognized as the
'father of modern branding,' and American Marketing Association
of New York inductee to the Marketing Hall of Fame®

'In every industry, the old is going away faster than the new can replace it - marketing included! *The New Marketing* fills the gap with a breakthrough toolkit that will help marketing students and professionals succeed and become change makers.'

Beth Comstock, author, Imagine it Forward,
and former Vice Chair, GE

'The transformation of the digital landscape has made nearly every marketing textbook obsolete. But in this one, you can learn what's really happening now, from people who are researching and practicing at the bleeding edge.'

Zoe Chance, Assistant Professor of Marketing,
Yale School of Management

'*The New Marketing* provides important and timely information for a new generation of MBA students in this evolving world of marketing technology.'

Lei Lei, Dean, Rutgers Business School—Newark
and New Brunswick

'*The New Marketing* disrupts outdated marketing education by empowering students and professionals with the knowledge to help them own the future.'

Dan Schawbel, New York Times bestselling author,
and Managing Partner of Workplace Intelligence

'How do you help marketing students in a time when everything is changing so fast? You look into the future. The authors do just that. They have authored a future-forward textbook that helps students learn how to succeed now.'

Brian Solis, Digital Anthropologist, Futurist,
8x bestselling author

'The gap between marketing practice and marketing education has never been more pronounced, as the advertising, marketing and brand industry transforms at breakneck speed. There is an unprecedented need for a textbook that addresses the changes and offers to MBA students the most updated and thorough look at what they need to learn now to achieve in today's—and tomorrow's—radically different digital landscape. This book delivers.'

Jenny Rooney, Communities Director and
Chair of the CMO Network at Forbes

'This is a must-read book for the modern marketer who wants to understand and successfully navigate the fast moving digitally networked marketing landscape of today.'

Sengun (Shen) Yeniyurt, PhD
Marketing Department Chair and Dean's Research Professor
Co-Editor in Chief, Rutgers Business Review
Rutgers Business School

ONLINE RESOURCES

The New Marketing is accompanied by online resources for instructors, students, and practitioners to help support teaching and learning. These resources are available at: https://study.sagepub.com/burgess

FOR INSTRUCTORS ONLY

- **Save time** and **fully integrate** the text **into your teaching** each week by using the extensive **PowerPoint slides** prepared by the authors for each chapter.
- **Easily upload the resources** listed on this page into your institution's **learning management system** (e.g. Blackboard, Canvas or Moodle), and **customize** content to suit your teaching needs using the **resource pack**.

FOR INSTRUCTORS, STUDENTS, AND PRACTITIONERS

- **Improve your knowledge** of the **key emerging themes and topics** by watching **exclusive, expert short videos per chapter** created by the authors, together to be viewed as a master series titled: *The New Marketing: Masters Series*
- **Boost your understanding and skills base** further by using the click through links to complete the authors' popular **LinkedIn Learning courses** covering further topics related to *The New Marketing*.

Remember to **post online about these resources** and the book generally using the hashtag: **#NewMarketingNewTimes**

Students piled into the auditorium, deciding where to sit. The back row filled up first, followed by the rows closer to the front. Soon almost every seat in the center section was taken.

'Testing. One, two, three', a staff member said, followed by a gentle tap, tap, tap on the microphone.

Anticipation filled the room as students looked inquisitively toward us onstage, where we were making final preparations for our presentation, 'How to Break into a Career in Digital Marketing', at Rutgers Business School Marketing Bootcamp. The bootcamp, which is held annually, is designed to provide both full-time and part-time first-year MBA students interested in a career in marketing with a general overview of the field and its various career paths.

We'd made the drive to Rutgers' Newark, New Jersey, campus earlier that morning – a brisk October day, which greeted us with just a touch of frost on our windshield. On the drive, we rehearsed our presentation, as well as our responses to student questions. Would they be similar to the ones we received at last year's Marketing Bootcamp? Or, would the 2015 crowd have a whole new set of questions for us?

Our answer came about halfway into our presentation, when a student in the back row stood up, raised his hand, and asked, 'Can you talk about why I should pursue a career in marketing?'

'Great question', Mark responded, pausing from his presentation. 'Well, we've been talking a lot about *what* marketers do, and *how* they do it. So, to answer your question, let's focus on the *why* of it all, and what that means to you.'

Mark then went on to explain our core beliefs as marketers. The days of 30-second commercials, intrusive ads and spam are over – forcing smart marketers to think differently. Today, marketing is about providing valuable and relevant information via a new approach called *content marketing*. It's about integrating all marketing activities across channels. It's about building relationships and earning the customer's trust. It's also about focusing on doing more than selling products. To borrow a phrase from the American Marketing Association, it's about creating magic. Revenue is still critical for sure, but today's brands understand that they must stand for more – and that *purpose* has become a crucial competitive advantage.

'So, here's my advice', Mark said to the student. 'If you want to be part of the shift from traditional marketing to digital, to work for a brand whose goals and values match your own, and to create magic for both a business and for yourself, then you should become a marketer.'

WELCOME TO THE NEW MARKETING

Advances in technology, data, and intelligence have shifted marketing into a new era of transformation.

In a hyper-connected world that is changing at warp speed, marketers recognize the need to shift from traditional marketing methods to a new way that can help them better navigate the unpredictable environment. For traditionalists, this change has posed a challenge. Many have tried to incorporate new tactics into the old models they grew up with, only to be frustrated with the results.

Today, marketing stands at the threshold of tremendous opportunity. However, all around the world, marketers young and old – both brand-new MBA students and seasoned professionals alike – are struggling to understand their place in this strange new landscape. They want to develop new skills that will make them more employable, more adaptive, and more promotable. *The New Marketing* holds the key to crossing that threshold, embracing the promise of the digital age, and transforming your brand in the process.

NEW THINKING FOR NEW TIMES

To be sure, this isn't going to be easy. Today's marketers must learn to walk a fine line, focusing on authentic, personalized human experiences in a plugged-in, data-driven world – and they must do so in a way that is frictionless, that is empathetic, and that creates value for both the brand and customer.

But how? As you'll see in the following chapters, the answer is a little bit art, a little bit science. In *The New Marketing*, you will learn new thinking for new times –such as how to bridge the gap between human intelligence and artificial intelligence (AI), how to leverage content marketing and brand storytelling, and how to root all branding efforts in purpose, authenticity and trust.

To communicate these concepts in ways that are both accessible and actionable, we approached these challenges first as experienced marketers and consultants working on high-profile projects for major brands. As both industry vets and the cofounders of Blue Focus Marketing®, we've seen the dramatic transformation the marketing landscape has undergone, and we understand firsthand what that has meant for both marketing as an industry, and marketing as a profession.

Second, we approached marketing transformation as authors, global speakers, educators and consultants. Our first book, *The Social Employee*, examined how changes in digital and social media had not only revolutionized the workplace, but also how brands connected with their customers. We then shared those lessons in presentations around the world that even included a TEDx Talk on '*The Rise of the Social Employee*', and in dozens of workshops conducted for the American Marketing Association, and in the online courses we authored for LinkedIn Learning. In addition, Mark specializes in developing and teaching MBA, Executive MBA, and graduate courses, including digital marketing, content marketing, consumer behavior and marketing strategy for several leading universities, both in the classroom and online.

The New Marketing is the next step in our journey, a powerful new textbook that cracks the marketing code in our hyper-focused digital age.

To help us crack that code, we've invited some of the best and the brightest in the business to share their thoughts and experiences – not only on where marketing *is*, but also where it's headed. The following pages are brimming with contributions from CMO trailblazers, martech disruptors, behavioral economics luminaries at Yale, and leading marketing thinkers at Northwestern University's Kellogg School of Management, Stanford and Wharton. We are grateful to their contributions, and we hope you will use these experts as your GPS for navigating in a digital world mastering the craft of marketing in an era marked by rapid transformation.

GET READY FOR THE FUTURE

We have divided the chapters into what we consider the key concepts of *The New Marketing* – concepts such as content marketing and storytelling, using AI in marketing to gain strategic advantage, customer experience, customer journeys, brand purpose and trust, social employee advocacy, influencers, consumer behavior and neuroscience, data-driven buyer personas, the new content distribution mix, privacy and personalization, personal branding, and a new integrated marketing framework that we call Brand Choreography®. Each chapter provides valuable lessons that stand on their own, but each is also only part of the picture. In *The New Marketing* ecosystem, the more diverse your knowledge and your skill set, the better prepared you will be for an unpredictable future.

Just what is that future? We can't be certain – no one can predict the future. However, we *can* explore some of the wild and exciting possibilities. To that end, we'll conclude every chapter with a *Future Gaze*, an in-depth look into emerging marketing trends with some of marketing's greatest minds.

Ultimately, our exploration of the past, present and future of marketing, as well as our focus on both cutting-edge strategies and tried-and-true foundational method-ologies, is all to serve one goal: helping MBA students and marketers of all ages and experience to become the adaptive, future-ready leaders this industry needs. If you're up for the challenge, then let's get started.

PART 1

MARKETING TRANSFORMATION IN A DIGITAL WORLD

1

CHALLENGES FACING THE NEW MARKETING ORGANIZATION

Learning Goals

- Analyze the concept of marketing transformation and the need to redefine marketing as a strategic asset to drive business growth.
- Build a broad working overview of the current challenges facing marketers as a profession.
- Adopt a marketing mindset that allows for success in the short-term and promotes growth in the long-term.
- Analyze what marketers can do to create success in the present while still preparing for a changing future.
- What is the role of the CMO in the future?

The people who are crazy enough to think they can change the world are the ones who do.

Rob Siltanen[1]

In the fall of 1989, Universal Pictures released *Back to the Future Part II*, the follow-up to the smash 1985 hit starring Michael J. Fox and Christopher Lloyd. Throughout the first act of the film, protagonists Marty McFly (Fox) and Doc Brown (Lloyd) find themselves 30 years in the future – in the faraway year of 2015 – where they struggle to navigate the technological and culture shock of this strange and advanced era.

Back to the Future Part II's vision of the future was instantly iconic and recognizable, capturing the imagination of audiences and futurists alike. In the decades since the film's release, fans have delighted in pointing out all the incongruities between creator Robert Zemeckis and Bob Gale's eighties-inspired vision of 2015 and the actual 2015 that came to pass. Even today, with 2015 quickly receding in the rearview mirror, you don't have to poke around the internet for long before you come upon someone playfully lamenting, 'Where's my hoverboard?' or 'Where's my flying car?'

Still, while many of *Back to the Future Part II*'s predictions still haven't come to pass (personally, we're still waiting for those instant pizza ovens), the movie actually got quite a bit right. The Hill Valley, California, of 2015 has plenty of features familiar to us today, such as flatscreen TVs, video conferencing, smart clothing, wearable tech, thumbprint ID scanners, augmented reality (AR), and even the Chicago Cubs finally winning the World Series (even if it took them an extra year to pull it off in the real world).

Just like in science fiction, when it comes to predicting the future of marketing, we inevitably end up with a mixed bag of results. However, as any marketer would attest, the best way to paint an accurate picture of the future is to understand what's happening in the present.

Today, advances in technology, data and analytics have shifted marketing into a new era we call *marketing transformation*. In our ever-changing and hyper-connected world, marketers are recognizing the need to shift from traditional marketing methods toward a new approach that can help them better navigate an unpredictable environment.

For traditionalists, this shift has posed a challenge. Many have tried to incorporate newer approaches into the old models they grew up with, only to be frustrated with the results. However, to succeed at marketing transformation, the marketers of both the present and the future must learn to shift toward a more integrated, digital, personalized and AI-driven approach that creates frictionless, empathetic, customer experiences across all relevant touchpoints.

Welcome to *The New Marketing*.

Think of this chapter as your roadmap for the chapters ahead. Here we will explore the six big challenges facing modern marketers and the specific considerations those challenges involve. In later chapters, we'll dive into each of these current marketing trends in greater detail. Here, our goal is simply to help you get your bearings, understand the current marketing landscape, and begin to navigate through it.

CHALLENGE #1: CONTENT MARKETING

Content marketing is the process by which brands create, curate and share engaging, informative brand-related content as a way of building brand value and generating leads in the digital marketplace – and it's a big part of any marketing future. Unfortunately, many brands either lack a content marketing strategy entirely or struggle to execute the strategy they *do* have. For many brands, their content marketing struggles boil down to one or more of the following issues.

Many modern brands find themselves stuck at a crossroads between traditional methods and modern approaches. They want to change, but they're unsure how to go about it. This has led to a proliferation of marketing *consulgencies* – consulting and agency hybrids – who are leading the way in teaching brands how to adapt to a new future.

Spamming Customers

As we'll explore in the following chapters, at the core of good content marketing is brand storytelling, which enables marketers to make an emotional connection with customers. The goal is not just to put content out there, but also to encourage your audience to share and engage. By providing them content that connects and has *value*, marketers can make huge leaps toward earning their audience's trust.

No Distribution Network

As more organizations learn to flood channels with content, standing out from the pack is getting harder than ever. In some ways, the basic approach to distribution remains the same – that is, brands still want to leverage a combination of paid, owned and earned media (the POEM approach) to connect with their audience. Today, however, measurement and modification are everything. The most successful brands have embraced a process of micro-optimizations at the end of each phase of the customer journey in order to better attract attention.[2]

Matching the Content with the Audience

Modern brands have embraced the concept of longtail marketing – selling large volumes of a niche product to a specific audience. However, in order for that to work, marketers must be able to understand, target and reach that audience so they can market more efficiently.[3]

Leveraging Content to Become a Social Brand

Most brands in the twenty-first century agree that, whether you're a business-to-business (B2B) or business-to-consumer (B2C) brand, it's essential to create a social media presence to engage with your target audience and guide them along the customer journey. The question is, how do you do that successfully and in a way that resonates with your audience?

As you'll see in the chapters that follow, the top three answers are content, content, and content. That said, having a plan for sharing that content is paramount. The best social brands have a clearly defined social media and content sharing strategy, and they know how to create content in a variety of different forms (i.e. video, images, blogs), which audiences to share that content with, and what channel they should share it on. Finally, they know that without outstanding customer engagement and service, the best content in the world is effectively moot; a complete brand creates value through every stage of the funnel.

Optimizing for Voice Search

Some of you may be wondering, 'What could voice search possibly have to do with content marketing?' As more and more brands are discovering, *a lot*. Consumers are increasingly turning to their in-home or in-hand smart devices – powered by Apple's Siri, Amazon's Alexa, or Microsoft's Cortana – to answer their questions, order useful products, plan trips, and so on.

Solving the Content Marketing Puzzle

Speaking broadly, the big challenge posed by content marketing is that it exists outside of the old status quo. To succeed with their content marketing efforts, marketers need to shift from outdated, traditional marketing approaches and embrace the new opportunities provided by content marketing. To learn how brands are meeting this challenge, see Chapters 6, 7 and 12.

CHALLENGE #2: CONSUMER BEHAVIOR

The rise of the internet and the digital age didn't just change how we access information; it also fundamentally changed the way we behave as consumers. To succeed in today's landscape, the modern marketer must understand what those changes mean and how to anticipate and adapt to changing consumer behavior. To do that, they'll need to overcome the following consumer behavior-related challenges.

The Rise of Brand Purpose

Marketing has shifted away from the attention economy and toward the *emotion economy*. To thrive in this new paradigm, it's not enough to deliver a product or service.

Like Nike with their embrace of controversial football player Colin Kaepernick, brands must be willing to stand for a cause or a concept that their target buyers will believe in. Many refer to this as *purpose-driven marketing* – creating a customer experience (CX) around core values rather than product features as a way of attracting and retaining customers.

The Customer Journey

Marketers have put forth many different models for understanding and managing the customer journey over the years. From the well-worn AIDA model (attention, interest, desire and action) to McKinsey & Company's Customer Decision Journey,[4] brands have certainly had their pick of models to help understand their relationship to their customers. However, with changes in the consumer landscape come changes in how we fundamentally understand the customer journey.

In Chapter 4, we will discuss newer customer journey models, including the New Consumer Odyssey™ and Gartner's New B2B Buying Journey. Also, with so many different customer journey models to choose from, we'll also discuss whether customer journeys are becoming too much of a maze.

The Need for New Marketing Research Methods

In many ways, the internet represents the greatest market research tool that brands have ever had access to. But while the problem used to be that brands didn't have access to *enough* customer information, today the challenge is that there might be *too much*. Where do brands even begin to understand their audience?

As we'll see in the chapters that follow, marketing researchers are applying a variety of different approaches, from breakthroughs in neuroscience to pioneering work in social listening. In fact, some organizations, such as Omnicom's sparks & honey, go even further, helping clients become culture-centric, informing their innovation strategy by how culture is evolving in the here and now, and identifying the disruptive trends that create business transformation opportunities for the long-term future.

Understanding the Differences between B2B and B2C Customers

It's not enough to know whether your brand is B2C- or B2B-focused. It's also important to understand what that means from a strategic marketing perspective. While certain marketing fundamentals remain constant across B2C and B2B applications, many other approaches differ. Understanding those differences begins with understanding your buyers and the fundamental forces driving their behavior. Put another way, the importance of creating dynamic and accurate buyer personas may be more important now than ever.

The Need to Better Develop New Product Ideas and New Concepts

The rise of digital tools and information technology has accelerated the pace of innovation. Today's organizations are bringing good products to market faster than ever before. This is a great boon for the consumer, but it puts new pressure on brands both young and old to keep up. To meet that challenge, brands are putting a greater emphasis on approaches such as *design thinking* to generate new and exciting product ideas. Marketers play a substantial role in this process, working with team members across the organization to ensure the product is not only innovative, but that its design, packaging and features align with the organization's mission, vision and values.

For more on the consumer behavior challenges marketers are working to address, see Chapters 2, 3 and 5.

CHALLENGE #3: NEW CHANNELS AND PERSONAL BRANDING

Since the rise of social media, organizations have become increasingly aware that a strong brand is a *social* brand – engaged, relatable and, above all, human. To build social brands, marketers have learned that the top-down approach by itself no longer works. While branded channels, pages and content are essential, so too are other voices within the organization, from the CEO all the way down to the mailroom.

Of course, creating a unified brand identity out of a plurality of voices is no easy task. Brands hoping to leverage the power of other voices from within the organization certainly have their work cut out for them with the following challenges.

Leveraging Influencers

Authenticity and content that resonate with consumers have never been more important in a world of fake news and decreasing brand loyalty, brand trust and effectiveness in advertising. For these reasons, influencer marketing – fueled by micro-influencers and celebrity mega-influencers alike – is rapidly becoming a new marketing channel, particularly due to the strong potential to reach young people. The vast majority of consumers trust recommendations from other people and seek content that helps them make purchase decisions.

Brand Building from the Inside Out

An organization's employees arguably know what their brand stands for better than anyone else. After all, they live and breathe the brand's mission, vision and values day in and day out. The depth of knowledge and experience available within an engaged workforce is a tremendous resource for any brand. However, in too many organizations, this resource is going untapped. To build their brands from the inside out, organizations must learn to adopt a culture of the *social employee*, leveraging their skills, knowledge and authentic personalities as the new marketing channel.

Growing a Personal Brand

While social employees may represent the new marketing channel, they don't just appear within an organization overnight. Employees interested in growing their personal brand in service of their organization thrive when they are given effective guardrails, trained on best practices, and otherwise given the tools to succeed. It's important for any marketing team, then, to provide these basic building blocks for success – how to build a personal marketing plan, how to create and curate helpful content, and how to craft a high-quality profile on professional networking sites like LinkedIn.

Counteracting Brand Distrust

A series of high-profile data scandals gave rise to the General Data Protection Regulation (GDPR) in the European Union, as well as other regulations in the United States. The purpose of such regulations is to encourage brands to use better data hygiene practices – and ultimately restore public faith in brands' use of sensitive data. Social employees and influencers alike must be aware of the regulatory environment in which they work and be sure to communicate in ways that are both authentic and legal.

To help you learn to think like a brand and prepare for the future, see Chapter 9.

CHALLENGE #4: INTEGRATED MARKETING STRATEGIES

In simplest terms, integrated marketing is the idea that brands should present a unified, cohesive and coherent front across all media channels, all brand touchpoints, and all customer and stakeholder interactions. However, while the value of such an approach is readily apparent – a brand that is clearly and consistently understood in the marketplace – putting it into action can be much more difficult, due in part to the challenges we will cover next. In Chapter 10, we will explore our modern integrated marketing framework called Brand Choreography.

The Rise of New Media Options

The number of media choices available to consumers is growing at a remarkable pace. New social channels, information hubs and streaming services are popping up seemingly every day. Facing this growth, many brands worry that they need to be everywhere at once. Especially in an era of shrinking marketing budgets and the need to justify return on investment (ROI), this is an impossible task. Luckily, it's also an unnecessary one. As we'll discuss later, a good integrated marketing approach isn't concerned with how many channels a brand appears on, but rather on *how well* they establish a presence on their channel of choice.

Harnessing the Power of Mobile

When smart mobile devices first hit the scene in the mid-to-late 2000s, marketers praised the innovation, but did little to embrace it. Today, with mobile devices becoming the primary means of consumption for a growing number of users, mobile simply can't be ignored. In fact, it's a cornerstone of any effective digital marketing strategy. The question is, how can brands position themselves in order to fully harness its power?

The Connected (but Closed-off) Customer

Especially among younger generations – namely Millennials and Generation Z – customers are increasingly connected across a variety of devices and channels. However, regardless of what form of media they might be consuming in a given moment, whether TV, social media, or something else, consumers all have one thing in common: they hate intrusive advertising. Brands looking to craft a successful integrated marketing approach must acknowledge that many in their target audience will do whatever they can to block out brand messaging.

Lack of Consistent Messaging

Many marketers and marketing teams lack an integrated marketing strategy. As a result, they're essentially running blind, trying to find their place in a complex media landscape with too many options, for too many devices, in a too-dynamic marketplace. The result? Inconsistent messaging. However, through a process we call Brand Choreography, we will lay out a seven-step roadmap for integrated marketing success.

The Rise of Big Data

Big Data refers to the rise of data collection and analytics processes in the twenty-first century. Much has been written about the value of Big Data, and many leading brands have seen considerable success in learning how to harness its power. However, for the brands that are learning how to navigate the world of Big Data, simply knowing where to start can be overwhelming. Throughout this book, we'll champion an approach to Big Data that focuses on addressing specific needs and answering specific questions to keep brands on target and – most importantly – on budget.

Siloed Workforce within the Company

Workers in a siloed company often feel more like competitors than colleagues. Because they often compete internally for resources, they withhold valuable information, tools and processes that could help the entire brand succeed. To de-silo their workforce, brands must embrace what we call the social ecosystem.

For more on the challenges posed by integrated marketing strategies, see Chapter 10.

CHALLENGE #5: ARTIFICIAL INTELLIGENCE (AI)

Artificial intelligence (AI) has many possible applications for businesses, from supply chain management and manufacturing to marketing and sales. However, many business leaders believe that AI will have its biggest impact in the world of marketing – making up as much as two-thirds of the total AI opportunity.[5]

Market Segmentation

The old methods of segmentation aren't going to cut it. Brands need to understand precisely who their target buyer personas are – and they must do so quickly and accurately. A persona enables you to create a compelling message strategy by providing an informed context about who they are, what they struggle with, and how they make decisions and interact with a brand. AI can help power those efforts through a process known as *micro-segmentation*.

How to Use Data to Improve Marketing Efforts

We live in the era of Big Data. The question is, how do we learn to use that data in a way that helps us establish and achieve important metrics and key performance indicators (KPIs) in a way that brings a return on investment (ROI)?

Using Personal Data Responsibly

Consumers and business leaders alike have become increasingly concerned over the safety of their data – who has access to the data, how it is being used, and whether it's safe.

Keeping up with an Ever-Changing Marketplace

Agile marketing has become a must in the modern marketplace. But marketers can't go it alone if they hope to keep up. Deployed correctly, AI can help show them the way.

Personalization

AI and machine learning will soon make personalization – and even *hyper-personalization* – a reality. Driven by AI, these personalization efforts can help create a frictionless customer experience all throughout the customer journey. According to McKinsey & Company, personalization will blur the line between the real world and the digital world as physical spaces come to be increasingly digitized through the rise of augmented reality (AR) tools. Brands will also begin deploying advanced analytics to build a more personalized end-to-end customer journey: one in which the individual's pain points and needs are anticipated and understood through a scaled-up approach to brand empathy.[6]

For more on the challenges and opportunities posed by AI, see Chapters 2, 4, 5, 11 and 12.

CHALLENGE #6: SHIFT TO MARKETING TECHNOLOGISTS AND THE GROWING IMPORTANCE OF DIVERSITY IN BUSINESS

The tech explosion of the early twenty-first century has created a tremendous amount of opportunities for marketers. However, as is often the case, with those opportunities also come new challenges. To counteract these challenges, marketers of the future must not only be aware of the upside their new tools and processes bring, but also the potential drawbacks.

Emergence of the Marketing Technologist

According to Scott Brinker, VP, Platform Ecosystems, at HubSpot, a marketing technologist is a hybrid role that straddles the line between IT and marketing. The marketing technologist is technically savvy, but they use those skills specifically to build, evaluate and operate marketing software and systems. 'Since everything in marketing is now powered by software', Brinker says, 'it's important to have someone on the team who understands the dynamics of technology management.'

However, while the marketing technologist is essential to any modern marketing team, their role must be clearly defined. 'Customers are humans, not machines', Brinker says. 'The danger with too much automation in marketing is that we can lose the human connection between our company and our customers.' In other words, while these technologists can help open the door to more effective marketing processes, they must learn to do so in a way that doesn't dehumanize the brand.[7]

Diversity in Business

Another challenge that arises from an increasingly data-led and tech-focused approach to marketing is accounting for accidental bias. Any system, algorithm, or process is only as good as the people creating it. If those creators – whether knowingly or unknowingly – have biases for or against certain groups, those biases will be reflected in whatever they produce. While diversity is understandably a complex issue, the solution begins by creating diverse marketing teams, which will in turn benefit the entire organization.

For more on the challenges of data-led marketing, see Chapter 11.

EMBRACING THE FUTURE OF MARKETING TRANSFORMATION

At this point, you have a broad idea of the current marketing landscape and the challenges awaiting even the savviest marketers in the future. The question is, where do we go from here? How do we as marketing professionals rise to the challenges of today to create better brands of the future?

Throughout the rest of this book, we will help you answer those very questions – and many more. Before we get started, however, let's turn once again to *Back to the Future*. By the end of the final movie in the series, *Back to the Future Part III*, our heroes Marty McFly and Doc Brown have travelled all throughout time – to the future of 2015, the past of 1885, and finally back to their present of 1985. Throughout their adventures, these characters saw a world in flux, one where even the smallest change could have a tremendous ripple effect on their entire timeline – even their very existence.

By the end of *Back to the Future Part III*, everyone is back safely in their present time, and with the proper timeline restored (more or less). While reflecting on the wild adventure their lives had become and pondering where they might go from there, Doc Brown offers Marty and his future wife, Jennifer, one last bit of encouragement: 'Your future hasn't been written yet. No one's has. Your future is whatever you make it. So make it a good one.'

That's our goal with this book. When it comes to predicting the future, no one has a perfect track record. Some of the predictions in this book are all but certain to come to pass, while others may take on an as-yet undetermined form as new advances and voices enter the conversation. We can't know which is which because, as Doc Brown famously said, the future hasn't been written yet.

Ultimately, it's not a matter of being right with every prediction – who could have predicted Starbucks would phase out all physical newspapers in 2019?[8] – but of being proactive and prepared for whatever may come your way. By the end of this book, we expect that you will have built a strong foundation for becoming the kind of proactive, prepared marketer able to tackle an ever-changing world head-on.

Future Gaze

William Putsis, Professor of Marketing, Economics, and Business Strategy at the Kenan-Flagler Business School at the University of North Carolina at Chapel Hill, and Yale Faculty Fellow for Executive Programs, and author of *Compete Smarter, Not Harder* and *The Carrot and the Stick*

Marketing has gone through many different evolutions of the past few decades. With the advent of the internet and other digital technologies, many have referred to the current period of change as 'the Fourth Industrial Revolution'. But what's next? Where do we go from here? What will the world of marketing look like five, 10, or even 20 years from now?

We put these questions to William Putsis. The answers are rooted in today. For instance, certain marketing fundamentals, which Putsis refers to as 'legacy marketing', still hold water today – whether it's the four Ps (price, product, promotion and place), STP (segmentation, targeting and positioning), or the three Cs (company, customers and competitors). Even in a changing world, any one of these bedrock approaches is still a valuable lens through which to view a brand's marketing needs.

Looking toward the future, Putsis notes that different brands will have different needs. 'Companies like Alphabet [Google], Apple, Amazon, and all the big tech companies need to be concerned more with the broader market opportunities and what gives them the competitive advantage that's sustainable in the future', Putsis says. This includes the ability to own data rights, the ability to have a dominant position in emerging technologies like AI, and the ability to perform advanced analytics on blockchain and other new technology.

Chief among those is the ability to own data rights. In an era where big brands like Facebook have lost considerable trust as a result of the Cambridge Analytica scandal (see Chapter 11), Putsis sees a new path forward for companies. 'Winning business models in the future will not be focused on selling data or using data for an individual company's advantage', Putsis says. Instead, they will be focused on using customer data – their movements, habits, or search queries – to provide better offerings that serve their customers and provide value. In other words, they will no longer profit on the data per se, but rather on how they can use that data to help their customers. As Putsis notes, such an approach blurs the traditional lines between marketing and strategy. 'They have to be blurred', Putsis says. 'What gives you a competitive advantage that's sustainable in a market is exactly what you have to market on.'

(Continued)

Second, Putsis says, is 'the idea that we can never be fast enough to allow to market'. Approaches like artificial intelligence can't just be buzzwords that brands leap at; they must also be strategic. 'So instead of having to do analytics', Putsis says, 'find the conclusion from those analytics and then develop a marketing strategy, campaign, or branding approach moving forward.' In other words, analytics shouldn't be undertaken for analytics' sake, but rather in service of meeting specifically defined marketing goals. In Putsis's view, such an approach should be undertaken automatically as part of a marketing team's standard operating procedures.

Finally, the future of marketing will require a rethinking of the role of the chief marketing officer (CMO). Traditionally, Putsis says, the role of the CMO was more about managing the brand and managing the position of the company both moving forward and within the company. Moving forward, however, Putsis believes that the role of the CMO must become more strategic – perhaps even combining the role of the chief strategy officer (CSO) with the role of the CMO. Says Putsis, 'The CMO needs to increasingly take on the role of what used to be delegated to strategy, and they need to have a single seat at the table.' While Putsis notes that many organizations are working to create more segmented, specialized roles within an organization, such as chief digital officer, he sees more value in a broadening and combining of roles in the C-suite instead.

To put the changing marketing landscape in context, Putsis quoted Microsoft co-founder Bill Gates: 'We always overestimate the change that will occur in the next two years and underestimate the change that will occur in the next ten. Don't let yourself be lulled into inaction.'[9] To give an example of what he means by referencing this quote, Putsis used the idea of 5G internet. In the first few years of its rollout, its impact will be minimal. However, within five to 10 years, it will have become seamlessly integrated into our way of life as part of the growing Internet of Things (IoT). That's why, as Putsis sees it, in order to prepare for an ever-changing tomorrow, marketers must be prepared to embrace and adapt to those changes today.

CHAPTER ANALYSIS QUESTIONS

1. What is marketing transformation?
2. What are three challenges facing marketers today?
3. What are some of the possible solutions to those challenges?
4. What can marketers do to create success in the present while still preparing for a changing future?

NOTES

1 Goodreads.com. (2020). A quote by Rob Siltanen. [online] Available at: www.goodreads.com/quotes/597615-the-people-who-are-crazy-enough-to-think-they-can [Accessed 28 Jan. 2020].

Shah, A. (2019). Introducing the new tenets of digital marketing. [online] Albert. Available at: https://albert.ai/blog/introducing-the-new-tenets-of-digital-marketing/ [Accessed 4 Sep. 2019].

Ibid.

Court, D., Elzinga, D., Mulder, S. and Vetvik, O. (2009). *The Customer Decision Journey.* [online] McKinsey & Company. Available at: www.mckinsey.com/business-functions/marketing-and-sales/our-insights/the-consumer-decision-journey [Accessed 18 Sep. 2019].

Chui, M., Henke, N. and Miremadi, M. (2019). Most of AI's business uses will be in two areas. [online] Available at: www.mckinsey.com/business-functions/mckinsey-analytics/our-insights/most-of-ais-business-uses-will-be-in-two-areas [Accessed 4 Sep. 2019].

Boudet, J., Gregg, B., Rathje, K., Stein, E. and Volhardt, K. (2019). *The Future of Personalization – And How to Get Ready for it.* [online] McKinsey & Company. Available at: www.mckinsey.com/business-functions/marketing-and-sales/our-insights/the-future-of-personalization-and-how-to-get-ready-for-it?cid=eml-web [Accessed 11 Sep. 2019].

Brinker. S. (2019). Personal communication. [10 Feb.].

Purdue, M. (2019). Starbucks to end newspaper sales in September, including USA TODAY. [online] *USA Today.* Available at: www.usatoday.com/story/money/2019/07/12/starbucks-end-newspaper-sales-september/1720290001/ [Accessed 11 Sep. 2019].

Putsis, W. (2019). Personal communication. [27 July].

2

SEEING REAL-TIME INTO THE CONSUMER'S MIND

Learning Goals

- Illustrate the importance of knowing your customer.
- Critique the value and drawback of using traditional focus groups and online focus groups to generate consumer insights.
- Analyze a new approach to develop cultural insights that can transform thousands of daily data points into forward-thinking insights.
- Analyze the reasons why consumer neuroscience has become a game-changer for marketers seeking more valuable consumer insights.

People don't think how they feel, they don't say what they think, and they don't do what they say.

David Ogilvy[1]

The family pet has a special place in our global culture. Whether they're a hiking partner, a playmate for the kids, or just a sympathetic face meeting us at the door after a long day at the office, a loyal dog or cat can enrich our lives like nothing else. The fact that organic dog food, pet spas, and a billion-dollar animal toy industry all exist reveals just how deep our connection is to our furry friends.

But what about the pets who don't have a good home – or any home at all? What happens to them?

The vast majority end up in shelters – where most don't survive long. According to the American Society for the Prevention of Cruelty to Animals (ASPCA), approximately 6.5 million cats and dogs arrive in shelters every single year in the United States. While a small percentage of this group includes strays that are eventually reunited with their owners, only 3.2 million – 1.6 million dogs and 1.6 million cats – are adopted each year. The result of this is inevitable but tragic: each year millions of companion animals are euthanized.[2]

To address the grim statistics, the Ad Council, Maddie's Fund and The Humane Society launched the Shelter Pet Project, an advertising campaign developed by DraftFCB to raise awareness and to increase the number of pet adoptions in the United States and reduce the number of companion animals that are killed. The goal of the project is to encourage pet lovers to make shelters and rescue groups the first place to go when they want to adopt a pet.[3]

The results of the ad campaign were encouraging; nevertheless, campaign organizers felt they could do even more to get the word out and help save the lives of more shelter pets. In order to stretch their success even further, in 2014 campaign organizers enlisted help from the Consumer Neuroscience arm of Nielsen, the well-known media ratings and data analytics company.

The Nielsen researchers' mission was to analyze a campaign ad from the Shelter Pet Project, determine its strengths and weaknesses, and help organizers create a stronger, more resonant ad that would encourage more people to adopt shelter pets – and thus save more lives. Driving their efforts were a combination of cutting-edge tools from the world of neuroscience – such as electroencephalograms (EEGs) and eye tracking devices – which they would use to target audience responses.

For their initial analysis, the Nielsen researchers decided to test one of the campaign's most popular video ads, 'Meet'. The star of the 30-second TV spot was Jules, a small, cuddly white-and-black shelter dog. As Jules trots happily around, entering and leaving the frame while his tongue wags and his paw raises as if to shake hands with the viewer, short lines of text cross the screen explaining that 'there's a shelter pet who wants to meet you'. A narrator declares the same, and adds a few additional lines directing viewers to the Shelter Pet Project's website. The ad was simple, attractive and effective, judging from campaign data. But could Nielsen researchers make it even better? (See Figure 2.1).

Using information gleaned from their tools, the researchers pinpointed both the parts of the ad that engaged viewers most strongly and those where viewer interest dragged. They determined that Jules truly was the star of the show: viewer engagement peaked any time he was on-screen. Ad text providing information about the campaign and its website also produced high engagement – that is, whenever Jules wasn't stealing the show. Jules's unforgettable cuteness, it turned out, drew viewer

Jules strongly engages when on screen

Viewers disengage when Jules exits, and strongly re-engage when he interacts with the camera

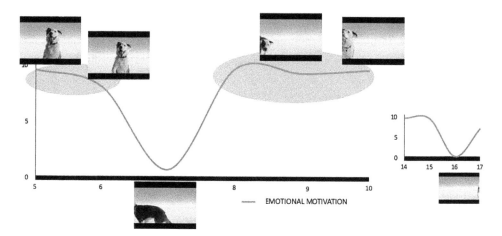

Figure 2.1   Jules strongly engages when on screen.

Source: Nielsen Consumer Neuroscience.

attention away from the ad text and its call to action. To fix this, Nielsen suggested two things: separating the ad's text into its own, Jules-free screen, and cutting the ad down to just 15 seconds so it could pack a more powerful punch (see Figure 2.2).

Were the researchers right? The proof would be in the pudding. After the leaner, meaner (but no less cuddly) Jules ads were rolled out, the Pet Shelter campaign recorded

Problem: too much of a good thing?

Eye tracking indicates Jules competes with messaging, branding, and call-to-action

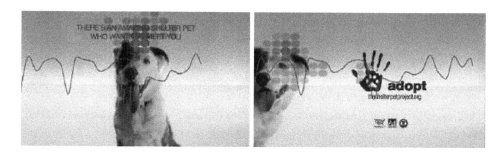

Competition for Message   Competition with Brand and CTA

Figure 2.2   Too much of a good thing.

Source: Nielsen Consumer Neuroscience.

a 133% increase in website visits and a 28% rise in searches through the 'Pet Finder' pet adoption portal.[4] Nielsen, it seems, had effectively understood the Pet Shelter campaign's audience.

Additional data provide further evidence of their success. Between 2011 and 2017, the ASCPA recorded an 18.5% increase in shelter adoptions and a remarkable 43% decrease in the number of euthanized companion animals.[5] Although correlation isn't necessarily causation, and it's difficult to directly tie Nielsen's efforts to these impressive figures, it's certainly plausible that their intervention helped get the Pet Shelter campaign closer to its goal of saving more animals.

WHERE BRAINS, SCIENCE AND MARKETING MEET

Joe Willke, President, BASES and President, Nielsen Consumer Neuroscience, presided over the analysis of the 'Jules' spot. According to Willke, 'consumer neuroscience is the application of tools and techniques to actually measure nonconscious processing typically in the domains of attention and emotion, and memory activation and in an experimental design to a stimulus, like a video ad or a package. Then [we] deliver those insights to our clients.'[6]

From their perch, Willke and his colleagues have the most promising intelligence and tools at their fingertips. With this state-of-the-art technology, they work to help companies satisfy two critical needs:

1. More accurately anticipate consumer needs; and
2. More effectively target consumers through more powerful, better-designed marketing and advertising.

In other words, they work to help marketers get inside their target audience's heads. Through the application of neuroscientific approaches, Willke and his colleagues teach companies to respond more effectively to what consumers want, helping them to stay relevant and profitable.

At Nielsen, 'Video Ad Explorer', the tool Joe Willke and his team use to evaluate the effectiveness of ads, relies on five metrics to gauge responses from subjects (see Figure 2.3):

1. Electroencephalograms (EEGs)
2. Biometrics
3. Facial coding
4. Eye tracking
5. Self-reporting

VIDEO AD EXPLORER OFFERS THE MOST POWERFUL, MOST COMPLETE SOLUTION USING BEST-IN-CLASS TECHNOLOGIES

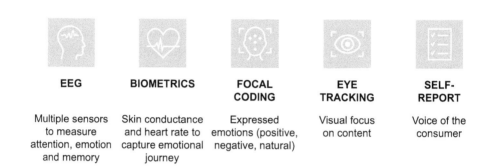

EEG	BIOMETRICS	FOCAL CODING	EYE TRACKING	SELF-REPORT
Multiple sensors to measure attention, emotion and memory	Skin conductance and heart rate to capture emotional journey	Expressed emotions (positive, negative, natural)	Visual focus on content	Voice of the consumer

Figure 2.3   Video Ad Explorer offers the most powerful, most complete solution using best-in-class technologies.

Source: Nielsen Consumer Neuroscience.

Taken together, Willke says, these tools can provide deep insights into an ad's likelihood of success or failure. 'The ability to get granular and find moments where things are working well and moments for optimization is very important for our clients because we're no longer in the business of saying, "Go, no go", or "This ad's not working and we don't know why, throw it out"', says Willke. 'We build better ads. In every ad, there are going to be moments that are working and in almost every ad there are moments that aren't optimized.'[7]

According to Willke, people interact with brands in two ways: rationally and emotionally. Rational interactions are those that are tangible – say, the touch of a soft tissue, the crunch of cereal, the sturdiness of a work boot. Emotional interactions, on the other hand, are 'the essence or feeling' that comes from interacting with a brand. If we feel good about ourselves while wearing a particular jacket, or if seeing a brand makes us feel comfortable, we are having an emotional reaction. Rational interactions are plain to observe and measure, but emotional ones – which come from our brain – are obviously more difficult to understand. That's where Willke and his fellow neuroscientists come in. By concerning themselves with the non-conscious, they hope to better gauge whether a brand or a product creates a positive emotional reaction (see Figure 2.4).

While neuroscience is still a relatively young discipline – especially in its application to market research – it shows considerable promise. But before we explore its ins and outs, let's start from the beginning and take a quick tour through the evolution of consumer listening. We'll begin with the classic, tried-and-true window into consumers' minds: focus groups.

WE INTERACT WITH BRANDS IN TWO KEY WAYS

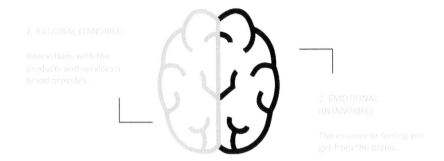

1. RATIONAL (TANGIBLE)

Interactions with the
products and services a
brand provides.

2. EMOTIONAL
(INTANGIBLE)

The essence or feeling you
get from the brand.

Figure 2.4   We interact with brands in two key ways.

Source: Nielsen Consumer Neuroscience.

WHAT'S MY MOTIVATION?

For most of modern marketing history, the gold standard for finding out what your customers want has been the focus group. For this we can thank Ernest Dichter, the Austrian-born Sigmund Freud acolyte often referred to as the 'father of motivation research'. Dichter's clients included some of America's largest corporations, including Chrysler, Exxon, General Mills, Coca-Cola and Sears, and hundreds of others. Dichter was one of the first researchers to put the consumer 'on the couch', so to speak, using Freudian methodologies to uncover the unconscious motivations driving consumer behavior. His most well-known innovation, the focus group, was simple and economical enough for businesses across the country to conduct on their own, and it eventually became a widely used tool for gathering consumer intelligence.

Thanks in part to Dichter, companies no longer had to guess what their customers wanted. With the help of a moderator, focus groups gave market researchers the ability to directly interact with their target audience. A well-designed focus group session can produce organic, information-rich conversations as respondents discuss their reactions to a product or service.

FOCUS GROUPS IN THE DIGITAL AGE

Now that IT infrastructure has spread to nearly every corner of the earth, the focus group is no longer confined to the office headquarters or rented boardroom. According to Zain Raj, chair and CEO of market research firm Shapiro+Raj, companies seeking consumer intelligence have been able to expand their reach across the globe 'to people who otherwise were not available to us'. This has had benefits for both companies and consumers. 'Because they were not at the table, they weren't marketed [to]. . . . So, it's allowed us to take our qualitative posture and expand it geographically', Raj explains.

Additionally, advances in artificial intelligence have made it possible to view transcripts of online focus group discussions as they are happening, enabling moderators to tailor their questions or approach while the focus group is still in session, whereas previously in a traditional focus group they could only hand deliver a note to the moderator sent from the client behind the glass while the session was in progress, or review their study subjects' replies after the fact. Such an advancement has made focus groups more interactive and directed, says Raj, yielding even better insights. 'What technology is starting to do is allowing [lines of enquiry] to happen real time versus later.'[8]

Online focus groups offer more flexibility than do traditional focus groups, especially for participants who may have difficulty attending in-person sessions. Given that many in this group are part of highly targeted consumer demographics – parents, working professionals, and the like – offering an online option may certainly be a worthy investment to marketers. Additionally, the privacy inherent in online groups may encourage participants to disclose information about themselves they wouldn't be comfortable sharing in a face-to-face setting, an asset when the discussion involves sensitive topics. For instance, a 2017 asynchronous online focus group conducted through Facebook that surveyed young adult smokers found that 'this data collection method may be particularly appropriate to inform development of social media interventions for health behavior change'.[9]

Additionally, the more soft-spoken participants in large or poorly moderated focus groups are at risk of being dominated or drowned out by more assertive participants. In an attempt to remedy this, the traditional focus groups Shapiro+Raj commission are limited to six participants. Such an approach allows moderators to better 'engage with each of those respondents and, more importantly, give each of the respondents time to engage with each other', says Raj.[10]

Online-only focus groups have their own unique issues. Technical difficulties – always a risk – can slow participants and moderators down and affect performance and finding a truly appropriate group mix can be challenging. To many marketers, however, the upsides outweigh the downside:

- Because of their convenience and lower cost, online groups enable companies to survey many more people in a single session than a traditional, walk-in group.
- The larger sample sizes of online groups translate to more representative data sets.
- Advances in technology may continue to make focus groups even more reliable and useful to researchers.

According to Zain Raj, many other benefits are likely still to be discovered. 'We are just scratching the surface.'[11]

Sidebar

Author Insights from Attending Over 300 Focus Groups

by Mark Burgess

Throughout my career, I have had the pleasure (and pain) of attending over 300 focus groups on consumer and business products and services. The simple lesson I've learned from spending literally hundreds of hours behind the two-way glass is this: if a marketer wants to know how customers and prospects feel about their brand – if a marketer truly wants to understand their audience – they must *actually* listen to them. While marketers must always work to strike a balance between qualitative and quantitative results, there is simply no substitute for learning their target audience's opinions about brands, ad campaigns, new products, logos, etc. in real-time.

Live is Best

Attending a focus group in the flesh offers an entirely different experience than reading a typed report. Yes, it's good to create a record of the group's conversations, but simply put, nothing compares to viewing groups live. Listening to and observing respondents' facial expressions and body language as they react to campaigns or new product concepts is an invaluable experience in itself.

Even senior executives must be reminded of this fact from time to time. Every time I've convinced an unhappy senior executive to take some time out of their busy schedules to attend a focus group, their response has always been similar: 'Wow, our customers really think that?' 'I've never seen anything like this.' 'Our CEO should see this.'

Strategy Matters

Strategy is just as important as group dynamics. The shrewdest marketers, for instance, strategically deploy focus groups to save their brand from making a costly mistake. On several occasions, I've worked with clients who were under a very short deadline and needed a final 'disaster check' before selecting an ad campaign to shoot. In these situations, we often presented three to four TV campaigns to a group using animatics – which are essentially moving storyboards with an audio/visual component – as the stimulus. The goal was to make sure the campaign that was chosen to shoot was basically problem-free. From a purely directional standpoint, the focus groups we assembled provided a valuable opportunity to suss out the best (and least objectionable) of the choices. With the play clock ticking and with millions of dollars in media and production expense at stake, this insurance investment was well worth it.

GOING BEYOND THE GROUP

If Dichter's focus group represents the earliest prototype of consumer listening, Omnicom's 'cultural consultancy', sparks & honey, could be considered version 3.0. (Full disclosure, Cheryl Burgess, author, is on sparks & honey's advisory board.) Located in the overlapping center of a Venn diagram that includes a cutting-edge market research company, consulting firm and marketing agency, sparks & honey has made its name forecasting consumer trends. 'We translate culture into real-time opportunities for brands', CEO Terry Young explained in an expansive 2018 *Deloitte Insights* case study on the company.[12]

A component of the sparks & honey proprietary Active Learning System Q™ (see Figure 2.5) is their 'culture briefing' (see Figure 2.6), a wide-ranging daily dispatch whose mission is to identify and decode the zeitgeist at the moment – and, it's hoped, the future. The briefing is generated by a rotating group of employees, who use the Q™ intelligence platform to sift through important or percolating culture 'signals' from the last 24–48 hours.[13] 'A signal is a manifestation of culture (fast and slow) in our daily lives. It can be anything from a tweet, song, or meme that's spreading fast, to popular news articles, research papers and patents filed, to changes in public policy or emerging tech.'[14] The signals are debated in an open studio discussion every day at 12 EST as a pattern recognition exercise to develop hypotheses and potential business implications. The more perspectives offered, the company believes, the more accurate their forecasting and strategic recommendations will be as you highlight opinions and tensions from all different viewpoints.

Over the past eight years, sparks & honey has developed a powerful set of tools and processes for decoding the complexities of culture – building and training the data that serve as the backbone of the Q™ cultural intelligence platform, now available as a SaaS platform for enterprises.

The consultancy works with the C-suite of organizations in the public and private sector to transform the way they view and leverage cultural change.

Key benefits that the sparks & honey Q™ platform delivers for users include:

- A Method for Disruption Proofing. The platform includes in-language data from more than 45 countries, and with millions of signals being added every day, Q™ can master any shifting landscape by understanding a trend's past, current zeitgeist and mathematically predicting its future – helping businesses place smarter bets on their future.
- Data at the Speed of Culture. Q™ sources signals through a robust data pipeline (ranging from news articles, academic discoveries, patents and VC activity, to social media posts and more) and validates it through AI-powered scoring and contextualizing tools to turn months of laborious and costly research into mere hours of analysis.
- A Built-in, Tested Trends Framework. sparks & honey has built and refined its proprietary trends-set, the Elements of Culture, over eight years into a dynamic and quantified language to understand and talk about culture at a macro and micro level while also ensuring a single knowledge base for all users across an organization.

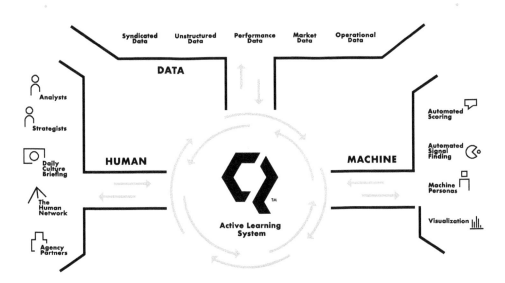

Figure 2.5   The Q™ Active Learning System works by (1) making change visible through systematic codification, (2) tracking and scoring signals, (3) accelerating responsiveness to signals and real-time system calibration, (4) enabling scalable collaboration and real-time knowledge creation through the culture briefing.

Source: sparks & honey.

sparks & honey's search through thousands of human and machine inputs is expansive and relentless. 'The consultancy's "culture newsroom" operates 24/7, 365 days a year', writes *Deloitte*. 'With a mission to "open minds and create possibilities in the now, next and future for brands," s&h aims to be a filter for, and presenter of, ideas that influence and shape culture.'[15] Apart from its consulting work for companies, sparks & honey produces 'culture forecasts', comprehensive reports (made freely available to the public) predicting future trends. Representative report titles include 'Generation Z 2025: The Final Generation' and 'Rebranding Marijuana', an analysis of the burgeoning cannabis industry, and 'Precision Consumer 2030'.

sparks & honey was recognized in The Drum's Top Agencies of 2019 list. The Drum described sparks & honey as 'a "cultural consultancy" offering in-depth analysis of the digital world'. They also stated that 'the agency promises its clients nothing short of bottled lightning – the ability to transcribe the cultural zeitgeist into hard numbers and trackable metrics'.[16]

If you look for it, traces of sparks & honey's model can be found in Dichter's focus group. But instead of relying on a small assortment of people to provide insight, its subject includes the wider culture itself – and everyone participating in it. Through its sophisticated data mining and well-calibrated ear, it has extended consumer listening to a whole population, pushing the art and science of consumer research to evolve further.

Figure 2.6   The daily culture briefing at sparks & honey's interactive studio in New York.

Source: sparks & honey.

When attending a sparks & honey cultural briefing in New York City in December 2019, Cheryl Burgess shared with the audience that the Q™ database was useful to her efforts to write *The New Marketing*. 'I can't tell you what a gift Q™ was to us – it provided access to global trends, insights, and experts at the tap of a few keys. It saved us countless hours of research time. It also helped to elevate the quality of our work by uncovering ideas we hadn't considered and helped identify experts.'

GETTING TO THE SOURCE

In any era, focus groups have proven not only useful marketing research tools, but also adaptable. However, if you want to get a more complete understanding of what is happening in a consumer's brain, it pays to go straight to the source – literally. With its reliance on academic research tools, neuroscience can give you a more granular understanding of how someone's brain reacts to various stimuli, including advertisements and other marketing content. While neuroscience isn't yet in wide use, it may well take up a bigger share of the market research pie as its technology matures and costs go down. And when it does, we may well be entering a new phase of consumer research.

Before we continue, some definitions are in order. Let's start with neuroscience, which refers to the study of neurons – nerve cells – and the nervous system; it's a hard science that's considered a subset of biology. It's from this that neuromarketing is derived. While descriptions of neuromarketing differ from person to person and company to company, we'll defer to Dr. Thomas Zoëga Ramsøy, founder of the applied neuroscience company Neurons Inc., and author of *Introduction to Neuromarketing & Consumer Science*. Ramsøy defines neuromarketing as 'a part within marketing that studies the effect of marketing stimuli on consumers' sensimotor, cognitive, and affective (emotional) responses'.[17] Within neuroscience, certain subfields have a greater application to neuromarketing than others.

The premise of consumer neuroscience is that we don't always know what we want, how we feel, or why we like or dislike a product. Hence, neuroscience can be used to get around some of the comparative weaknesses of focus groups and surveys, which both rely on self-reporting. Taking measures of brain activity, on the other hand, may reveal information about what *drives* self-reported attitudes, such as liking or purchase intent. We may say one thing, and we're thinking another.

The importance of an emotional connection cannot be understated. Though you may not be aware of it, many companies have incorporated some amount of neuroscience-derived data into their branding. Take colors, for example. Brands like Coca-Cola, Target and Netflix have all built their brands around the color red, because research shows that we associate that color with boldness, excitement and energy. Brands who want to promote feelings of strength, honesty and trust, such as LinkedIn, American Express and IBM (a.k.a. 'Big Blue'), all rely on the color blue.

We had similar goals when we chose the name Blue Focus Marketing. Our mission from the beginning has been to build trustworthy brands that engage audiences with integrity and confidence. To do that, we knew that we had to choose a brand identity for ourselves that our clients would associate with these positive traits – whether consciously or otherwise.

BUILDING A BETTER AD

The marketplace, of course, is the final arbiter of ad success, so no matter how positively people claim they respond to an ad, the truth will win out once sales figures come back. In Thomas Ramsøy's view, a successful neuro-analysis can actually serve as something like a crystal ball, helping marketers anticipate responses well ahead of time. In fact, he says, neuroscience often leads to much more accurate predictors than self-reporting. It can better shed light on what consumers truly respond to, even if they don't know it themselves – the holy grail of any market research study. 'The neuro scores that we get, they tend to be much more predictive of market responses than self-reported liking and other types of responses. And I think that's one level of contribution from neuro – typically a better predictive score on market responses', he says.[18]

Much of this is due to neuroscience's ability to isolate granular moments that connect with the audience in some meaningful way, as well as moments where brands and advertisers may be losing their intended audience. In fact, in conversations with researchers working in neuroscience, the notion of 'granularity' comes up repeatedly. Says Joe Willke:

> I think there's a certain unique value and ability to take very specific granular insights. I got three emails in my inbox today from reports last week. . . . clients are just thrilled they were able to understand their advertising at the level of depth we were able to create and come up with concrete actionable recommendations.[19]

There is a reason for this. According to Thomas Ramsøy, researchers use neuro essentially as a measurement device, capable of quantifying core marketing questions like:

- How many people are actually paying attention to this ad?
- How many views did the ad actually get?
- How long did the ad hold their attention?

In other words, neuromarketing pushes beyond the question of whether the audience saw the ad and seeks to understand whether they engaged with it. 'Do they actually respond to it?' says Ramsøy. 'Do they show a sign of increased cognitive processing, so they are actually engaged and understand what's going on?' Neuroscience can answer these questions with surprising accuracy and specificity, allowing marketers to pinpoint the exact moments where an ad held or lost a viewer's attention, and to then adjust accordingly.

That said, success with neuroscience isn't guaranteed. If deployed by inexperienced hands, the science can flag false positives. 'It sounds simple but, it turns out to be really hard to do right, because there's lots of ads that are engaging on an emotional level but don't actually say anything or aren't connected to a brand', says Joe Willke. 'They advertise nothing, or often what we see is they advertise the category and not your brand specifically, or sometimes specifically the competitor.'[20]

Neuroscience may not have widespread adoption just yet, but its impact is growing, and it's only a matter of time before it becomes a routine component of consumer insight research. According to a 2018 survey commissioned by the Association of National Advertisers that gauged industry beliefs about consumer neuroscience, 73% of survey respondents said they were 'familiar or very familiar' with consumer neuroscience.

That number alone doesn't tell the whole story. According to an article discussing the survey (penned by Dr. Carl Marci), 80% of the surveyed companies that had revenue growth over the previous year were in the 'familiar or very familiar' camp, suggesting some sort of link between an open mind when it comes to new technology and revenue growth. Further, among the cohort of respondents who attributed their reve-nue growth to using neuroscience techniques, each 'saw an average 16-percent increase, which equates to about $80 million in revenue [among this group of respondents]'.[21]

The survey also reported that 10% of survey participants think consumer neurosci-ence is just a fad, 64% think it will complement 'traditional techniques', and 8% think it will actually replace traditional marketing techniques.[22] We tend to agree with the 64% who see neuroscience as a complementary tool and an ever-expanding marketing toolbelt. While neuroscience and neuromarketing will no doubt continue to establish themselves as powerful marketing practices, we find it unlikely that they will ever replace traditional methods entirely.

Future Gaze

By Kevin Randall, brand strategist and contributing writer for *The New York Times*

Can a robot recognize human feelings? The question prompted by the science fiction film classic *2001: A Space Odyssey* is being pursued by a growing branch of computer science known as 'affective computing'. MIT Media Lab's affective computing field 'addresses machine recognition and modeling of human emotional expression, includ-ing the invention of new software tools to help people gather, communicate, and express emotional information and to better manage and understand the ways emo-tion impacts health, social interaction, learning, memory, and behavior'.[23]

As AI becomes more attuned to interpret emotions, it's taking on a role in product design, advertising, customer service, even mental health or occupational treatment, says brand strategist Kevin Randall. An application might take the form of 'having our iPhones spit back, "Oh, how are you feeling today?" in a Siri-type voice'.[24] Randall cites the work of pioneering companies such as Affectiva, which was spun out of MIT Media Lab. Its core offering uses facial expression and emotion analytics for measur-ing consumer reactions to ads. Its newest automotive technology senses the faces, voices and moods of drivers and passengers to help prevent distraction and improve both safety and the overall in-vehicle experience.

Says Affectiva co-founder and CEO, Rana Kaliouby, who has helped recast and commercialize affective computing into a booming 'emotion AI' category:

Emotion AI enables marketers to gain a deeper understanding of consumers' emotional engagement with their content. Today we are surrounded by 'smart' technology, but it is missing the emotional and social skills needed for mean-ingful interactions between consumers and brands. Emotion AI like Affectiva's

(Continued)

teaches marketers our likes and dislikes based on unfiltered and unbiased emotional reactions to, for example, advertising content and TV programming. Armed with this insight from Emotion AI, companies can adjust their strategies to produce content that resonates with their target audiences. Research has shown that emotion analytics can predict key success metrics such as sales lift and purchase intent.[25]

Cogito, another emotion AI company hatched out of the MIT Media Lab, helps physicians understand patient emotions during phone calls through voice analytics. Talk about deep listening!

Where is this category going? 'These innovators are swimming in a sea of tech titans who see emotion AI as a key puzzle piece for fulfilling larger ambitions', says Kevin Randall. 'Apple bought Affectiva's only real competitor in the facial emotions AI space to augment Siri. Google and Amazon are busy filing patents in voice emotions recognition. And with a growing client, partner and investor list, Affectiva is now expanding the category to "Human Perception AI" which includes understanding our complex cognitive states, human activities and interactions and objects we use. So rather than asking you how you're feeling, tomorrow's robot assistant will proactively tell you your mood or health, advise and connect you to things you want or need based on your Emotion or Human Perception AI inputs.'[26]

Still, Randall cautions that as these technologies and their efficacy continue to improve, the public concern over their ethical use and consumer privacy will intensify.

CHAPTER ANALYSIS QUESTIONS

1. Why is it important to understand your customer?
2. What are the advantages of consumer neuroscience over focus groups?
3. When it comes to advertising, what does 'engagement' look like?
4. What is affective computing and what are the implications for marketers?

NOTES

1. Sakr, S. (2011). Market research and the primitive mind of the consumer. [online] BBC News. Available at: www.bbc.co.uk/news/mobile/business-12581446 [Accessed 20 Feb. 2019].
2. ASPCA. (2019). Shelter intake and surrender: Pet statistics. Available at: www.aspca. org/animal-homelessness/shelter-intake-and-surrender/pet-statistics [Accessed 17 Feb. 2019].

3.   Inspiration Room. (2009). The Shelter Pet Project. Available at: http://theinspirationroom. com/daily/2009/the-shelter-pet-project/ [Accessed 9 Jan. 2020].

4.   Nielsen Neuro Shelter Pet Case Study. (2019). [Slides provided to the authors].

5.   ASPCA. (2017). ASPCA releases new data showing remarkable progress for homeless dogs & cats [10 March]. Available at: www.aspca.org/about-us/press-releases/asp-ca-releases-new-data-showing-remarkable-progress-homeless-dogs-cats [Accessed 17 Feb. 2019].

6.   Willke, J. (2019). Personal communication. [16 Aug.].

7.   Ibid.

8.   Raj, Z. (2018). Personal communication. [13 Dec.].

9.   Thrul, J., Belohlavek, A., Hambrick, D., Kaur, M. and Ramo, D. (2017). Conducting online focus groups on Facebook to inform health behavior change interventions: Two case studies and lessons learned. *Internet Interventions*, 9(1), pp. 106–111.

10.   Raj, Z. (2018). Personal communication. [13 Dec.].

11.   Ibid.

12.   Hagel, J., Brown, J.S., Wooll, M. and de Maar, A. (2018). sparks & honey culture briefing group: Embracing a diverse world to sense and make sense of cultural signals. *Deloitte Insights,* 7 March. Available at: www2.deloitte.com/insights/us/en/topics/talent/busi-ness-performance-improvement/sparks-honey.html [Accessed 17 Feb. 2019]

13.   Young, T. (2019). Personal communication. [29 Jan.].

14.   sparks & honey (2017). Our daily briefing is going live. *Medium*, 26 July. Available at: https://medium.com/sparksandhoney/our-daily-briefing-is-going-live-76ba2a604ece [Accessed 17 Feb. 2019].

15.   Hagel, J., Brown, J.S., Wooll, M. and de Maar, A. (2018). sparks & honey culture briefing group: Embracing a diverse world to sense and make sense of cultural signals. *Deloitte Insights*, 7 March. Available at: www2.deloitte.com/insights/us/en/topics/talent/busi-ness-performance-improvement/sparks-honey.html [Accessed 17 Feb. 2019].

16.   The Drum. (2020). New Year Honours: The Drum editorial team's agencies of 2019 [7 January]. Available at: www.thedrum.com/news/2020/01/07/new-year-honours-the-drum-editorial-teams-agencies-2019 [Accessed 8 Jan. 2020].

17.   Ramsøy, T. (2014). *Introduction to Neuromarketing & Consumer Neuroscience*. Neurons Inc ApS, p. 3.

18.   Ramsøy, T. (2018). Personal communication. [18 Dec.].

19.   Willke, J. (2019). Personal communication. [16 Aug].

20.   Ibid.

21.   Marci, C. (2018). Deeper insights, ROI and the future of consumer neuroscience [8 August]. *GreenBook*. Available at: https://greenbookblog.org/2018/08/08/deeper-in-sights-roi-and-the-future-of-consumer-neuroscience/ [Accessed 17 Feb. 2019].

22.   Ibid.

23. MIT Media Lab. (2019). Advancing wellbeing by using new ways to communicate, understand, and respond to emotion. [online] Available at: www.media.mit.edu/groups/affective-computing/overview/ [Accessed 17 Feb. 2019].

24. Wharton Business Radio. (2017). Marketing Matters: May 31, 2017. [podcast] Marketing Matters. Available at: https://shows.acast.com/wbr-guest/episodes/kevin-randall2 [Accessed 17 Feb. 2019].

25. Kaliouby, R. (2019). Personal communication. [24 Jan.].

26. Randall, K. (2020). Personal communication. [13 Jan.].

3
ARCHITECTING DATA-DRIVEN BUYER PERSONAS

Learning Goals

- Analyze why buyer personas are essential to marketers.
- Analyze the steps involved in creating a buyer persona.
- Understand the value of social listening and monitoring tools in persona development.
- Identify customer pain points and provide solutions to them.
- Recognize AI's value and promise in micro-segmentation to fine-tune your personas.

It is a capital mistake to theorize before one has data. Insensibly one begins to twist facts to suit theories, instead of theories to suit facts.

Sherlock Holmes[1]

In The Who's classic 1978 song 'Who Are You?' listeners are challenged to take a hard look at themselves. Over a hypnotic, echoing chorus, the legendary British rock group repeats the song title again and again, practically demanding an answer to their question. The band's insistent call for the examination of motivation and identity applies to many aspects of life, marketing included. This is especially true when it comes to buyer personas. For those unfamiliar with the term, a buyer persona is an expertly crafted profile of your target customer. As HubSpot writer Sam Kusinitz explains, 'A buyer persona is a semifictional representation of your ideal customer based on market research and real data about your existing customers.' Effective personas, Kusinitz writes, take into account 'customer demographics, behavior patterns, motivations, and goals'.[2] In a nutshell, knowing who you're selling to makes it a lot easier to sell to them.

Developing strong buyer personas better enables you to provide an authentic, impactful customer experience. Personas help you get inside the mind of your buyer, building empathy for their needs, concerns and pain points. They're so useful, in fact, that in addition to creating personas for their buyers, the most successful marketing departments also construct personas for those who influence their buyer's purchasing decisions. For example, a university focused on attracting high school seniors could start by building a persona for prospective students, and then follow up with personas for any parents, teachers, or coaches who might influence their students' decisions.

Buyer personas put a face to all of that demographic and market data you've painstakingly researched and collected. However, since your job as a marketer is to sell to people and not data points, personas can help you develop a winning messaging strategy meant for actual humans.

'Marketers fundamentally need to figure out a way to walk in the customer's shoes, or live in the customer's home', asserts Zain Raj, chair and CEO of market research firm Shapiro+Raj. This is much easier said than done, however, as Raj's experience consulting for a large retailer illustrates. The company, a longtime powerhouse in the retail sector that had been struggling for a few years, brought in Raj to help them target their customers with more precision. They had amassed key information about their market, but it consisted mostly of demographic data points that didn't actually reveal anything deep about the lives of the people who bought from them. Says Raj, 'We went in, and my first question was, "Guys, who's your customer?" And they didn't have a clue. They gave me all the data: "My top percentile makes $110,000, blah, blah, blah." I'm like, "Yeah, I know all that – but who are they? How do they live?"'[3]

When Raj suggested that companies need to 'live in their customer's home', he wasn't speaking in metaphor. He actually arranged to stay with a family in the retailer's target market for three days. Talk about getting to know your customer!

While getting such an intimate glimpse into our customers' lives may not be a realistic option for most of us, a thoughtfully constructed buyer persona can be a powerful, easy-to-use tool for helping to define and refine your target market. It serves as a roadmap, laying out your customer's pain points, media consumption habits, and other relevant information that affects their purchasing decisions.

THE SEVEN STEPS TO BUILDING A STRONG PERSONA

In this section, you will learn our seven-step approach to creating strong buyer personas:

1. Gather buyer data
2. Assemble your team
3. Get to know your buyer
4. Evaluate pain points
5. Craft your persona
6. Revisit and revise your persona
7. Validate your persona

By taking a systematic approach, your marketing team will be able to define and target their ideal buyers with remarkable precision. Before we dive in, however, it's important to start with the end result in mind. The following are two examples of what a completed buyer persona might look like.

The first example depicts a customer in the business-to-business, or B2B, sector. The B2B sector consists of trade and communications between businesses, rather than between a business and an individual consumer. For instance, businesses in the tech sector offering software or enterprise solutions to other companies.

Example 1 depicts a B2B target, 'Sam Smart-Tech'. Sam is the VP of Purchasing at a global manufacturing company. He's a heavy web user, values vendor responsiveness, loves golfing, and enjoys listening to The Fray and Maroon 5 (see Figure 3.1).

The second example depicts a consumer in the business-to-consumer (B2C) sector. This includes transactions between brick and mortar retailers and consumers as well as online shoppers.

Example 2, created for a B2C target, offers a profile of 'Ellen Entrepreneur', a 28-year-old marketing consultant who needs a reliable computer for personal and business (see Figure 3.2).

Now that you understand what the end result might look like, let's walk through the process step by step. While we'll be providing our own examples as we move along, if you want to get the most out of this exercise, you may use this same process to create a buyer persona for a B2C customer of your own.

Step 1: Gather Buyer Data

Just like Sherlock Holmes needs good, reliable information to solve a mystery, marketers require accurate data to help them figure out what customers are saying about

B2B Persona Profile

Example 1

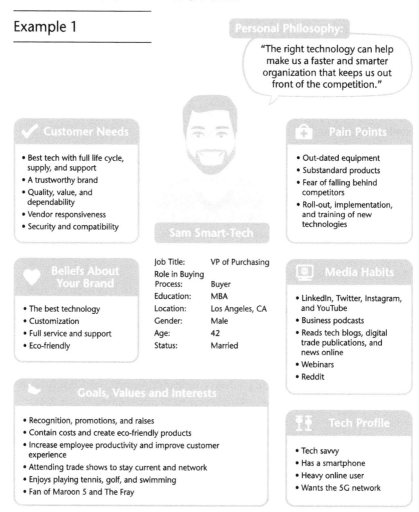

Personal Philosophy:
"The right technology can help make us a faster and smarter organization that keeps us out front of the competition."

Customer Needs

- Best tech with full life cycle, supply, and support
- A trustworthy brand
- Quality, value, and dependability
- Vendor responsiveness
- Security and compatibility

Pain Points

- Out-dated equipment
- Substandard products
- Fear of falling behind competitors
- Roll-out, implementation, and training of new technologies

Sam Smart-Tech

Beliefs About Your Brand

- The best technology
- Customization
- Full service and support
- Eco-friendly

Job Title:	VP of Purchasing
Role in Buying Process:	Buyer
Education:	MBA
Location:	Los Angeles, CA
Gender:	Male
Age:	42
Status:	Married

Media Habits

- LinkedIn, Twitter, Instagram, and YouTube
- Business podcasts
- Reads tech blogs, digital trade publications, and news online
- Webinars
- Reddit

Goals, Values and Interests

- Recognition, promotions, and raises
- Contain costs and create eco-friendly products
- Increase employee productivity and improve customer experience
- Attending trade shows to stay current and network
- Enjoys playing tennis, golf, and swimming
- Fan of Maroon 5 and The Fray

Tech Profile

- Tech savvy
- Has a smartphone
- Heavy online user
- Wants the 5G network

Figure 3.1   B2B persona profile – Example 1.

Source: ©2020 Blue Focus Marketing®. All Rights Reserved.

their brand, their competitors, or their industry to help determine their target buyer. Your data might come from independent observation, or from studying buyer demographics, psychographics, purchase behavior, or social media activity.

'Now in the digital space, you have the ability to learn so much more about people and what they're doing and how they're interacting with their brand, with your brand, and how they're leading their life', says Tim Calkins, Clinical Professor of Marketing, Kellogg School of Management, Northwestern University. That said, a little bit of

B2C Persona Profile

Example 2

Personal Philosophy:

"I love challenges and finding new ways to grow my business. My full-time job has me on the road a few days a month. I'm a mother to an active 6-year-old and I need a computer that keeps up with me."

Customer Needs

- Good value
- Fast and simple to use
- Tech support and security
- Software for business and personal use
- Compact and sleek design with a long battery life

Pain Points

- Heavy, difficult to use computers
- High prices
- Security and privacy
- Eco-unfriendly brands

Ellen Entrepreneur

Occupation:	Marketing Consultant
Income:	$65,000
Education:	BA
Location:	London, England
Gender:	Female
Age:	30
Status:	Married

Beliefs About Your Brand

- Understands their needs and offers solutions
- Dependable and easy to use
- Simplifies their life
- Cool designs instill confidence in front of clients

Media Habits

- Facebook, Twitter, Instagram, LinkedIn, and YouTube
- Netflix/no cable
- Business podcasts
- Uses text and email
- Business blogs

Goals, Values and Interests

- Marketing like a boss
- Growing her business
- Likes brands that are eco-friendly and cares about women's rights
- Loves traveling, pop music, dogs, and a healthy lifestyle
- Fan of Bastille and Paul McCartney

Tech Profile

- Not super tech savvy yet
- Has a smartphone
- Loves social media
- Enjoys shopping online

Figure 3.2   B2C persona profile – Example 2.

Source: ©2020 Blue Focus Marketing®. All Rights Reserved.

vigilance goes a long way. Having access to so much information, Calkins says, 'makes the job of a marketer, I think, sort of more robust but also a lot more challenging, because you've got to make sense of all of this data that's out there'.[4]

One increasingly valuable tool for collecting data is social listening. This process involves tracking online comments about your business – both positive and negative – through review sites like Yelp and Google Reviews, or over social media platforms like Twitter, Instagram and Facebook. Customers offer plenty of frank, unfiltered insights into their preferences and buying habits through these sites. If you look carefully, you will uncover valuable information about your target market. Researchers in a 2017 study found that 'Analyzing trends and the temporal dynamics of information . . . in social tags helps marketers identify managerially interesting changes within top-of-mind brand associations. Such information enables marketers to take steps to proactively manage their brand equity by detecting trending keywords.'[5]

When it comes to social listening, brands can either perform this work in-house, or they can work with social listening providers like BuzzSumo. To get a feel for how social listening works, let's take a closer look at the world of Twitter. This platform offers marketers an invaluable social listening platform. Twitter users tend to be blunt and to-the-point, in part because they're working within a strict 280-character limit. This offers marketers easy-to-interpret insights without having to wade through overly wordy or unnecessary information, as they might find in a lengthier Yelp review. On Twitter, all marketers have to do is search for hashtags and keywords relevant to their brand, and they'll find a treasure trove of useful information.

This interplay between brand and audience is readily apparent during one of the highest-profile marketing events of the year: the Super Bowl. Every year, the Super Bowl is the most-watched television event in the United States. Ads that air during the game are often especially creative and daring, and many viewers are just as interested in the ads as they are in the teams on the field.

During the 2019 Super Bowl, Kia ran an emotion-stoking ad set in West Point, Georgia, where the car manufacturer has a plant. 'We're not famous', begins the narrator, a young boy in a cowboy hat speaking in a somber, heavy Southern drawl. 'There are no stars in a sidewalk for us. No statues in our honor. We're just a small Georgia town of complete unknowns.' Clips of local Kia workers assembling cars appear on the screen, and orchestral music swells as the boy tells the town's humble but inspiring story.[6]

'Great marketing comes from targeting and finding customer insights, and Kia's Super Bowl ad does both', said Tim Calkins. 'Kia is tapping right into this insight with its Telluride spot. The ad speaks to the mainstream, in a tone that is empathetic and true. The core message: working people, the people who build the Telluride down in Georgia, are incredible. And they build an amazing car.'[7]

The public also responded favourably. One Twitter user replied, 'OMG made me want to run out and buy a Kia!' Both Calkins and the reviewer were clearly touched by the ad's message. It was a good start for Kia, but to truly gauge whether or not the ad was positively received, Kia would have to take the time to sift through many more responses the commercial received.

Vigilant social media listening can also lead to valuable opportunities for connecting with your target market. In the winter of 2017, Southwest Airlines' marketing team noticed a lot of chatter on Facebook and Twitter about how airlines handle harsh winter weather and realized that they had a great engagement opportunity on their hands. They acted quickly, sending a team to Denver International Airport in the middle of January to shoot a video showing how the airline deals with winter weather and keeps planes safe – all through the lens of an employee jokingly referred to as 'The Bucket Man', who would work tirelessly to de-ice the planes. By demystifying the process of weatherizing its planes, Southwest used social listening to underscore its commitment to safety – an important value for most consumers – while simultaneously entertaining viewers.[8]

Neglect what your customers have to say at your peril. As evidence, look no further than one of the most iconic brands on Earth: Lego. For many years Lego dominated its unique position in the toy space. But in the early 2000s things changed. Lured by the opportunity to collaborate with hit movie franchises to create toys with more bells and whistles and electronics, the company put its core product offerings on the backburner. The result was a loss of $300 million in 2003 that nearly bankrupted the company. Disaster was only averted when Lego accepted that its customers – and their parents – liked Lego just the way it was.[9] It took hard conversations with focus groups to help them realize how far they had strayed from their mission. 'With focus groups you can listen [to consumers] or you can really listen, and I think we taught ourselves to really listen', said Lego Systems President Soren Torp Laursen in a 2015 interview with Bloomberg News (for more on focus groups, see Chapter 2).[10]

As you consider how to make social listening work for you, consider the many tools available to your brand. Whether you're monitoring comments on social platforms like Facebook and Twitter, making use of a focus group, or hiring a dedicated social listening service, the important thing is to identify the tools that meet your branding goals and that bring external voices into internal conversations. From there, the opportunities for growth are endless.

Step 2: Assemble Your Team

Building a persona needn't be a solitary task. In fact, the more minds you have on it, the better. After you've gathered plenty of useful data, put together a team that is excited to comb through it looking for insights. Good persona brainstorming sessions produce a lively environment where participants are open to all ideas. The more conversations you can generate, the more nuanced your personas will be. This isn't a time for conformity; you should encourage group participants to be candid (but respectful) as you zero in on your targets. Think of your persona-building sessions as fact-finding missions. If you're doing things right you will naturally run into a few dead ends, and that's okay. Don't be discouraged!

Create an environment that's ripe for participation by asking your team to leave their phones at the door and to be prepared to speak. Once everyone is in place, you can proceed to the next step.

Step 3: Get to Know Your Buyer

The persona you create should not reflect the entirety of your customer base. If it does, then the persona you came up with is too general and needs to be refined. You are better off having several tightly focused personas than one all-encompassing super-persona. Returning to our earlier example, if you're a university, it would not be helpful to create a persona that reflects the needs, consumption habits and pain points of both a typical student and a typical parent, since most 18-year-olds are looking for very different things out of their college experience than their parents are. A persona that reflects both of these targets would be unrealistic – and therefore useless.

As you construct your persona, think of yourself as an investigator. Ask lots of simple, direct questions that will help you figure out who your customers are and what they care about. This is where conversations between team members come in handy. Everyone can chime in, playing off one another until a realistic persona with needs, concerns and motivations emerges.

Here are some useful questions to get the ball rolling:

- What is their name?
- What do they look like?
- What do they do for work?
- What do they do for fun?
- What are their buying habits?
- What are their hopes, dreams and aspirations?
- How can your brand reach them at different points in the buying stage?
- Is your customer B2B or B2C?
- Who or what influences their buying decisions?
- What are their pain points, and how can you alleviate them?

Answering these questions shouldn't be guesswork. Use the data you collected from step 1 to make your answers as specific as possible.

Step 4: Evaluate Pain Points

To create a truly authentic persona, you must know not only what your target buyers want in a product, but also what could prevent them from buying it. These are pain points – barriers to sales that keep them from pulling the trigger. Pain points can be just about anything, both large and small. One buyer's pain point might be using a website that has poor navigation making it difficult for customers to find the information they are seeking. To address and eliminate pain points, look for any avoidable barriers in the purchasing process and eliminate them.

For instance, imagine that you're an online shoe retailer. Sales have been good the past couple of years, but lately you've noticed them slipping. After some research, you discover an interesting trend. Your site still generates a lot of traffic. In fact, most prospective buyers actively engage with your digital storefront, filling up their carts with shoes and related products. But then something happens: a large percentage of buyers abandon their carts, leave your site, and take their business somewhere else.

Whatever the reason is that they're abandoning their carts, that's their pain point. Now, it's up to you to figure out what's causing that pain point and then to resolve it as quickly as possible.

First, brainstorm some possible causes. Why are so many people getting so close to buying, only to change their minds?

Possibilities include:

- A poorly designed, non-user-friendly checkout system.
- High prices compared to competitors.
- Inferior incentives or buyer rewards programs. Perhaps your customers are going somewhere else for more enticing deals or loyalty programs?

These are all promising possibilities, but just like our old friend Sherlock, it's important to gather more information before jumping to any conclusions. The most successful brands diligently collect consumer data, which are invaluable when attempting to identify a customer pain point. Common information streams include:

- Customer feedback. Are you encouraging your customers to tell you about your brand – and are you making it easy for them to do so? If so, when and how often? What kinds of questions are you asking?
- Consumer behavior. Where do visitors go after leaving your site without a purchase? Are they going to your competitors' sites instead?
- Industry trends. What about industry data? This is a great way to determine whether your challenges are part of a larger trend, or unique to your brand.

Let's continue with our shoe retailer scenario. After reviewing customer feedback, you learn that your buyers have a positive view of your brand overall but give you lower marks on price. This seems odd, because your prices are generally lower than your competitors.

What could explain this discrepancy? Perhaps you aren't asking customers the right questions, or perhaps your process for collecting feedback isn't generating honest responses. Here again, social listening may be valuable.

To get a handle on how your customers and potential customers really feel, you could:

- Seek out conversations about your brand on channels like Twitter, Facebook, or Instagram. Ask questions when appropriate, but remember that you are there to listen.
- Find out what others in your market are saying about your brand. Industry or consumer blogs can be very helpful for identifying problems with your website or brand.
- See what consumers are saying about you and your competitors on review sites such as Yelp or Google Reviews.

After a little digging, you emerge with a valuable insight: prospective buyers love your product selection, especially your exclusive offerings. This is nice to know, but this information alone doesn't solve the mystery – if anything, it deepens the mystery. Curious, you begin monitoring the reviews and conversations around your competitors. Through these conversations, you find the missing piece of information: customers love your competitors' shipping and return policies.

It looks like you may have found your pain point. While your prices and product offerings may be superior to those of many of your competitors, your shipping and returns policy leaves something to be desired. When your buyers go to check out and discover these unexpected costs, they abandon their carts and go to your competitors instead. Address this pain point and you will make life easier for your customers, and better for yourself.

Step 5: Craft Your Persona

Now that you've collected data about your target customers through research and social listening, assembled your persona-building team, and identified the customers' pain points, it's time to create your persona. As you build it, feel free to use the example-personas presented earlier in this chapter for reference. Your own persona should include all of the elements contained in each of the previous four steps, though any other information you've generated may be helpful as well.

EXERCISE

Pain Points: A Closer Look

Brainstorming a target buyer's pain points helps you build empathy by forcing you to view the world from your customer's perspective. During this exercise, you are a hotel. To better understand your customers' pain points, you will assume the persona of a marketing director named Susan. Read the description of Susan and then fill out the chart listing her potential pain points.

Figure 3.3   Persona: Susan, business traveler.

Source: iStock photo/Szepy.

Name: Susan

Gender: Female

Age: 30

Marital status: Married, with one child

Occupation: Marketing director for a B2B company

Frequent business traveler

Likes to exercise

Likes to earn travel rewards

Treasures her new iPhone

Owns a Welsh Springer Spaniel

(Continued)

EXERCISE

Understanding Susan's Pain Points

Identify some of the pain points Susan may experience on her next business trip.

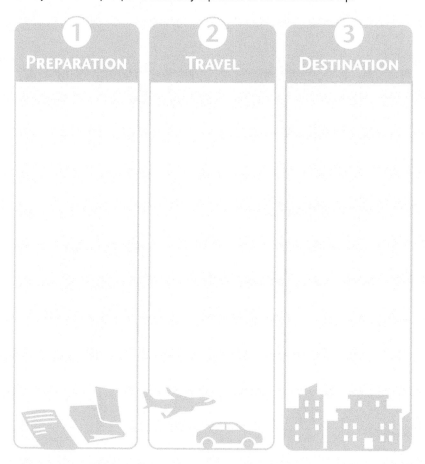

Figure 3.4   Exercise: Understanding Susan's pain points.

Source: ©2020 Blue Focus Marketing®. All Rights Reserved.

Remember that the process is the point. From the previous five steps, you might go into this step thinking that you have a pretty good idea of your target persona, only to find that, as you fill out your worksheet, your ideal target is completely different from your original conception. If so, congratulations – you are getting closer to figuring out your customer.

Step 6: Revisit and Revise Your Persona

Buyer personas must constantly be updated and maintained in order to sustain their accuracy and usefulness. As the market, society and technology change, people do too, and the likelihood of your target buyers exhibiting the same persona attributes year after year is next to nil. The more open to adaption you are, the better positioned you'll be to respond to changing customer needs, market conditions and pain points. So even if you and your team devise a strong persona, don't get too comfortable. You will need to update it before you know it.

In fact, given how quickly customer tastes are presently changing, we recommend revisiting these seven steps at least quarterly. You should never be afraid to let new information challenge your assumptions.

Step 7: Validate Your Persona

Now it's time to take your new persona for a test run. How will you do this? By marketing to your persona, of course. This is the moment of truth when you will rely on all of that research, social listening and team conversation to yield actionable results.

If you notice an increased interest in your products, as measured by either sales or customer engagement, then you'll know that your persona-building has been a success. If the needle doesn't move, or if sales or engagement decreases, then go back and revise your persona.

Another way to validate your persona is by using surveys to gather both qualitative (i.e. emotions, feelings and opinions) and quantitative (i.e. tests, surveys and statistics) data. Statistical clustering techniques can also help to identify your personas, as well as the variables that differentiate them.

Sidebar

The Power of Segmentation

One of the benefits of a good buyer persona is that it can enhance your market segmentation. In marketing, segmentation refers to the targeting of a subset of customers within a larger market. For example, a company that makes expensive diaper bags wouldn't target all moms – just ones with higher disposable income. Their target

(Continued)

demographic probably only makes up a small share of the overall diaper bag market, but it's a potentially lucrative share. Segmenting your market is a mainstay marketing practice, and for good reason. In *Marketing 4.0*, authors Philip Kotler, Hermawan Kartajaya and Iwan Setiawan write, 'Segmentation and targeting are both fundamental aspects of a brand's strategy. They allow for efficient resource allocation and sharper positioning. They also help marketers to serve multiple segments, each with differentiated offerings.'[11]

Segmentation is no less relevant in the current era, but buyer personas generated in a digital world ensure that even better information drives your decision-making. For instance, relying on persona data to segment the market is seen as a highly productive marketing strategy. In a 2018 poll commissioned by the Content Marketing Institute, nearly four out of five respondents said that they either had segmented demand-generation activities using a persona or planned to do so in the future.[12] Here's where all of those hours spent reading online reviews and Twitter chatter really pay off. By zeroing in on those potential customers who are predisposed to buy what you're offering, you will increase awareness of your products as well as your sales.

Segmentation is likely to get increasingly granular in the years to come. As algorithms and modelling enable companies to sort customer and target information with previously unimaginable levels of precision, more and more focused profiles will emerge. 'By yielding accurate, brain-like associations and insights . . . an AI can automatically craft rich profiles of a marketer's optimal prospects, resulting in far more accurate lead generation for sales teams and outbound marketing', writes *MarTech Today* contributor Venkat Nagaswamy. 'The marketer can then serve up digital experiences fine-tuned to maximize relevance to prospects and customers. An AI can continually update these personas in real time, so engagement strategies and messages stay relevant over time.'[13]

Content and marketing messages will be tailored to target buyers at every step along the customer journey, says Pini Yakuel, CEO of Optimove, a company that creates personalized marketing software. 'We can use historical data and machine learning models to say, "Okay, which message is likely to yield the highest return on a customer like [you] by knowing who you are as a customer?"' The answer, he says, lies in 'which persona or microsegment [you] belong to'.[14] It's all about hitting the right person at the right time with the right message – and micro-segmentation will help you do that. Instead of one or two buyer personas, you could end up with a dozen or more. And if the evidence overwhelmingly suggests that male Capricorns with brown hair between the ages of 43 and 45 who live in the Northwest represent an untapped target demographic for your product, well, then that's who you'll approach.

As the old saying goes, the only constant in life (and buyer personas) is change. So always be ready to ask, 'Who are you?' – and know that the answer you receive today may not be the same as the one you get tomorrow.

Future Gaze

Personalizing with Transparency

By Behavioral Economist Ravi Dhar, George Rogers Clark Professor of Management and Marketing at Yale School of Management

If marketers had the perfect answer to the question of how to personalize without raising privacy concerns – and therefore losing their customers' trust – they would likely already have a cushy consulting gig with Facebook by now. Suffice to say, privacy is a huge issue, and one with no clear solution.

One of the biggest challenges in solving the privacy issue is defining it. Ask ten different people what privacy means to them, and you'll get ten different answers depending upon the context. Some people are happy that Google can scan their email, see that they have an appointment across town, and then recommend the best route. However, those same people may take issue when they begin receiving targeted ads from loan sharks when they begin searching online for debt consolidation options. If just one person, depending on the context, thinks about their own privacy differently in different situations, how are marketers supposed to come up with a solution that satisfies *millions* of potential customers – especially when those customers span generations of different thinking?

There may never be a perfect solution, but an increasing amount of research indicates that transparency is key. Marketers need to be frank with their customers. 'This is what we do with your data', or, 'This is what we *will* do with your data'. This kind of message doesn't have to be complicated. Nobody's going to read a four-page document spelling out every possible scenario. Simply notify the customer how their data will be used in a broad context, and they will be grateful for the show of good faith.[15]

CHAPTER ANALYSIS QUESTIONS

1. What is the purpose of a buyer persona?
2. What are your personal pain points, and how do they affect your purchasing behavior?
3. What are the advantages of social listening over more traditional market research techniques?
4. What questions would you ask your customers to get to know them better?

NOTES

1. Conan Doyle, A. (1891). *A Scandal in Bohemia*. London: G. Newnes.
2. Kusinitz, S. (2019). The definition of a buyer persona [in under 100 words]. [online] Blog. hubspot.com. Available at: https://blog.hubspot.com/marketing/buyer-persona-definition-under-100-sr [Accessed 29 Mar. 2019].

3.   Raj, Z. (2018). Personal communication. [13 Dec.].

4.   Calkins, T. (2018). Personal communication. [3 Dec.].

5.   Nam, H., Joshi, Y.V. and Kannan, P. (2019). Harvesting brand information from social tags. *Journal of Marketing*, 81(4), pp. 88–108.

6.   YouTube. (2019). *Kia 2019 Super Bowl Commercial | BEST SUPERBOWL ADS.* [online] Available at: www.youtube.com/watch?v=YW76sMf0kZw [Accessed 3 Apr. 2019].

7.   Calkins, T. (2019). Making sense of Kia's curious Super Bowl ad. [online] Available at: http://timcalkins.com/super-bowl-advertising/making-sense-kias-curious-super-bowl-ad/ [Accessed 1 Mar. 2020].

8.   Rutherford, L. (2019). How Southwest Airlines uses social listening to produce compelling videos. [online] *PR News.* Available at: www.prnewsonline.com/social-southwest-videos [Accessed 3 Apr. 2019].

9.   Knowledge@Wharton. (2019). Innovation almost bankrupted LEGO – until it rebuilt with a better blueprint. [online] Available at: http://knowledge.wharton.upenn.edu/article/innovation-almost-bankrupted-lego-until-it-rebuilt-with-a-better-blueprint/ [Accessed 3 Apr. 2019].

10. YouTube. (2019). *Lego Story: What the Company Learned From its Mistakes.* [online] Available at: www.youtube.com/watch?v=gvLVsIZQbZI [Accessed 3 Apr. 2019].

11. Kotler, P., Kartajaya, H. and Setiawan, I. (2017). *Marketing 4.0.* Wiley, p. 47.

12. Rose, R. (2019). Are you generating demand or just identifying it? [online] Content Marketing Institute. Available at: https://contentmarketinginstitute.com/2018/10/generating-demand-research/ [Accessed 3 Apr. 2019].

13. Nagaswamy, V. (2019). Kiss your personas goodbye (and say hello, AI)! [online] *MarTech Today.* Available at: https://martechtoday.com/kiss-personas-goodbye-194454 [Accessed 3 Apr. 2019].

14. Yakuel, P. (2019). Personal communication. [6 February].

15. Dhar, R. (2019). Personal communication. [30 August].

4

PERSONALIZING THE CUSTOMER JOURNEY AND ACTIVATING BRAND PURPOSE

Learning Goals

- Analyze what a brand is and how it helps businesses stand out in a competitive world.
- Illustrate the importance of building brand trust.
- Demonstrate why purpose-driven brands are more valuable than their competitors.
- Analyze essential brand-building tools.
- Analyze the evolution of the customer journey from purchase-only to AI-driven customer experience.

People don't buy what you do. They buy why you do it.

Simon Sinek[1]

For the four co-founders of the trendy eyewear startup Warby Parker, financial success was never the ultimate goal. 'We started Warby Parker to solve problems', said co-founder Dave Gilboa in a 2014 promo for the company. 'We wanted to transform an industry that we thought was broken . . . and we thought we could do things in a better way. But we also wanted to start a for-profit business that had a positive impact on the world.'[2]

Through the company's Buy a Pair, Give a Pair program, they have done just that. For every pair of glasses or sunglasses a customer buys, Warby Parker pledges to put a pair of prescription glasses in the hands of someone who can't afford them. To make this happen, the company partners with non-profit organizations around the world, from Guatemala to India, to provide people in need of corrective lenses with a free or low-cost solution. Closer to home, Warby Parker has been collaborating with government agencies in New York City and Baltimore to fund eye exams for school children and give them the glasses they need. As Gilboa and his fellow co-founders see it, the company's twin goals of business success and making a positive impact on the world go hand in hand. Their purpose-driven mission helps attract positive attention to the company, which further drives growth and helps them invest in their mission to create positive change.

Through their efforts, Warby Parker has created an unforgettable brand. Customers in the market for eyewear know exactly what Warby Parker stands for: quality, value and the common good. While customers have plenty of other options for buying stylish and inexpensive eyewear, few, if any, are as attractive to consumers as the Warby Parker brand.

BEGIN WITH THE BRAND

What is a brand? While it might seem obvious at first, ask a few different people to define 'brand', and you will likely end up with a few different responses. To help alleviate this ambiguity, we surveyed several highly respected marketers and branding experts.

- **Walter Landor, branding pioneer and founder of Landor, the brand management company**: 'A brand is a promise. It delivers a pledge of satisfaction and quality.'[3]
- **Daniel Binns, CEO of Interbrand**: 'It's the means by which a consumer or a customer interacts with a company. It is the filter between the business and the customer. . . . All of the interactions that somebody has with a company defines their brand.'[4]
- **Russ Klein, CEO of the American Marketing Association**: 'From a consumer point of view, a brand is a method for establishing a familiarity and trust. [It is] somewhat of a warranty on the product or service that is involved. The other important aspect about a brand is that it has meaning. Some call it the space in your mind. From a brand-owner standpoint, a brand is, number one, an asset.'[5]
- **Kevin Randall, brand strategist and contributing writer for *The New York Times***: 'A brand is a relationship among company, employee, and customer that creates value through shared utility, purpose, and trust.'[6]

While each of these definitions is unique, they all touch on a common theme. Whether you conceive of a brand as a promise, a reason to believe, or the sum total of the entire customer experience, the bottom line is that it is a signal to the customer. It tells them exactly what they are getting themselves into, for better or for worse. The more reassuring and authentic your message, the more valuable your brand will be, and the more people will show their appreciation for it through sales and loyalty.

The trick, however, is getting your branding efforts right. For all the benefits of good branding, bad branding has the opposite effect. Bad branding confuses people and leaves them unsure about the value they'll receive. They need to know, in simple terms, exactly what's being offered and what your promise is. Otherwise they'll move on to a competitor who can tell them exactly what they're getting. For example, imagine you're at a restaurant. When you open the menu, you see a hundred different dishes listed – each more incongruent than the next. Among your options are Italian, Chinese, Greek, Czech, and even Peruvian fare! The restaurant owners may think that offering a smorgasbord of delights is a smart move. In reality, however, this shotgun approach suggests that the owners are unsure of what their kitchen staff is good at, too concerned with appealing to all kinds of customers, or both. The result is a muddled mess. Even if the restaurant does a few things really well (say, the pasta carbonara is to die for), its highlights will be lost and buried beneath a sea of lesser options. In other words, when it comes to brand awareness, clarity is crucial. Customers must be able to identify your value quickly and effortlessly.

On the other hand, good branding doesn't just help customers – it benefits companies, too. A good brand offers a guiding vision for your company that informs every decision you make, whether by a CEO or an entry-level employee. According to Interbrand's Daniel Binns, for many successful companies, every decision that's made extends from the brand promise:

Increasing[ly] what we see is that brand is the filter from which business decisions are made. [A brand] permeates everything, from how you treat and manage your employees and build a culture internally, to the products and services you offer, to how you're going to market, to how you're acquiring your companies and products.[7]

Southwest Airlines offers a famous example of this. According to the Southwest website, their official company vision is 'To become the world's most loved, most efficient, and most profitable airline.'[8] With every customer interaction, Southwest employees must consider whether their actions fulfill the company vision. With this guiding vision in mind, they set out to do exactly that. As a result, the company regularly scores miles ahead of other airlines in customer satisfaction surveys.

Sidebar

'You Don't Join Us. We Join You.'

Former McKinsey & Company partner and current Aetna CMO David Edelman offers a quick meditation on how he's been helping the Aetna brand stay relevant

Transforming a brand that's over 160 years old requires bringing a deep understanding of one's heritage into solving the needs of the future market. We saw a serious gap in healthcare, where people feel that everything is a one-off transaction that leaves them with all the burden of continuity. Aetna's long heritage of support in the local community, plus people's understanding of our role as a health payor, led them to feel we should fill that gap as a health partner. Hence, we developed our position of helping people on their path to better health, with the tagline 'You don't join us, we join you.' Focused on holistic care, connecting a person's journey, and transforming the cost structure to ensure health care is affordable are at our core. But it has to be more than words, so I have had to work hard across our business functions, setting brand standards, aligning initiatives, measuring impact on experience. It never stops, but with such a brand direction, we are all energized to make it happen.[9]

THE POWER OF TRUST

No amount of branding, however clever or entertaining, can take the place of an authentic relationship. 'The reason brands exist is because in one form they are trust marks', says Rishad Tobaccowala, chief growth officer for Publicis Groupe. 'So, when you see a brand logo, you trust that it will deliver on the capability of promises it made as a product, service, or utility – that it actually works.'[10]

Think of some of the best-loved brands out there, companies with high levels of customer satisfaction and perceived value. Subaru, REI, Southwest Airlines, Costco, Zappos, Trader Joe's: customers buy from these companies knowing that everything they purchase is guaranteed to be reasonably priced and of a high quality. They trust that if something goes wrong, the company will work with them to fix the problem. For these companies, 'trust' isn't just a marketing hook – it's an animating value.

None of these brands became beloved institutions overnight. It takes a lot of hard work to gain your buyers' trust. However, once you have, then your ideal customers won't hesitate to buy from you. 'People can spot the inauthentic a mile away', says Daniel Binns. 'You could try and pretend to be something that you're not and don't really believe in. People pick up on it so quickly, and then they lose trust.'[11]

The Edelman PR agency considers trust to be such a vital part of business and governance that for the past 20 years they've commissioned an annual report known as the Edelman Trust Barometer to gauge trust levels around the world. So why such an emphasis on trust?

As Edelman's global strategy director, David Armano naturally spends a good deal of his time thinking about trust. While he acknowledges that in many ways the modern world is marked by widespread distrust, he also sees opportunities for businesses that prove themselves as honest:

> [For] traditional institutions, like government, I think this past year we've seen the highest level of distrust. Now, on the flip side, what's really interesting, is that we've seen an increase [in trust], almost across the board, when it comes to companies . . . with the exception of the tech sector, which used to have much higher levels of trust. . . . In general, we've actually seen a willingness for people to be more trusting of private organizations.

> When you take into consideration what's going on societally . . . there's a lot of distrust in government. But, you also in parallel see at least a willingness to look at alternative sources to help solve a problem, brands being included. What we see here is actually both the responsibility and a really big opportunity for companies to step it up in that space. And that's actually a trend that we've really been following on very closely, and doing work in.[12]

Many other surveys and articles bear this out. In a report by PricewaterhouseCoopers Canada, commissioned on 2018 Canadian holiday shopping trends, researchers found that Millennial and Generation Z customers were more likely to buy from companies whose values they shared and whom they felt like they could trust. Companies looking to appeal to these demographics should take heed of this conclusion from the report: 'As they fight to differentiate themselves in a crowded marketplace, retailers may find brand trust is their most powerful, not-so-secret weapon.'[13]

Like building trust with people in your life, building trust with your customers can take a long time. Some of the country's most trusted brands have been around so long they've spawned urban legends purporting to show how great they are. See: the Nordstrom tire story. According to this story, which dates from the 1980s, one day a Nordstrom customer tried to return a set of snow tires to a Nordstrom location. Despite the fact that the clothing retailer doesn't carry snow tires – or tires of any kind – the clerk gave the man a refund for the price of the goods. In a 1988 interview, Nordstrom representatives told *The Washington Post* the story is apocryphal and they have no record of this incident ever happening. The fact that it's become such an oft-repeated legend just goes to show how willing people are to believe an incredible story about Nordstrom's customer service.

True or not, it's clear that consumers think very highly of the company. Either way, this urban legend is an excellent example of the old axiom that while there's no substitute for consistent excellent service over time, there are strong branding strategies you can employ to help build up credibility with consumers on a more short-term basis.

WHAT'S YOUR PURPOSE?

One promising and increasingly popular strategy is to develop a *brand purpose*. Both established firms and new companies trying to differentiate themselves have found this to be a rewarding approach.

As with the term 'brand', people define 'brand purpose' in different ways. For many companies, brand purpose refers to pursuing some greater social good. Warby Parker's brand purpose is to help disadvantaged people obtain prescription lenses; their Buy a Pair, Give a Pair program helps them fulfill that purpose.

According to Rishad Tobaccowala, this change-the-world approach is especially popular with companies created by Millennials. 'They basically always have a purpose. These brands tend to [first] be very transparent on how they make money. Second, for every product you buy, they give. They also tend to have very strong ESG [environment, sustainability, and/or governance] capabilities.' Essentially, he is saying that 'purpose means you think [about] more than just a commercial transaction'.[14]

That said, for brand purpose to register with customers and for trust to be built, the brand can't just pay lip service to a high-minded mission – it must live the values that it advertises. According to Russ Klein of the American Marketing Association:

> I think that in many cases you're seeing companies and brands inauthentically try to wrap themselves in purpose, so-called purpose, that are nothing more than sort of retrospective, artificial creations that, frankly, can be deceptive. Now, do people favor companies that are more aggressive, or more explicit about their corporate citizenship, and their moral compass? Yes! Those are important too, but I guess my point is that social impact is not a strategy. I believe it is a responsibility.[15]

For others, 'brand purpose' refers to something more abstract: the core of a company's identity or justification for existing in the marketplace. Larry Fink, the founder and CEO of BlackRock, one of the world's largest asset management companies with holdings valued at over $6 trillion,[16] defined his company's stance on purpose in the following way:

Purpose is not a mere tagline or marketing campaign; it is a company's fundamental reason for being – what it does every day to create value for its stakeholders. Purpose is not the sole pursuit of profits but the animating force for achieving them.[17]

Susan Credle, global chief creative officer of advertising firm Foote, Cone, and Belding, offers a similar description. 'A brand purpose is really about knowing why you exist in this world. I think sometimes the brand purpose can be incredibly rational. If I'm a communications company, "Why is this company important to the communication's business?"'[18]

Credle's mention of 'the why' brings to mind the classic 2009 book by Simon Sinek, *Start with Why*, as well as his viral 2011 TEDx Talk, *How Great Leaders Inspire Action*. Because of his unique ability to frame a company's motivations, the former ad agency employee was able to revolutionize thinking in the business world and have a profound impact on the field of marketing. 'Any organization can explain what it does, some can explain how they do it, but very few can clearly articulate why', Sinek writes in *Start with Why*. 'WHY is not money or profit – those are always results. Why does your organization exist? Why does it do the things it does? Why do customers really buy from one company or another?'[19] Helping customers identify a brand's mission, vision, and/or purpose is at the heart of Sinek's *why*.

As Rishad Tobaccowala pointed out, many young or young-ish companies have found their purpose in donating to causes. Their attempt to signal to the world that they care about more than just making money (though of course they – and their investors – care plenty about that too) has helped them define themselves in opposition to the business mentality of previous generations, when simply being successful was considered purpose enough.[20]

From the beginning, the popular skincare startup Glossier has promoted a series of YouTube videos featuring real-life influential customers doing their makeup routines with Glossier products. This '#GetReadyWithMe' effort aligns with the company's mission to 'democratize beauty'.[21] According to the company's 'About' page, 'Glossier, Inc. was founded in 2014 on the belief that beauty isn't built in a boardroom – it happens when you're a part of the process.'[22] Or, as Glossier CEO and founder Emily Weiss said in a 2019 interview, 'Every single person is an influencer.'[23]

Brand purpose isn't just for upstarts. Legacy companies such as Patagonia have come to fully embrace the ethos of purpose. In the spring of 2019, the company sparked a flurry of articles after announcing that it would no longer sell branded apparel to companies unless they were B Corps (companies whose commitment to environmental or social causes meets specific certifiable standards; examples include Ben & Jerry's and Athleta).[24]

Nevertheless, not everyone needs to build their company around a brand purpose, says Tim Calkins, Clinical Professor of Marketing, Kellogg School of Management, Northwestern University. 'Some people say everybody should be out talking about how they're saving the world, and I just don't agree with that at all. I think for some brands it's really important. You take a brand like Patagonia, and purpose is core and fundamental to the brand. But there's lots of other brands [where] purpose really doesn't drive the decision', he says. Calkins uses the example of United Airlines to make his point. 'People fly United because the flight goes at the right time and it's a good price and they usually don't whop you on the head. It's not about purpose in that case.'[25]

Even so, having strong brand purpose can help companies connect better with consumers and differentiate themselves in a crowded marketplace. Many customers want to know that the firms they do business with care about the same things they do. Again, to quote Simon Sinek, 'People don't buy what you do, they buy why you do it.'[26]

BUILDING A BRAND

So far in this chapter, we've explained what a brand is, the importance of building brand trust, and how establishing a brand purpose can help companies stand out in an increasingly socially conscious marketplace. In this section, we'll get back to basics and begin exploring how to build a brand.

It all starts with the *brand value proposition* (BVP). If a brand has a soul, then the brand value proposition lies buried within its inner reaches. The BVP is the catalyst for the consumer's purchase – their reason for buying, or, as Sinek might put it, the customer's *why*. To get better at identifying BVP, take a few moments to analyze your personal buying habits. When you're at the grocery store and thirsty for a nice, cold glass of orange juice, do you reach for the nearest generic product, or do you scour the display case until you find Tropicana? When you're ready for your next smartphone, do you search endlessly online or do you go directly to an Apple store where experts can help you make the right decision? What sorts of products and services delight you and consistently provide a WOW experience? (To learn more about the WOW, see Chapter 5.) Chances are they have a strong brand value proposition. Now, consider how you will offer that to your customers.

A winning BVP requires solid brand trust. Why else would someone pay for something unless they are confident it will deliver exactly what's promised? When you study iconic brands such as Starbucks, Amazon, or American Express, it becomes apparent that their success is the result of many years of high-quality service. Consumers trust that these brands will deliver on their promises. This trust didn't accumulate by accident.

These brands made long-term decisions about how they would win in crowded, highly competitive categories. They determined what they wanted to stand for and geared their internal and external actions to deliver on this, as opposed to creating ad hoc strategies and decisions on the fly. By deeply understanding and responding to the desires of important segments of your target market, an effective BVP can be a real differentiator.

A powerful BVP creates organizational alignment because it offers a simple guiding philosophy that can be shared and understood by all. The BVP drives activities across the firm and can drive messaging architecture. As a result, it becomes much easier to transmit a company's values – and the value they provide – in every internal and external interaction. (For more on creating a winning brand value proposition, see Chapter 10.)

The SWOT Analysis

Another useful business strategy tool is the SWOT (Strengths, Weaknesses, Opportunities, Threats) analysis. Though its exact origins are somewhat unclear, it appears to have developed in the 1960s or 1970s in the world of academic management research. Once regarded primarily as a theoretical exercise, today the SWOT is enjoying new life as a must-use business tool essential to modern companies.

Conducting a SWOT analysis for your brand is straightforward: just evaluate your strengths, weaknesses, opportunities and threats one by one. As simple as this exercise may be, a deep examination of each of these vital aspects of your brand can yield invaluable insights. When's the last time you honestly assessed your brand's weaknesses, or what competitor brands do better than you?

Having conducted SWOT analyses for many different types of businesses, we have found that the key to getting good results is to solicit input from a wide swathe of people across your company. This includes the leadership group as well as the marketing, customer service, product development, HR and IT sectors. Because the marketing department is the engine that drives revenue for the firm, they should manage the process, but a holistic approach is needed to candidly recognize the strengths and weaknesses of your business and identify opportunities for addressing and minimizing threats. Total honesty is the best policy here; employees should be encouraged to put everything on the table and not be shy about weighing in on the company's weaknesses. This is not a task to delegate to your ad agency, but it's not a bad idea to invite them to participate.

The situation analysis you created for your marketing plan should drive the SWOT analysis. In turn, the results you glean from your SWOT analysis should fuel your firm's marketing strategy – it's that important. Treat the 'opportunities' section of the SWOT analysis like a brainstorming session. (For bonus points, consider leveraging the brainstorming process used at the award-winning design company IDEO, which we cover in detail in Chapter 5.) Remember that great ideas can come from anywhere; the old saying 'the best idea is the boss' should prevail during your analysis. (For a deeper dive into conducting a successful SWOT analysis, see Chapter 10.)

Define Your Brand

Defining your brand purpose requires serious reflection. To help clients down this path, Susan Credle advises, 'Interrogate the past, understand the present, and antici-pate the future.' Here's how she broke this process down for us:

> Interrogating the past is really about understanding the essence of the founder's story. Why was this company originally created? What equities have been built? What values have been consistent over time? A true brand purpose will start to emerge. Understanding the present is pretty much where everybody lives in marketing today. Positioning the business for success in the short term.
>
> Anticipating the future is really looking hard at where the business might go. If you're in the car business, 'What's the future of the car business? Is it really a commitment to mobility? Are you actually in the business of data? What does the future look like, and where's this business going to go?' Looking at the past, the present and the future often will lead a company to a clear purpose that people want to wake up and serve every day.[27]

David Armano has also spent a lot of time helping companies identify and activate their purpose. Numerous Edelman surveys have taught him that 'what a company stands for, what a brand stands for' has a significant impact on how many consumers – including Gen Xers and Boomers – engage with those companies.[28] Accordingly, establishing an authentic purpose that aligns with their values (and, of course, those of their custom-ers) should be an important goal for brands. To that end, Edelman's Cultural Purpose Platform tool (see Figure 4.1) is a useful tool to have, offering a detailed guide to creat-ing a relevant purpose and making the most of it.

The following chart from David Armano at Edelman describes the need for brands to develop a cultural purpose platform that can be aligned to an activation process. Begin by determining goals, objectives and KPIs (key performance indicators). Then launch the platform with selected audiences across multiple channels and platforms. Finally, in the activation phase, seek feedback and participation from selected audi-ences to influence iterations of the platform over time.

Figure 4.1   Planning and programming a Cultural Purpose Platform from alignment to activation.

Source: Cultural Purpose Platform Methodology, Edelman and David Armano.

Getting META

Examining how other countries and cultures do things can often provide valuable perspective on prevailing trends in almost any field of expertise. When it comes to branding, this is no less true. One such fascinating development is the META (Maintain, Evolve, Transform, Approach) model, a marketing philosophy developed between Prophet, a global consulting firm, and Alimama, the official marketing platform of the Chinese e-commerce and retail colossus Alibaba.

Historically, Chinese companies haven't prioritized branding. This was because of both Chinese consumer preferences – which have tended to value availability and price above all else – and the companies' interest in maximizing short-term transactions. In the past, the idea of cultivating a brand and differentiating oneself via a strong BVP carried little appeal. However, as the Chinese economy has matured, and more and more highly recognizable global brands have been making inroads into the United States, things have begun to change. The META model was created to help Chinese and global firms better position themselves for long-term success in this rapidly changing ecosystem.

Essentially, META is a rubric for marketing behavior that has been adapted to the distinctive characteristics of the Chinese marketplace. For example, as part of its 'Maintain' category, which relates to maintaining brand positioning, the model dictates that brands must first position themselves in a way that addresses specific local needs. Just being recognizable, or having a reputation for excellence, isn't enough. According to Jay Milliken, a senior partner at Prophet, this model's flexibility is the point: 'It is built as a universal concept applicable for all brands and focuses on *why* and *what* – it does not further go into executional details of *how* in each component – brands need to identify their own ways of transformation instead of using a one-size-fits-all model or process.'[29]

The chart in Figure 4.2 offers a glimpse into how the META model compares to traditional branding models.

The Old Customer Journey

Once you're satisfied with your brand and brand purpose, it's time to start thinking about the *customer journey*. By 'journey', we're not talking about a daring adventure through the Amazon. We're referring to all the interactions a customer has with your brand on their way to a purchase and beyond.

For most of the twentieth century, the customer journey didn't change much. Potential customers either sought out a product they needed or were informed about

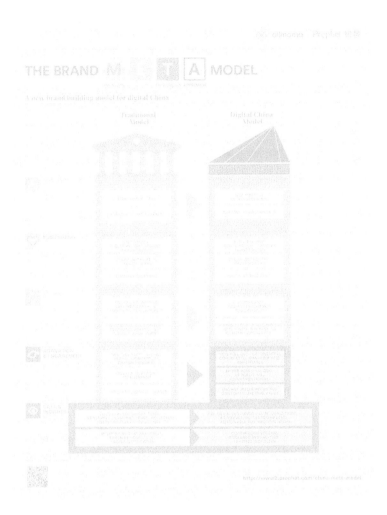

Figure 4.2   The META model, which stands for the Maintain, Evolve and Transform Approach, applies the core components of traditional marketing but changes how these concepts are achieved.

Source: Prophet HK Limited.

a new product via advertising or through the advice of a trusted friend or family member. In the early twenty-first century, however, the tech revolution shifted an enormous amount of commerce and marketing online, disrupting the old order. As we get further into the twenty-first century, this trend has only accelerated. A 2015 article published in Wharton's online business analysis journal states that 'There is one critical tool for successful digital transformation – smart customer journey mapping.'[30]

The AIDA Model

Once upon a time, marketers followed a communication model called AIDA, an acronym that stands for Awareness, Interest, Desire and Action. Meant to describe the different steps customers take on their way to a purchase, this model is still used in many marketing circles today. However, while it may offer a useful starting point for thinking about how customers behave, in certain ways it feels outdated and irrelevant, as it doesn't account for the modern-day customer experience, which has changed drastically over a short period. (For more on the customer experience, see Chapter 5.)

The McKinsey Model

Let's move on to a newer model that was intended to address this vital missing ingredient: the Customer Decision Journey, introduced by McKinsey in 2007. This model represents a leap forward from AIDA, identifying five elements in the customer journey: Consideration, Evaluation, Purchase, Experience and Advocacy. By including customer experience and loyalty (advocacy) as distinctive journey points, this model demonstrates that an excellent customer experience can lead to additional sales (loyalty) and create customers who are advocates for the brand.[31] The McKinsey model offered an important update to the AIDA template.

THE NEW CONSUMER ODYSSEY™

To ensure a consistent brand experience, marketers need to understand brand touchpoints and how they work. Examples of such touchpoints might include a satisfying call with tech support, discovering a helpful mobile app, reading a reassuring fact on a product label, or having a rewarding in-store experience.

Because brands live or die through the connections they make (or don't make), we recommend an approach to branding that counters pervasive *media fragmentation*, to enable you to focus on the most relevant touchpoints for your brand. In our Consumer Odyssey chart (see Figure 4.3), we provide examples of some potential touchpoints and our view of the buyer's journey. This winding road begins with awareness and consideration of products and services, passes through the purchase process, and then moves on to the retention and advocacy stages. As more consumers use new technologies to capture micro-moments throughout their busy days, brands must work to identify the most *relevant touchpoints* where their brands can interact with customers. This chart is not intended to be an exhaustive list of potential touchpoints, but rather a helpful starting point.

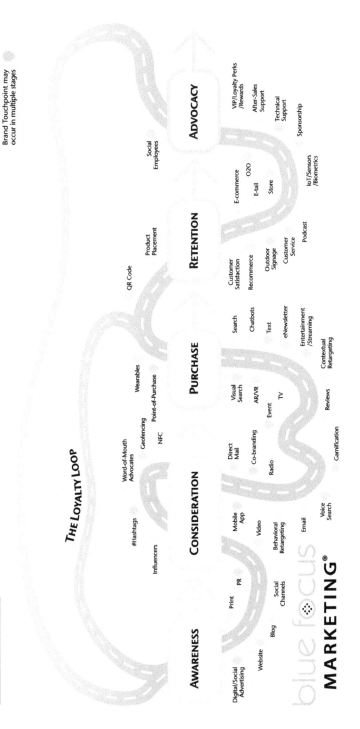

Figure 4.3   Consumer Odyssey™ by Blue Focus Marketing®.

Some observers, like LinkedIn Learning senior director of marketing Blake Buisson, argue that the modern customer journey is actually more of a maze with the purchase at the center. In this scenario, brands solve their customers' problems by enabling them to interact with dozens of brand touchpoints – each of which represents a turn in the right direction – before arriving at the purchasing stage, or end, of the maze.

These touchpoints make use of many forms of media, ranging from traditional to digital. Such a diversity of possible media options, coupled with the consumer's high degree of control over their own journey, makes it a wise strategy to deploy as many social media and digital channels as possible. When it comes to touchpoints, the more the merrier. The goal is to (1) be where your consumers prefer to be, and (2) experiment with a large number of touchpoints and tactics. Blogs, infographics, case studies, web articles, videos, e-newsletters, mobile apps, and more – one or several of these may just grab a potential customer at the opportune moment.

Sidebar

Is the Customer Journey Becoming a Maze?

Most people are familiar with the *funnel model* of marketing. An old standby, it portrays the customer journey as a series of graduated steps that transform potential customers from unaware to converted. The journey begins when the customer is first made aware of the product. After that, you capture their interest. Several steps later, success: they finally make a purchase. The funnel has long been a proven method for converting sales. But how does it hold up in the current world – and how relevant will it be in the years to come?

Blake Buisson of LinkedIn Learning has thought a lot about this. While he continues to see a place for the steps that make up a typical funnel, he feels strongly that the customer journey has become a much less straightforward path. In the digital-first age in which we find ourselves, getting a customer from awareness to purchase may be a long, winding road. 'I still think marketers need to think about a journey', he says. 'I coach my team on seeing the world more as a scatter plot than as a line. And directionally if we can get the most traction where there's the most dots on the framework then we're winning.'[32]

While the shape of the journey has changed, and will surely continue to do so, Buisson suggests not throwing the baby out with the bathwater, so to speak. Right now, there may be thousands of touchpoints for a consumer to interact with, but it's still worth applying the best practices of the past – when opportunities were much more limited – to current conditions. There's a huge spectrum of opportunity, with journeys that are all-funnel at one end, and journeys that are all-chaos at the other. 'When I talk to younger marketers, I'm like, "Hey, look at a funnel. There's truth to it. But then look at this really confusing sort of circuitous maze. There's also truth to that." And the reality is that most customers live in the middle.'[33]

Consumer Odyssey, maze, journey, scatter plot, map, labyrinth – call it what you will. The main point is that it's a new world for both customers and sellers, and companies able to figure out the most seamless way to help customers make their purchase will be best positioned for success.

IBM has been at the forefront of using technology to improve customer journeys. This includes anticipating what a user is searching for through adaptive content, chatbots and call center assistance. By tracking a customer's digital footprint through all of their interactions with a company, IBM is able to use creative software to tailor specific journeys just for them. This process requires 'really creating and shifting a set of skills for marketing into the domain of more technical areas like data, data analytics, [and] data mining', says Katrina Troughton, managing director, IBM Australia/New Zealand.[34]

According to Jodie Sangster, chief marketing officer at IBM Singapore, customer experience will soon be *the* brand differentiator. 'It's not about pushing out a message', she says. 'It's about understanding every single one of those customer touchpoints, how you can then enhance those customer touchpoints to make that customer experience exceptional at every turn.'[35] Based on her extensive experience analyzing customer journeys, she created her own engaging visualization of the process, which she calls the Customer Life Cycle (see Figure 4.4). This diagram also shows how technology and AI can be used at each stage of the customer life cycle to enhance customer experience.

Things aren't any different in the B2B world, either. In 2018 global research and advisory firm Gartner publicized its findings that B2B buyers progress through a series of six "jobs" before coming to a decision: Problem Identification, Solution Exploration, Requirements Building, Supplier Selection, Validation, and Consensus Creation. According to the Gartner press release publicizing these findings, "while nearly every successful B2B purchase progresses through the first four jobs, customers simultaneously address "validation" and "consensus creation" throughout the entire process. In effect, these two jobs are always on, even while customers are working to complete the other four jobs in the process." (For what it's worth, "Gartner research shows that most B2B buyers will revisit nearly every "buying job" at least once before they make a purchase. The result: a customer buying journey that resembles more of a maze than a linear path." Stop us if you've heard this before.) The title of the chart illustrating Gartner's interpretation of the B2B buying journey, reproduced in Figure 4.5, says it all: "A Long, Hard Slog".[36]

A 2016 paper in *The Journal of Marketing*, titled 'Understanding customer experience throughout the customer journey', validates Troughton and Sangster's views about the importance of customer experience: 'Creating a strong customer experience is now a leading management objective. According to a recent study by Accenture (2015; in cooperation with Forrester), improving the customer experience received the most number one rankings when executives were asked about their top priorities for the

Figure 4.4 Customer Life Cycle.

Source: ©Jodie Sangster and Slidemaster.com.

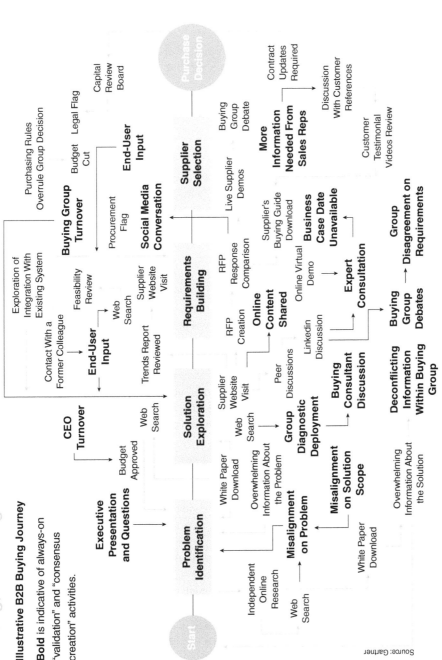

Figure 4.5 Gartner "A Long, Hard Slog," Illustrative B2B Buying Journey.

Source: Gartner Press Release, "Gartner Says the Marketing-to-Sales Handoff Should No Longer Exist," October 9, 2018, https://www.gartner.com/en/newsroom/press-releases/2018-10-09-gartner-says-the-marketing-to-sales-handoff-should-no-longer-exist.

next twelve months.' Additionally, many well-known companies, including KPMG, Amazon and Google, 'now have chief customer experience officers, customer experience vice presidents, or customer experience managers responsible for creating and managing the experience of their customers.'[37]

Future Gaze

Using AI to Create a Better Customer Journey

Engaging potential customers at prime touchpoints can be challenging. But it's important to know when a touchpoint fails. As behavioral analytics become increasingly sophisticated, our understanding of why touchpoints aren't working – or worse, actively thwarting potential sales – is likely to get stronger and arrive more quickly. Powered by AI, these analytics can help you pinpoint choke points or areas where consumers seem to have given up on their journey.

Individual findings can reveal important information regarding improvements you should make. In the future, top-notch data science and advanced software may be able to detect predictive patterns across the entire customer journey. With more and more refined data inputs, AI can and will help tighten a customer journey until its touchpoints are all in the right places and ready to go. A robust, AI-vetted customer journey coupled with a meaningful brand purpose is a powerful combination, and the embodiment of David Edelman's call to use impact measurements to create an optimal connection with your customer. Jodie Sangster believes[38] that 'having AI as your eyes and ears across your digital channel will ensure that your customer experience is seamless'. In many ways, AI is becoming the electricity that energizes our marketing plans.

But how does one get started with AI? (see Figure 4.6). According to Sangster, this is the number one question marketers ask her. 'You should begin as you would with any other customer journey: by mapping out realistic customer steps. After this, scrutinize each step and decide which is likely to yield the highest return on investment (ROI) if enhanced with AI.' Sangster suggests starting small: something that offers 'the quickest win' is more likely to get buy-in from leadership. The point is to begin with a concrete, solvable problem in mind and then figure out the best AI tool to address it, not vice versa.

A natural outcome is that your marketing and tech departments will begin to converge as your goals increasingly align. 'We believe that marketing and marketing professionals need to better understand far more about the technology that is [going to] underpin the future of looking at engagement and customer journeys than they [do] today', warns Katrina Troughton, and it's hard to disagree.[39]

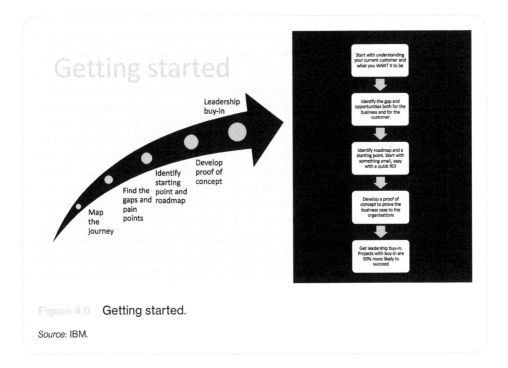

Figure 4.6   Getting started.

Source: IBM.

IN SUMMARY

- A brand is a promise that helps businesses stand out in a competitive world.
- Cultivating a high degree of trust in your brand is difficult but extremely valuable.
- Having an authentic brand purpose is an increasingly vital way to differentiate your brand and add more value than your competitors.
- Brand-building tools such as the SWOT analysis and META model offer helpful ways to build up and evaluate the strength of your brand.
- The customer journey is evolving from a linear purchase-only path into an AI-driven experience that can reach customers at any point.

CHAPTER ANALYSIS QUESTIONS

1. What makes a strong brand – and a weak one?
2. Why have a brand purpose?
3. Why does brand trust matter?
4. What can a SWOT analysis tell us about a brand?
5. How will customer journeys be different in the future?
6. When it comes to customer journeys, what does it mean to describe customers as 'in a maze'?

NOTES

1. *How Great Leaders Inspire Action*. (2009). [video] Directed by S. Sinek. TEDxPuget Sound.
2. YouTube. (2014). *Warby Parker | One Million*. [online] Available at: www.youtube.com/watch?v=a1PTDXOgIF0 [Accessed 1 Jul. 2019].
3. MarketingTech. (2013). [online] Available at: www.marketingtechnews.net/news/2013/jul/17/why-traditional-marketing-theories-dont-apply-to-mobile-apps/ [Accessed 11 Nov. 2019].
4. Binns, D. (2018). Personal communication. [12 Dec.].
5. Klein, R. (2019). Personal communication. [30 April].
6. Randall, K. (2019), personal communication. [8 May].
7. Binns, D. (2018). Personal communication. [12 Dec.].
8. Southwest Airlines. (2019). *Purpose, Vision, Values, and Mission*. [online] Available at: http://investors.southwest.com/our-company/purpose-vision-values-and-mission [Accessed 16 April 2020].
9. Edelman, D. (2018). Personal communication. [16 Dec.].
10. Tobaccowala, R. (2019). Personal communication. [7 March].
11. Binns, D. (2018). Personal communication. [12 Dec.].
12. Armano, D. (2019). Personal communication. [5 April].
13. PwC. (2019). Brand trust: The retailer's not-so-secret weapon. [online] Available at: www.pwc.com/ca/en/industries/retail-consumer/brand-trust.html [Accessed 1 Jul. 2019].
14. Tobaccowala, R. (2019). Personal communication. [7 March].
15. Klein, R. (2019). Personal communication. [30 April].
16. Reuters. (2019). BlackRock profit beats estimates as assets rebound above $6 trillion. [online] Available at: www.reuters.com/article/us-blackrock-results/blackrock-profit-beats-estimates-as-assets-rebound-above-6-trillion-idUSKCN1RS0W0 [Accessed 1 Jul. 2019].
17. BlackRock. (2019). Larry Fink's letter to CEOs. [online] Available at: www.blackrock.com/corporate/investor-relations/larry-fink-ceo-letter [Accessed 1 Jul. 2019].
18. Credle, S. (2019). Personal communication. [13 Dec.].
19. Sinek, S. (2009). *Start with Why*. Portfolio.
20. Tobaccowala, R. (2019). Personal communication. [7 March]
21. Sunnucks, J. (2017). The founder and CEO of Glossier is on a mission to democratize beauty. [online] *Medium*. Available at: https://medium.com/thrive-global/woman-made-emily-weiss-68150ad8c142 [Accessed 2 Jul. 2019].
22. Glossier.com. (2019). What is Glossier – About us. [online] Available at: www.glossier.com/about [Accessed 16 April 2020].
23. YouTube. (2019). *Glossier CEO Emily Weiss on Recode Decode with Kara Swisher at the 92nd Street Y | Full interview*. [online] Available at: www.youtube.com/watch?v=Ud7cuULtfrw [Accessed 1 Jul. 2019].

24. Forbes.com. (2018). The rise of B Corps highlights the emergence of a new way of doing business. [online] Available at: www.forbes.com/sites/michelegiddens/2018/08/03/rise-of-b-corps-highlights-the-emergence-of-a-new-way-of-doing-business/#1feaf50c2ed2 [Accessed 1 Jul. 2019].

25. Calkins, T. (2018). Personal communication. [3 Dec.].

26. Sinek, S. (2019). *How Great Leaders Inspire Action*. [online] Ted.com. Available at: www.ted.com/talks/simon_sinek_how_great_leaders_inspire_action [Accessed 1 Jul. 2019].

27. Credle, S. (2019). Personal communication. [13 Dec].

28. Armano, D. (2019). Personal communication. [5 April].

29. Milliken, J. (2019), personal communication. [06 May].

30. Knowledge@Wharton. (2015). Customer journey mapping – The heart of digital transformation. [online] Available at: https://knowledge.wharton.upenn.edu/article/customer-journey-mapping-is-at-the-heart-of-digital-transformation/ [Accessed 1 Jul. 2019].

31. McKinsey. (2017). Ten years on the consumer decision journey: Where are we today? [online] Available at: www.mckinsey.com/about-us/new-at-mckinsey-blog/ten-years-on-the-consumer-decision-journey-where-are-we-today [Accessed 1 Jul. 2019].

32. Buisson, B. (2019). Personal communication. [5 April].

33. Ibid.

34. Troughton, K. (2019). Personal communication. [8 April].

35. Sangster, J. (2019). Personal communication. [8 April].

36. Gartner Press Release. (2018). Gartner says the marketing-to-sales handoff should no longer exist. [online] Available at: www.gartner.com/en/newsroom/press-releases/2018-10-09-gartner-says-the-marketing-to-sales-handoff-should-no-longer-exist [Accessed 12 Nov. 2019].

37. Lemon, K. and Verhoef, P. (2016). Understanding customer experience throughout the customer journey. *Journal of Marketing*, 80(6), pp. 69–96.

38. Sangster, J. (2019). Personal communication. [8 April].

39. Troughton, K. (2019). Personal communication. [8 April].

PART 2

BUILDING THE CONTENT MARKETING SUPPLY CHAIN

Learning Goals

- Apply the design thinking process to solve problems related to customer experience.
- Analyze the value of WOWing a customer via enhanced customer experience.
- Demonstrate how to identify and address gaps in a desirable customer experience.
- Analyze the power of simplicity in marketing.
- Identify future trends in customer experience.

EXCELLENT customer experience depends entirely on EXCELLENT employee experience! If you want to WOW your customers, FIRST you must WOW those who WOW the customers!

Tom Peters[1]

It was the early 1980s, and Dennis Boyle had a problem to solve.

He was a mechanical engineer working at David Kelley Design, a recently founded Palo Alto product design firm. Apparently, there was a new company in the area named after a fruit and they needed something called a 'mouse'.

The company's name, of course, was Apple. They explained to David Kelley Design what the purpose of a mouse was, and then they asked them to build one for the Apple Lisa computer that could be sold for $10. This would become the first mouse on the commercial market.

The mouse had been invented in the mid-1960s by Stanford Research Institute co-founder and computer pioneer Douglas C. Engelbart. It had three buttons, was housed in a rectangular wooden box, and few people outside of Northern California's nascent computing scene had ever heard of it. 'There wasn't really any commercial mouse out there', remembers Boyle. '[Renowned computing research center] Xerox PARC had an internal mouse, but nobody had made one that was attached to anything that was being sold. So, we had to figure that out from first principles and try to understand how people would use it, and how to make it.'

With little to go on, Boyle and his colleagues looked to one of the few pieces of consumer electronics that had an external navigation device: the Atari video game console. 'We were playing the game from Atari called *Pac-Man* and we were using this big trackball that was on the console. So, we looked at that and how that worked, and we made it really small and flipped it over on its back and put that under a butter dish and moved it around on the table and experimented with how that looked and felt. And that turned into the Apple mouse.'[2]

The mouse Boyle's firm created wound up selling for around $17 – not quite the $10 Apple was targeting, but still a huge bargain compared to the cost of its predecessor. Due in part to the company's efforts, the mouse became an elemental part of computing. Apple – with the help of David Kelley Design – had succeeded in WOWing their customers.

FORM FOLLOWS FUNCTION

As Boyle's experience shows, high-quality design breeds success. It's no coincidence that Apple is currently one of the most highly respected and valuable companies in the world *and* considered a major design innovator. The value of good design applies to so many things apart from computing hardware and personal electronics – or even consumer products. A well-designed sermon will make a greater impression on congregants; a well-designed offensive strategy will help a football team rack up more wins.

Good design helps *WOW* people – that is, impress them so much that they can't help but appreciate you. The concept was first developed by the management guru and author Tom Peters in his 1994 book *The Pursuit of WOW! Every Person's Guide to Topsy-Turvy Times*. In the book, he makes the case for businesses and individuals to differentiate themselves by 'stepping out' and 'standing out' 'from the growing crowd of look-alikes'.[3] His philosophy continues to influence companies to this day. For example, retail giant Zappos's number-one core value is 'Deliver WOW through Service'.[4]

WOW-worthy design is also applicable to marketing. The simpler and more intuitive a retail website, marketing campaign, or content strategy, the greater the chance of a customer being converted. Savvy marketers know that design thinking is as relevant to their work as buyer personas, conversion rates, or social media platforms.

An effectively designed product or marketing campaign doesn't happen by accident. Good design is as much a science as an art, and the technically gifted engineers, artists and writers who bring a vision to life can only take you so far; the vision itself must be sound, or the project won't succeed.

In 1991, David Kelley Design merged with two other Palo Alto design firms to form a company called IDEO. Since its creation, IDEO – where Boyle is a partner and founding employee of David Kelley Design – has won hundreds of design awards and built a legendary reputation in the design world. One reason for this is the talent of their designers: IDEO hires a lot of smart, creative people. However, early on the company realized that raw talent isn't enough to arrive at an intuitive, effective solution. To help harness the collective wisdom of its employees, IDEO relies on a very unique approach.

While popping out bright ideas is easy enough, the trick is to follow certain guidelines. One of the most important is to hold off on judging any idea – no matter how zany it seems – until the end of the session. Every participant should be completely comfortable and willing to express their thoughts, even absurd ones, because the kernel of a good idea might be hiding inside of it. 'You really want to encourage people that anything goes, and to combine ideas that you're seeing in front of you', Boyle says. 'Suggest things that are ridiculous, illegal, or kind of dangerous, just because you want to push the boundaries. You want to encourage this sort of free-for-all, and sort of craziness in these sessions, because sometimes they again lead you to things that can be very useful and kind of outside your normal thoughts.'[5] This is the not-so-secret source of IDEO's success, or, if you will, their wellspring of WOW.

According to Boyle, IDEO's approach can be distilled into seven basic rules:

1. Defer judgment
2. Encourage wild ideas
3. Build on the ideas of others
4. Stay focused on the topic
5. One conversation at a time
6. Be visual
7. Go for quantity

Each guideline reinforces the others. Taken together, they can lead to truly groundbreaking solutions that take into account the most vital customer needs and pain points.

In your approach, Boyle recommends including employees from different parts of the company, not just the marketing division. Each contributor can provide a unique perspective drawn from their individual challenges, sparking insights that wouldn't arise in a more insular environment. Says Boyle, 'Having multidisciplinary teams work on innovation in general is the best way to approach this in our experience, [based on] our forty years of doing this. If you just have one discipline, you tend to have a very constrained and somewhat narrow approach to problem solving.'[6]

ARE YOU EXPERIENCED?

A design isn't exceptional simply because it looks nice or has a catchy slogan. It also has to work. In the end, functionality is king. The user's experience with a product is how they decide whether or not it meets their needs. This is true for physical products as well as digital ones, whether you're producing ski goggles or a website.

Sidebar

From Skype to the Spaghetti Tower Design Challenge

Peter Skillman, the director of UX Design for Amazon AWS, and former director of Skype and Outlook UX Design, has stressed a point about simplicity and a focus on the 'Core Job to Be Done' throughout his career. In 2017, Skype introduced a new feature and core navigation change to its video chatting platform called 'Highlights'. Highlights included Skype's version of the wildly popular Story feature on Snapchat, Instagram and Facebook. And, just like other social media platforms, Skype now allowed users to post and send pictures and videos adorned with stickers and text as the default view when entering the application. While these new features added functionality, they also produced confusion. The Skype interface increased from three to five tabs, and opening the app brought users to a new landing page that auto-loaded Highlights in place of immediate access to the phone dial pad.

Skillman arrived on the team the week it was announced and explains that the reception to these changes was less enthusiastic than the well-intentioned product managers expected. The mobile app store rating went to 1.9 stars out of 5 overnight. 'The core job to be done for Skype is calling and chat, and [the redesign] actually moved the calling tab to a new place, not at the bottom tab bar, but instead to the upper right. People couldn't figure out how to make a call.' In 2018, based on user feedback and some prodding from Skillman, Skype decided to get rid of many of the new features and return to basics. The response was immediately positive. Skype had tinkered with a successful design that perfectly met its users' needs. They had upended WOW. The solution, they found, was to design *less*, not more.

In deciding that this was the best way forward, Skillman employed what he calls the *sitmo* process.

A job to be done is a situation and motivation and an outcome. So I, in short form, always remind myself by saying 'sitmo': situation, motivation, outcome. For example, when I'm trying to create a PowerPoint, I want to include the best images and content so that I can feel proud of this work and communicate more clearly with my peers or the class. So, when you look at creating features, if you always focus on the core job to be done, it results in a different outcome than when you are just thinking about it from a feature standpoint.[7]

This is the essence of good (user-centered) design thinking. As a designer, you must put yourself in the shoes of the end user in order to satisfy them.

Research shows that designing experiences with humans in mind is good strategy. According to Salesforce Research's 2018 State of Marketing report, '84 percent of customers say being treated like a person, not a number, is very important to winning their business'.[8] Promisingly, many companies seem to realize this; the same report stated that '54 percent of high-performing marketing teams lead customer experience initiatives across the business'.[9]

Perhaps Skillman's favorite example of designing for success is the Spaghetti Tower Design Challenge (see Figure 5.1), which he discussed during a TED Talk in 2006. Since then, it has become a well-known parable in the business world. The challenge involves dividing an audience into multiple groups and then asking them to design a tower made out of nothing more than spaghetti, string, tape and one marshmallow. Whichever group creates the highest tower wins. That's it. Over the years Skillman has administered the challenge to audiences around the world, including

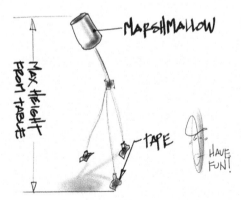

20 pieces of spaghetti
1 meter of tape
One piece of string
One marshmallow
Free standing
18 minutes

Sketch first...
or just start building

Figure 5.1   Peter Skillman's Spaghetti Tower Design Challenge.

Source: Peter Skillman Design peterskillmandesign.com; www.peterskillmandesign.com/#/spaghetti-tower-design-challenge/

(Continued)

CEOs and business school students at top-flight universities. The task sounds simple enough, but here's the rub: kindergartners routinely outperform the worst performing group of all, business school students and CEOs.

There are plenty of fascinating lessons to be mined from Skillman's experiment, but the biggest one may be that, as Skillman says, kindergartners 'don't waste time in status transactions. There's no discussion about who's going to be CEO of Spaghetti Corporation. They just jump in and do it.'[10] So, the next time you're faced with a design challenge, try thinking like a kindergartner. The results may surprise you.

Top five takeaways from the Spaghetti Tower Design Challenge:

- Attending business school (if it reinforces status transactions) won't help you design better.
- Keep your ego in check when brainstorming. Your job title doesn't make your ideas better than someone else's.
- Know when to stop talking and get to work. Even if what you come up with fails, it will fail less next time.
- To find a solution to a design challenge, look to your inner child, not your inner monologue. From John Cage: 'Nothing is a mistake. There's no win and no fail. There's only make.'[11]
- The first designs are rarely best, and the best designs are rarely first.

WHERE WOW MEETS CUSTOMER EXPERIENCE

To build the WOW into your products or services, you must first build it into the very fabric of your organization. That begins with understanding your customer and keeping the customer experience in mind from start to finish. According to Jodie Sangster, chief marketing officer for IBM Singapore, when you focus on the customer experience, you're not focused on pushing a message, but rather on how your customers experience your brand at every touchpoint. The more that experience is dialed in at every touch, the more exceptional the customer experience.[12]

So how do you make each touchpoint truly exceptional? In a word: data. According to Brendan Murray, VP of Enablement Services at the biometric software company iMotions A/S, the better the data, the easier it will be to meet each customer on their own terms. This is important, as no one likes to think of themselves as a 'generic customer' or part of a 'target demographic'. Most of us prefer to think of ourselves as unique people with unique needs – and to an extent, this is true. Therefore, Murray explains, the companies that can deploy technology to measure those individual needs and interests can better serve their customers by creating a personalized customer experience – whether that's a shopping experience, a web experience, or whether it's a direct experience with a product.[13]

Peter Hartzbech, CEO and founder of iMotions, also believes in the importance of zeroing in on how your product or service helps or hinders your customer. 'Ultimately, understanding the consumer experience relies on understanding the whole consumer: what grabs their attention, what connects with them emotionally, what makes them smile, and what do they remember and talk about?'[14]

Because marketers always have an ear to the ground, they are especially well-situated to answer this question. However, they can't create the ideal customer experience in a vacuum. A fully developed customer experience extends to every part of an organization, from product design to customer support. According to researchers Steven Chen, Ray Benedicktus, Yuna Kim and Eric Shih, this means that modern marketers must learn to play a dual role – part product manager and part product designer. Marketers able to occupy this dual role create a competitive advantage for their brand because they understand their product life cycle better, can facilitate communications with designers, and are well-positioned to organize activities that cross over with the design process in unique and useful ways.[15]

However, marketers can't create this WOW factor on their own. According to Katrina Troughton, managing director, IBM Australia/New Zealand, consumers have shifted from a view of products, pricing and features into the world of experience. The results, Troughton explains, is a generation of consumers who vote with their feet – if they have a lousy experience with a brand, they take their business elsewhere. This has created a shift in marketing that has affected the highest levels of the marketing department, with the traditional chief marketing officer morphing into more of a chief customer experience officer role, someone who understands the end-to-end customer experience with a brand.[16]

CUSTOMER CHOREOGRAPHY MAP

To help you visualize how customer experience and the customer journey intersect, we suggest creating a Customer Choreography Map using the following steps:

1. Start by choosing the experience journey that you want to map for your brand.
2. Set your experience journey stages, or moments of truth, at the top of the chart.
3. Map a typical customer's journey in the current state.
4. Now map out the ideal state – the experience journey that you would like all customers to have.
5. Your goal is to identify any gaps between the current state experience journey and your brand's ideal state journey.
6. Determine the cost of fixing these gaps and the potential return on investment in doing so.

The following Customer Choreography Map in Table 5.1 shows what this process looks like in action. Our purpose with this example is to illustrate two different journeys taken by our fictional persona, named Bob: (1) his current, problem-ridden journey; and (2) the journey that he would ideally like to take. By using this process, marketers will understand how to identify any gaps that must be addressed. The goal is to deliver a one-of-a-kind experience to every customer.

All about Bob

Persona: Bob

Age: 36

Status: Married

Occupation: Restaurant manager

Journey: To buy a new smartphone

Bob is unhappy with his current smartphone and cellular plan. He wants a smartphone with all the bells and whistles that comes with a plan that fits his high data usage.

At the moment, though, things aren't going too well for him; he is overwhelmed by choices and unhelpful salespeople. In an ideal state, Bob would be re-energized and guided toward a moment of WOW.

This is where our Customer Choreography Map comes in. Engaging with this simple process makes it easy to both identify the points in Bob's journey where things went wrong and to detect any gaps in his experience. With this information, a company that wants Bob's business will know exactly how to intervene and get closer to him than they are today. Let's get Bob on the path to WOW.

Table 5.1   Moments of Truth in the Customer Choreography Map

Current State

Discover	Evaluate	Buy	Experience	Loyalty
Bob is determined to find a better deal, a better brand, and a better phone. Bob is confused.	Bob visits store A, then store B, to get advice on phones and plans.	Bob goes to store to buy a new phone because the battery on his current phone is dying.	Negative experience from start to finish.	No loyalty benefits with this company. Honeymoon phase with new phone has ended.
Searches online for smartphones.	Sales reps are unfriendly and unhelpful. Long wait time.	Signs a new contract but does not feel confident with his choice. Still overwhelmed.	Unresolved billing issues.	Bob is determined to switch companies as soon as his contract expires.

Current State				
Discover	Evaluate	Buy	Experience	Loyalty
Not tech savvy, becomes confused, frustrated.	Notices high-pressure sales tactics in crowded stores.		Lack of good tech support.	
Overwhelmed by the glut of choices online.	Confused by number of plans and contract terms.		No training available.	

Ideal State				
Discover	Evaluate	Buy	Experience	Loyalty
Bob receives an email from his current carrier notifying him of discounts on phones and upgrades.	Bob follows the brand on Twitter and Facebook to receive additional info, which he retweets to friends in his network.	Bob visits retail store and is excited to buy his new phone.	Bob posts glowing reviews of his positive experience on his social channels.	Bob receives thank-you text and special offers for accessories.
Finds info on the carrier's website and Facebook page helpful.	Sees demos and unboxing videos on YouTube of preferred phone choice.	Receives expert advice in a low-pressure environment.	Store provides both online and in-store training sessions for new features and apps.	Joins robust loyalty program.
Watches YouTube videos posted by enthusiastic customers.	Visits store and finds friendly experts who are available to give helpful advice.	Phones and plans are easily explained.	Carrier website provides helpful product info that reinforces his purchase decision.	Bob writes a positive online review.
Reads reviews and content online to aid his search.		Less stress as the buying process is simplified.		Bob likes brand's Facebook page and tweets his experience.

Sidebar

Rutgers Class Field Trip to IKEA – From Theory to Customer Experience

The more employees are trained to see the world – and their company – through the eyes of their consumers, the better equipped they will be to WOW them. As a final project requirement for the marketing class he teaches at Rutgers University's Master of Business and Science (MBS) program, Mark takes his grad students to

(Continued)

IKEA in Elizabeth, New Jersey. The goal is to get the students to contemplate how design thinking applies in the real world. Few brands are more familiar with smart, human-centered design than IKEA, and an opportunity to get up close and personal with the company has great value. 'A key component of the Master of Business and Science (MBS) degree is experiential learning, and the IKEA trip reinforces the concepts that are discussed in the class', explains Rutgers' MBS program executive director and professor, Dr. Deborah Silver. 'Learning needs to be an active process, whether it is working on a science problem or understanding how marketing concepts are put into practice.'[17]

As Silver sees it, the goal is to train the next generation of individuals to assume key integrator and leadership roles in science-intensive industries. In so doing, Rutgers' MBS program is helping to fuel innovation, accelerate technological discoveries, and translate science-based research into practical applications and consumer offerings that drive economic growth. If a field trip to IKEA gives students a chance to sample some tasty Swedish meatballs in the process, then all the better!

Figure 5.2   Rutgers Master of Business & Science Experiential Marketing class field trip to IKEA, Elizabeth, NJ (4 April 2019).

Source: Photo by authors.

SIMPLICITY SELLS

Quick: What do Netflix, ALDI and Google all have in common? Well, aside from hundreds of thousands of employees and household-name status, they keep things simple. So simple, in fact, that in 2018 they were recognized as the top three performers in the Siegel+Gale brand consultancy's annual World's Simplest Brands ranking. After surveying more than 15,000 people in the US, Europe, Asia, India and the Middle East, Siegel+Gale announced the survey results along with some eye-opening findings about the benefits of simplicity. One particularly impressive statistic found that 'companies that fail to provide simple experiences leave an estimated share of $98 billion on the table'.[18]

If you were to ask most people what services these three companies provide, it's a good bet that they could tell you in a sentence or two. They have mastered their elevator pitches. How many of us can say that about our own companies?

At its core, design thinking is all about taking a human-centric approach to technology and business. Any feature you add should serve the end user in a completely obvious way; if it doesn't, it's time to get rid of it.

'There is no real downside to simplicity, as long as brand experiences align within the category', says Howard Belk, co-CEO and chief creative officer of Siegel+Gale. Belk continues:

> Historically, regulated and complicated industries like banking, insurance, and healthcare were prime candidates for simplification. Our latest studies show opportunities for many more categories to grow by simplifying brand experiences while delivering trusted services to consumers. Simplicity is not an either/or proposition, and there is proof that the winners are the ones who simplify services and experiences as a competitive differentiator, regardless of their business category.[19]

While it is true that there isn't much downside to simplicity, there is most decidedly a downside to needless complication. Consider the Juicero juicer, which offers a notorious example of simplicity and design thinking gone wrong. Released in 2016 amid much fanfare (and $120 million worth of venture capital backing), the $699 juicer came equipped with WiFi, specially engineered packets of pureed fruits and vegetables, a camera sensor to detect each packet's freshness, and a motor powerful enough to apply 8,000 pounds of force to them. A year after the juicer's launch, reporters from *Bloomberg* recorded a one-minute video that demonstrated that the packets could be crushed quite easily by human hands without the assistance of any expensive proprietary hardware. The video perfectly encapsulated the mounting criticism of the brand, and unable to shake off the growing chorus of bad publicity and consumer indifference, Juicero dissolved shortly afterward.[20]

The media and major tech blogs couldn't get enough of the story, offering head-lines such as 'The Parable of Juicero: A Tech Lesson for 2017' (The Ringer); 'The Juicero is an impressive piece of over-engineered hardware' (Boing Boing); 'Juicero teardown reveals the secrets of a wildly over-engineered juicer' (The Verge); and 'The Very Serious Lessons of Juicero' (*The Atlantic*). The product became a punchline that seemed to reflect all that was wrong with the tech world, wellness culture, and design for the sake of design.

Does a juicer really need WiFi? Just because it's *possible* to do something, does that mean that you *should*? Had the Juicero team reflected on Skillman's sitmo process, maybe they would have come up with a vastly different product or abandoned their flawed idea much sooner. No customer was WOWed by Juicero.

Fortunately, many brands seem to be learning that simplicity sells. A good example of this positive trend can be found in the world of consumer electronics. For a long time, devices were being offered with increasingly complicated user interfaces that didn't make much sense to most people. (Remember the old joke about how difficult it is to set the clock on a VCR? We do.) With the arrival of smartphones and tablets, however, competition to create more intuitive interfaces began to flourish. Now users can do just about anything with the tap of a single button or the swipe of a finger. The lesson? Sometimes sophistication isn't about adding more, but rather the opposite.

PillPack offers another instructive example. The company, which bundles custom-ers' daily prescriptions into sealed, single-serve packets, started in 2014. Boyle explains that PillPack was born from a troublesome problem. 'There are fifty to sixty million people in the United States that are on five or more medications. It's just a giant hair-ball of a problem, because you have this big bag of pill bottles and some are full, and some are half full and some are not full. It always ends up that way.'

Historically, customers would come up with their own workaround for this prob-lem, or they would buy one of those refillable seven-day slotted pill box trays and fill them up with their daily doses. These systems worked to an extent, but they were also accident-prone. Says Boyle, 'It's just a huge challenge for patients to stay on and take what they are supposed to when they're supposed to take it.'

With PillPack, the team at IDEO set out to make it easier for consumers to juggle their multiple medications. However, they didn't arrive at a solution overnight. 'There was this big attempt to make a better pill bottle, or combining these pill bottles', Boyle says. However, they realized that such a product wouldn't really solve the problem. It would just make customers work to keep their medications straight in a different way.

Eventually, the team took the project in a different direction and began consider-ing what it would look like to create an online pharmacy. They began looking at every aspect of the pharmacy experience – how the pill bottles looked, how physicians would fill prescriptions, and how patients would interact with that process. Then, instead of looking at customer fulfilment in the context of one prescription at a time, they began looking at all of the customer's prescriptions. 'What would be the physical embodiment?' Boyle says. 'What would we get every week, every two weeks, what would that look like, and feel like, and how would that work?'[21]

On the face of it, this value proposition is quite modest: to make medication-taking more convenient and accurate. But the practical and health consequences are enormous. Instead of fumbling around with various pill bottles each day, all a PillPack customer has to do is take what's in the packet, eliminating the risk of improper dosage. Now *that* deserves a hearty WOW.

PillPack is a perfect synthesis of integrated design thinking, user-experience focus, and building simplicity right into the product. Instead of trying to take something that already exists and add lots of needless bells and whistles, they focused intently on solving a common problem in the most straightforward way possible. For their efforts, the company was acquired by Amazon in 2018 for just under a $1 billion.[22]

Future Gaze

By Katrina Troughton, Managing Director, IBM Australia/New Zealand

Marketing isn't what it used to be. From data to AI to agile workflows, digital transformations are redefining what it means to be a modern marketer. All of which come together to create an ever-better customer experience. Customer expectations have changed – today, brand loyalty is won or lost by a single click or even an extra second. If you want to compete in this rapid digital world, you need to make your customers happy. Constantly. At IBM we help clients succeed in the data-driven economy and gain insights from both structured and unstructured data for better decision-making.

Marketing professionals tasked with designing differentiated experiences aren't competing with their industry competitors anymore. They're competing with Instagram, Lyft, and Netflix. Brands are fighting for attention against the best digital experience customers have ever had. The 'last best' shapes expectations.

As Maya Angelou said,[23] 'I've learned that people will forget what you said, people will forget what you did, but people will never forget how you made them feel.' While there are many trends, let me dive into the top three that I believe are going to drive future marketing innovation.

Innovation is Driving Rapid Change

The accelerated pace of technological innovation is driving rapid change in not just the skills that a marketer needs to invest in but also rethink the traditional hiring and

(Continued)

working model. Marketing programs will need to invest in new skills – both technical and soft – in order to level up their talent, which is key to maintaining the best customer experiences. Winning marketing structures will see the merging of design, data, engineering, product, and marketing teams into a variety of new structures, in addition to customer experience and sales teams – a cross-disciplinary marketers' function that can support a growing ecosystem of purpose-built marketing tools to match the uniqueness of every business model and customer base.

AI is no longer simply artificial intelligence but also augmented intelligence. Increasingly, humans will complement machine learning. According to recent findings published in World Economic Forum's *Future of Jobs* report[24], the value of soft skills like critical thinking [is] likely to increase as technology and automation continue to advance.

Using Tech to Deepen Personalization

From one-to-one to even deeper personalization, the marketer of today has to be able to sift through massive amounts of data and create actionable insights. The average marketing team uses over ninety marketing tools in their stack, leaving customer profiles and experiences fragmented. AI- and machine learning-based marketing tools will completely change the nature of how marketers make decisions and deploy campaigns. AI-based systems will make personalization easier for marketers by learning from every interaction and delivering the right content in the proper context of the customer's previous interactions with the brand.

Let's take a scenario – a marketer will receive an SMS alert from a marketing automation tool notifying him or her that a sizable number of customers are predicted to not renew their memberships in the next ninety days. The marketer will then produce multichannel content and campaigns that will be personalized by AI-powered tools with specific offers and content that are optimized in real time across each channel the customer engages in.

Now imagine a popular retail outlet, AI takes the in-store, one-to-one level of service and puts it online – the customer will now be at the center of every retail experience. It then personalizes shopping to unprecedented levels by allowing brands to tailor their content based on factors like the weather, favorite colors, buying trends, past purchases, and so much more. This personalization begins with the initial campaign and can go on to ensure that the products you see are never out of stock and arrive on a customer's doorstep at exactly the right time.

Establishing Trust through Data Management

Lastly, it's about establishing trust with our clients by responsibly managing their most valuable data. Data presents both an opportunity and a challenge because, while customers want personalized experiences, there's also the paradox of these same customers not wanting to share the personal information that would easily facilitate those experiences. At IBM, we believe that our clients' data is their data, and their insights are their insights. Marketers will need to reassess their marketing strategies and tools to account for every customer touchpoint and apply a set of ethical and market-accepted standards as a key measure alongside every action. This will help enterprises build an authentic brand and develop deeper customer loyalty.

The ultimate goal is to transcend a business's day-to-day transactions and transform the relationship between customer and business with an exchange of secured and trusted data that allows for deeper personalization of content from marketers to buyers and vice versa. I believe that marketers who take advantage of this will stay competitive by setting the tone of the conversation as the leaders of tomorrow.

CHAPTER ANALYSIS QUESTIONS

1. What is the purpose of design for customers? For marketers?
2. Why aren't good ideas enough to bring success?
3. How can identifying gaps in the customer's experience journey lead to change?
4. What is the value of simplicity?
5. How will the customer experience be different in the future?

NOTES

1. Peters, T. (2018). *The Excellence Dividend: Meeting the Tech Tide with Work That Wows and Jobs That Last.* Knopf Doubleday Publishing Group, p. 208.
2. Boyle, D. (2019). Personal communication. [6 March].
3. Peters, T. (1994). *The Pursuit of Wow! Every Person's Guide to Topsy-Turvy Times.* Penguin Random House, p. xi.
4. Christoffersen, T. (2019). Our common core: Deliver WOW through service. [online] Zappos.com. Available at: www.zappos.com/about/core-values-one [Accessed 26 Apr. 2019].
5. Boyle, D. (2019). Personal communication. [6 March].
6. Ibid.
7. Skillman, P. (2019). Personal communication. [10 March].
8. Salesforce.com. (2020). Customer expectations hit all-time highs. [online] Available at: www.salesforce.com/research/customer-expectations/# [Accessed 8 Jan. 2020].
9. Salesforce.com. (2018). Introducing the 5th salesforce state of marketing report: Here are the top trends redefining the profession. [online] Available at: www.salesforce.com/blog/2018/12/introducing-fifth-state-of-marketing-report.html [Accessed 8 Jan. 2020].

10. YouTube. (2019). *Peter Skillman Marshmallow Design Challenge.* [online] Available at: www. youtube.com/watch?v=1p5sBzMtB3Q [Accessed 26 Apr. 2019].

11. Gotham Writers. (2019). Tips from the masters. [online] Available at: www.writingclasses. com/toolbox/tips-masters/john-cage-ten-rules-for-students-and-teachers [Accessed 5 Dec. 2019].

12. Sangster, J. (2019). Personal communication. [14 Apr].

13. Murray, B. (2019). Personal communication. [22 March].

14. Hartzbech, P. (2019). Personal communication. [19 Jan.].

15. Chen, S., Benedicktus, R., Kim, Y. and Shih, E. (2018). Teaching design thinking in marketing: Linking product design and marketing strategy in a product development class. *Journal of Marketing Education*, 40(3), pp. 176–187.

16. Troughton, K. (2019). Personal communication. [25 March].

17. Silver, D. (2019). Personal communication. [8 Apr].

18. Muldoon, M. (2018). Netflix revealed as world's simplest brand. [online] Siegel+Gale. Available at: www.siegelgale.com/netflix-revealed-worlds-simplest-brand-according-annual-study-siegelgale/ [Accessed 26 Apr. 2019].

19. Belk, H. (2019). Personal communication. [3 Apr].

20. Nicholson, D. and Baker, H. (2017). Do you need a $400 juicer? [online] Bloomberg.com. Available at: www.bloomberg.com/news/videos/2017-04-18/do-you-need-a-400-juicer-video [Accessed 26 Apr. 2019].

21. Boyle, D. (2019). Personal communication. [6 March].

22. Lunden, I. (2019). Amazon buys PillPack, an online pharmacy, for just under $1B. [online] TechCrunch. Available at: https://techcrunch.com/2018/06/28/amazon-buys-pillpack-an-online-pharmacy-that-was-rumored-to-be-talking-to-walmart/ [Accessed 26 Apr. 2019].

23. Gallo, C. (2014). The Maya Angelou Quote That Will Radically Improve Your Business. [online] Available at: www.forbes.com/sites/carminegallo/2014/05/31/the-maya-angelou-quote-that-will-radically-improve-your-business/#39f11979118b [Accessed 16 April 2020].

24. Future of Jobs 2018. (2019). Workforce trends and strategies for the fourth industrial revolution. [online] Available at: http://reports.weforum.org/future-of-jobs-2018/workforce-trends-and-strategies-for-the-fourth-industrial-revolution/ [Accessed 26 Apr. 2019].

6

WINNING WITH CONTENT MARKETING AND STORYTELLING

Learning Goals

- Analyze how the power of storytelling can magnify your content strategy.
- Create a content marketing framework to develop engaging content.
- Demonstrate best practices for building an effective content strategy.
- Understand why brands should harness the power of video.
- Analyze how AI can be used to enhance your marketing impact.

Marketing is no longer about the stuff that you make but about the stories you tell.

Seth Godin[1]

Humans, it seems, are hardwired for stories. After eating, drinking and sleeping, storytelling may very well be the next most important human need. Why else would we go see the same paint-by-numbers action movies or romantic comedies over and over and over again? The characters, actors and locations may change, but the basic theme remains the same. Ditto your favorite country, rock, or pop songs.

It's no coincidence that the most long-lasting and influential written works are stories. *The Epic of Gilgamesh* describes the tale of a man desperately searching for meaning and eternal life. It dates from ancient Mesopotamia, circa 2000 BC, but it could just as easily describe the plot of a critically acclaimed new TV drama.

The most influential stories were more than just entertainment, however – they were intended to teach their listeners something. *Beowulf*, the Bible, the Bhagavad Gita, the Koran: none of these texts are simply a list of rules or demands. They are all books of stories, highlighting their lessons through parables, anecdotes, depictions of what to do (and what not do to) and case studies.

In 2010, we spoke about the power of storytelling with Fred Burt, a former managing director of Siegel+Gale. 'There's almost a cinematic quality [in *Beowulf*]', Burt said from London, his voice transmitting excitement across our international phone connection. His enthusiasm for the world's most famous medieval epic poem could not be contained. 'Grendel is swooping across the marshes, absolutely incandescent with rage against mankind. And then, the camera shifts.' Pausing momentarily, Burt resumed his lesson with a chuckle. 'A whole load of drunken Danes are swilling mead and thinking that the world is a great place. Then, again, it switches back to Grendel, as the monster gets closer and closer . . .' Even if you haven't read *Beowulf*, you can probably guess what happens next – though a well-told story will play up that moment for every ounce of suspense it can get.

Burt noted that the poem, which extols the virtues of self-sacrifice and heroism through a demonstration of good conduct, offered a crucial bridge between older folkways and the world we know now – a world in which symbols, letters and logos transmit meaning, and, with it, preferences and loyalty.[2] It had to have resonated with listeners, since it began as an oral poem, transmitted from generation to generation until, eventually, someone decided to write it down.

Simply put, good stories were 'sticky' long before the term was coined. And the very best stories transcend the confines of their intended audience. The world is a very different place than it was when *Beowulf* was recorded.

You don't have to be a medieval Dane to appreciate *Beowulf*'s tale of heroism, just as you don't have to be a practicing Christian to appreciate the Parable of the Prodigal Son. You just have to be human.

STORIES MAKE THE WORLD GO ROUND

Everything has a story it projects to the world – every country, every product, every person, every politician, every brand. There are no exceptions. A story is the difference between champagne and sparkling white wine, Xerox and photocopiers, Tiger Woods and pro golfers, the Real McCoy and its imitators.

A brand, then, might be best thought of as a condensed story that instantly transmits to consumers what they can expect. Take a moment to think about a few of the biggest, most well-known brands in the world. What ideas come to mind when you think of them? Tradition, consistency, value, fun? Or, conversely, cheapness, low quality, irrelevance? Whatever brand you think of, your perspective has undoubtedly been shaped by how the brand has conveyed its story, for better or for worse.

Coca-Cola and Budweiser are two of the best examples of brands with a compelling story to tell. Through cultivating a consistent, focused message, each company has come to be associated with certain positive stories and feelings. In a 2018 interview with the Content Marketing Institute, Kate Santore, a senior content marketing manager at Coca-Cola, explained what guides her efforts. 'At Coca-Cola, we want to create Coca-Cola stories and not stories by Coca-Cola. . . . If you read a script or even partner-created content and say to yourself, "Can I tell this story without Coca-Cola?" and the answer is yes, then it's not a Coca-Cola story.'[3]

Santore's focus on creating not just a story, but a *Coca-Cola story*, underscores a fundamental truth: telling a story may appear to be a simple matter, but the most memorable ones are the product of hard work and deliberate planning. Each successful story has a unity to it that requires careful thought and a laser-like focus on making its message clear. As Santore puts it, 'A story is a thread that connects all of the events. Sometimes that thread is long, like a film; or sometimes it is short, like a Tweet; or sometimes it's really tangled, like *Game of Thrones*, but it always connects.'[4]

The best tales tell what the veteran marketing strategist David Aaker calls a 'signature story'. Aaker, who is frequently referred to as 'the father of modern branding', believes so strongly in the power of stories and their marketing value he devoted an entire book – 2018's *Creating Signature Stories* – to the topic.

'A story is not a description of a set of facts (or features)', explains Aaker. Rather, a signature story 'is an intriguing, authentic, involving narrative that delivers or supports a strategic message clarifying or enhancing the brand vision, customer relationship, organizational values and/or business strategy. It provides visibility and energy to brands and persuades and/or inspires employees and/or customers over an extended time.'[5] Creating a signature story is a long-term, ongoing process. A signature story can't be conjured out of thin air, and it can't appear overnight. Consumers are increasingly savvy – and cynical – and will readily (and happily) sniff out fakes.

THE BEST STORIES TAP INTO EMOTION

Budweiser offers an instructive example of a signature story. Think about its famous Clydesdales, the strong, noble-looking equines that have appeared in so many of the company's annual holiday commercials and Super Bowl ads. At first glance, Scottish-bred draft horses might seem to have little relationship to malted beverages. But it's through the Clydesdales that Budweiser can tell its most compelling story.

The Budweiser Clydesdales have been around since 1933, when, according to Anheuser-Busch lore, August A. Busch Sr received a six-horse Clydesdale hitch from his sons to celebrate the repeal of prohibition.[6] Over the years, the handsome, strong, mission-oriented horses became a desirable metaphor for the Budweiser brand, and the company's marketing team prudently seized on this inspiring association. 'The Clydesdales are a great example of how a symbol can be the vehicle to help create a story and to keep it alive', says Aaker.[7]

As Aaker implies, it's not enough to just have any old story – you need to have one that says something. *The Epic of Gilgamesh, Beowulf* and the Bible haven't survived all these years just for their interesting plot turns – but because they tell us something important and provoke a deep response from us. They stoke our emotions.

This is no less true for brands. Budweiser has just a few (very expensive) TV moments to make a lasting impression on millions of viewers and convince them to purchase Budweiser products. Faced with this momentous task, they have brought out the Clydesdales. 'For Budweiser, the Clydesdales provide a symbol that is likable, masculine, loyal and a link to the brand's heritage', writes Aaker.[8]

Aaker is right, but Budweiser didn't make this choice on a hunch. Like all the best brands, Budweiser understands that customers who develop an emotional connection to brands are significantly more willing to purchase products or services from them and to consider factors beyond price.

START WITH THE WHY

'People don't buy what you do. They buy *why* you do it', explains noted thought leader Simon Sinek in one of the most-watched TED Talks of all time: *How Great Leaders Inspire Action.*[9] Sinek, a former ad agency employee and bestselling author of *Start with Why*, argues that the world's most successful brands build the question of *why* into every piece of marketing content they create. Apple dares customers and employees to 'think different'. IBM enlists stakeholders to create a 'smarter planet'. Mastercard provides the keys to 'priceless' moments that customers can cherish forever.

To put the *why* front and center, follow what Sinek calls 'The Golden Circle':

1. Start with the *why*.
2. Follow with the *how*.
3. Drive it home with the *what*.

This way, the hard task of developing an all-important emotional connection comes first. To figure out your *why*, Sinek says you should ask yourselves these questions:

- What's your purpose?
- What's your cause?
- What's your belief?
- Why does your organization exist?
- Why do you get out of bed in the morning?
- Why should anyone care?[10]

Once you figure out these answers, you can figure out your *why*. Knowing this is critical for telling your signature story.

'When a story is well told, [people] are able to feel connected, not just to the story, but to the storyteller', says Stanford Business School professor Jennifer Aaker (and daughter of David Aaker). 'When most of us think of advocating for ideas, we go to statistics. We go to convincing arguments, facts, and figures, but studies show that if we share a story, people are more likely to remember the message, be persuaded by it, [and] feel personally connected to it.'[11]

HOW CAN MARKETERS CREATE SIGNATURE STORIES?

When it comes to effective storytelling, it's increasingly clear that traditional advertising methods no longer cut it. Numerous studies have concluded that trust in traditional advertising has declined considerably in the twenty-first century. (To be fair, trust in general has also declined broadly across the United States.[12]) According to a 2018 survey conducted by the Havas advertising and PR agency, 74% of respondents said they wouldn't care if brands disappeared altogether.[13]

For better or for worse, the modern consumer feels more than empowered to voice their discontent. As easy as it is for someone to sing the praises of a brand, consumers are perhaps even more willing to share their negative experiences with those same online communities. Unfortunately for the brands on the receiving end, those negative messages tend to gain traction much more quickly than the positive ones. If all of this isn't enough to keep ad execs up at night, we don't know what else will.

While these numbers may be alarming, they're also deeply instructive. What they reveal is that the old ways have failed to keep up with the values of the current marketplace. Gone are the days when companies could simply wow their customers with stats and figures and then watch the sales roll in. 'Consumers can smell a sales pitch a mile away', concluded NewsCred Insight reporter Dawn Papandrea, citing a report by the Economist Group that found that 71% of respondents were turned off by content that seemed like a sales pitch.[14] Add to these dismal statistics, ever-evolving viewing habits and the rise of savvy, suspicious Millennial consumers, and it becomes clearer and clearer that the old ways will no longer work.

There is clearly a crisis of confidence in the advertising world. So what can we as marketers do?

WHAT IS CONTENT MARKETING?

Allow us to introduce content marketing. Simply put, content marketing is about sharing helpful information rather than pitching. Content marketing isn't a monologue – it's a dialogue. It's about interacting with buyers and helping to solve their problems. It's authentic. Great content fuels marketers' efforts to reach and engage buyers at every stage in the buying process, whether that content is a helpful how-to video, a sleek infographic, or a well-crafted blog post. It's not a hard sell.

Done right, content marketing can be a hugely important weapon in your marketing arsenal. Deliberate, high-quality content can help build a brand's signature story and attract consumers. As such, it has become the new currency of brand engagement in the modern marketplace – and one of the hottest topics on the minds of B2C and B2B marketers alike. At the center of an effective content marketing strategy, as David Aaker explains, is your brand's signature story: 'content is king in the digital age, and stories are the key to content', says Aaker.[15]

Let's talk a little more about definitions. In Chapter 1, we provided some common definitions for marketing. One is that 'marketing is a combination of art and science to achieve your business results'. The premise is that a brand can be outstanding on the scientific side (i.e. with analytics and measurement), but if the creative or artistic side isn't powerful, all the analytics in the world won't produce positive business results. The brand will fail.

This brings us to the definition of content marketing. Any web search will bring you multiple definitions of content marketing, but the most commonly cited comes from the Content Marketing Institute:

> Content marketing is a strategic marketing approach focused on creating and distributing valuable, relevant, and consistent content to attract and retain a clearly defined audience – and, ultimately, to drive profitable customer action.[16]

At Blue Focus Marketing®, we define content marketing as the creation and distribution of content across all relevant touchpoints to the right person at the right time and place. For content marketing to be successful, you must determine your audiences' media consumption habits and then create compelling content to meet or exceed their information needs.

What exactly do we mean by 'content'? In the broadest terms, we use the term 'content' to signify any media asset – whether traditional or digital – that is used in service of your organization or brand to provide value to your target audience. Examples include:

- How-to guides
- Magazines
- Blog posts
- Videos/commercials
- Newsletters
- Articles
- Interviews
- Podcasts

Perhaps the most exciting thing about content marketing is just how much it's driven by creativity. In fact, there is perhaps no other aspect of marketing that has as much potential for leveraging creativity than content marketing. The more creative your content and story, the more likely you are to reach and engage target buyer personas.

BUILDING AN EFFECTIVE CONTENT MARKETING STRATEGY

Though more and more companies are adopting content marketing strategies, the concept itself has actually been around for a while. In fact, chances are you've come across content marketing at some point and never realized what it was. American Express, for instance, published both *Travel + Leisure* and *Food & Wine* magazines, until selling them to 2013 to Time Inc. Though American Express is obviously a credit card company, they clearly saw a benefit in inspiring affluent consumers to travel and patronize high-end restaurants (and, presumably, use American Express cards while doing so).

This is the same rationale behind *MEL Magazine*, the quirky online men's magazine created by Dollar Shave Club, the shaving accessories startup founded in 2012 and then sold to Unilever for $1 billion five years later. What does a magazine have to do with razors? By publishing interesting features about 'sex, relationships, health, money, work, and culture from a male point of view',[17] *MEL* attracts the exact target audience Dollar Shave Club is trying to reach. In fact, Dollar Shave Club's content marketing efforts have gone way beyond just a magazine, which is no inexpensive endeavor. 'For [its] three million-plus customers . . . Dollar Shave Club is continually seeking ways to engage them with more than just sales pitches', writes *Entrepreneur* reporter Jaclyn Trop in a 2017 feature on company founder Michael Dubin. 'It has hired writers and editors to create *MEL*, an online men's lifestyle magazine; a funny pamphlet called "Bathroom Minutes," which comes in every delivery; and the company's podcast, which tackles topics such as "Why Is Everyone on the Internet So Angry?" and "Which Body Parts Can You Actually Grow Back?"'[18]

What story is Dollar Shave Club conveying through its various content channels? That it's a hip, funny, interesting brand that gets the modern man (well, at least those on the younger side). The critical point here is that the company's efforts are 'more than just sales pitches', as Trop put it. Content marketing is a long game.

'When candidate stories emerge, make sure that they are not just a list of facts (or features, data, or lists) but, rather, a narrative that appears intriguing, is perceived as authentic, engenders involvement, and has a strategy message', advise David and Jennifer Aaker. 'And make sure that it is managed like the asset it is.'[19]

BEST PRACTICES FOR PRODUCING HIGH-QUALITY CONTENT

Good content marketing demands a clear strategy. The content that you offer can't be random. Everything you put out must bolster your story in some way, even if the connection is indirect, as it is with Dollar Shave Club. An outdoor retailer such as REI, for example, might offer camping tips, interviews with accomplished rock climbers, or an article about the best places to cross-country ski. Whatever content you choose, you must ensure it aligns with your goals and inspires consumers to think of your company when they have a problem that needs to be solved. Deliberation is key.

It also, unsurprisingly, demands high quality. Poor-quality content can backfire and leave potential customers turned off. Content that could be perceived as offensive, condescending, or overly salesy is a recipe for lost customers. Today's consumers want helpful, easy-to-understand content – and they want it on their terms. If they sense you're just pitching your product and not adding value, they'll happily take their business somewhere else.

To get a more concrete sense of what successful content marketing looks like, it's worth examining some of the companies that are producing the world's best content. And there's no better place to look than at the winners of the 2018 NewsCred Top 50, an annual award given to 'companies [that] represent the best of content marketing today'.[20] Winners cut across categories and include insurance companies, tech firms, clothing retailers, car manufacturers, and more. Whatever they offer, their content has many things in common, including the following.

Arresting Visuals

Not every company can afford to fly a film crew out to Alaska and the Rockies, as Land Rover does as part of its Land Rover Stories, a documentary-style chronicle of travelling via Land Rover through some of North America's most stunning landscapes. But professional-looking video or photography and a smart-looking website make your brand shine and help catch a customer's eye.

A Challenge

Nike's Breaking2 campaign followed around a group of the world's fastest marathoners as they attempted to break the two-hour mark in a controlled race. It culminated in an event streamed live to 13 million viewers – all of whom got to see the shoe Nike created for the race, the Vaporfly Elite, up close and personal. (The winner missed the record by 25 seconds.) Visit Seattle, the Washington State city's tourism agency, recruited five filmmakers to make short features about the city as part of its 'Project Five by Five'. In a fun twist to the project, each filmmaker was tasked with chronicling the Emerald City in relation to one of the five senses, since, after all, challenges or directed tasks incite creativity – and crank up dramatic tension. Either way, they're a great way to get a viewer/reader/customer hooked.

Practical Advice

Fidelity, IKEA and the New York-based cosmetics startup Glossier may not seem to have much in common. But they all demonstrated a commitment to providing their customers and potential customers with tips and tricks to improve their lives. Fidelity's MyMoney blog and the IKEA Ideas blog were designed to educate consumers on finance and home decor, while Glossier launched a YouTube series showcasing morning makeup routines. If you can be useful to your buyers, they won't forget it.

A Personal Touch

Many of the content campaigns that made the Top 50 focus on just a few people, or a group of people, to tell a larger story. For instance, to call attention to its commitment to hiring more women in tech positions, GE created a fake ad that aired during the Oscars speculating what life would be like if scientist Millie Dresselhaus 'was treated like a celebrity'. The best content feels authentic and human, like it was created by people, for people, not by a big, faceless corporation.

A Good Story

Stop us if you've heard this one before, but it bears repeating: all of the content offerings in Top 50 campaigns expertly align with each company's story. Whether selling insurance, computers, or financial products, every company in the Top 50 is well aware of the message they want to convey to potential consumers, and they have crafted their content to reinforce it.[21]

THE SEVEN-STEP CONTENT MARKETING STRATEGY BLUEPRINT

You can have the best content in the world, but if you don't have a plan to properly execute it, you'll run into trouble. Fact is, great content marketing requires coordination. Juggling the various moving parts of a successful content marketing campaign takes effort, and there's always a risk that things can spiral out of control, resulting in an incoherent or ineffective message that fails to grab customers' attention.

After years of creating our own content and working with clients, Blue Focus Marketing® developed our Seven-Step Content Marketing Strategy Blueprint (see Figure 6.1) to help businesses streamline their content marketing process. This framework was presented by Mark Burgess to hundreds of marketers at American Marketing Association training events across the United States between 2012 and 2018. Scalable to businesses of any size, it offers a model for developing and distributing content that makes an impact. It helps brands amplify their message and enhance customer loyalty while reducing their marketing spend.

The work begins with a thorough understanding of your business goals and objectives. This is the foundation, and you should spend some time focusing on this area to develop an effective content marketing strategy. As you make your way through the process, remember that content is the currency of customer experience – and a good customer experience is all about being helpful to your customers. To make sure that we're always keeping our audience front and center, we're big fans of the '80/20' rule: focus 80% of your content on helping, informing, or otherwise piquing the interest of your customer, and the remaining 20% on your product or service.

Progressing from there, you can begin to implement the Seven-Step Content Strategy Blueprint. As you work through these steps, think supply chain across channels. As noted marketing thought leader David Edelman said in the foreword to our first book, *The Social Employee*, 'Building a content supply chain is becoming a new operations priority.' In other words, if you haven't started with your content marketing strategy yet, there's no better time than the present.

Figure 6.1 Seven-Step Content Strategy Blueprint.

Source: ©2020 Blue Focus Marketing®. All Rights Reserved.

Step 1: External Scan and the Content Audit

The process starts with a thorough understanding of the marketing landscape. A thorough scan includes collecting information about forces in the marketing environment: competitive, economic, legal, political, technological and sociocultural. Next, focus on a content audit to view your assets in the context of your business goals, determine priorities, and identify potential gaps. Here, remember that compelling content both informs your audience and serves your business goals. Ask yourself:

- Does your supply of content map to your customers' buying stages?
- Is it relevant to your target personas?
- Is it in sync with your brand value proposition (see next section)?

Finally, identify gaps that prevent your content from resonating with your audience.

Step 2: Identify Brand Value Proposition (BVP)

Effective content marketing links your BVP to your brand story. Ask yourself the following questions:

- What value do we deliver to our customers?
- Why do customers buy from us?
- Why should they care?

Once you have these answers, keep them somewhere handy – and refer to them often whenever you're planning out your next piece of content.

Step 3: Create Key Personas and Your Experience Journey

Who do you want to reach? At the core of your content marketing strategy is your target buyer persona. The better you know your buyers, the more compelling your messaging strategy.

Step 4: Create Content: Your Story

Next, focus on a good story. Not only are good stories more memorable, they can make the complex seem simple. Identify the core story at the heart of your brand, create narratives that feed this story, and customize your content to suit different touchpoints.

Step 5: Content Sourcing and Management

The more valuable content you produce, the better it is for your brand. When considering how to feed your content stream, carefully analyze all potential content development sources, including employees, customers, freelancers, ad agencies and crowdsourcing.

Remember, while quantity, speed and efficiency are important, don't cut corners on quality. Regardless of who produced it, each piece of content should represent the best your brand has to offer while delivering rich customer experiences.

Step 6: Your Content Team

Common roles in an effective content team include: content creators, channel managers, designers, content curators, editors and search engine optimization (SEO) specialists.

At many leading brands, content teams are driven by a chief content officer who works to ensure consistent integration across touchpoints.

Step 7: Publish Your Content

The most critical tool in your publishing arsenal is an editorial calendar. The best brands think like publishers, timing the release of content around product launches, brand milestones and current events in order to stay fresh and relevant.

Measure and Apply Results

Typical content marketing metrics include website traffic, reach, conversion rates, shares, engagement and other metrics contributing to leads and sales. As a marketer, you need to know if your content is generating leads and driving revenue for your business. Figure 6.2 lists the most common KPIs (key performance indicators) by content type to aid in analyzing the performance of a range of content types deployed by the marketer.

BLOG POSTS/ ARTICLES	EMAIL	SOCIAL MEDIA	VIDEOS	PODCASTS	PPC CAMPAIGNS
Website traffic	Open rate	Amplification rate	Views	Subscribers	Cost per click
Unique visitors	Conversion rate	Applause rate	Unique viewers	Backlinks	Click-through rate
New vs. returning visitors	Opt-out rate	Followers/ Fans	Average view duration	Downloads	Ad position
Time on site	Subscribers	Conversion rate	Subscribes	Social shares	Conversions
Avg. time on page	Churn rate	Landing page conversion rate	Impression click-through rate	Reviews/ratings	Conversion rate
Bounce rate	Click-through rate	Return on engagement	Shares		Cost per conversion
Exit rate	Delivery rate	Post reach	Comments		Cost per sale
Page views			Traffic sources		Return on ad spend
Page views per visit					Wasted spend
Traffic sources					Impressions
Geographic trends					Quality score
Mobile visitors					Total spend
Desktop visitors					
Visits per channel					

Figure 6.2   KPI's by Content Type.

Source: Content Marketing Institute, Jodi Harris author: KPIs by Content Type, 23 April 2018; https://contentmarketinginstitute.com/2018/04/measuring-content-performance/

Figure 6.3   Content strategy template.

Source: ©2020 Blue Focus Marketing®. All Rights Reserved.

Content Strategy Template

In our content marketing workshops, we developed a simplified template (see Figure 6.3) that helps marketers create a one-page content marketing strategy. Thinking about each core element, from buyer persona (Who) to support for the brand story (Why) to measurement (Metrics/ROI), will give marketers a holistic view of their content strategy and help them fine-tune their process.

Sidebar

Don't Just Plan: Choreograph

Great content is destined to be passed around, exciting potential consumers at any point in the buying process. But for this to happen, the content must be easy for people to find. Social media, of course, offer exciting new potential for creativity and quickly getting your message out to the world. But like any other process, distributing content via social media requires a level of finesse.

To help brands manage how they get their message out, Blue Focus Marketing developed the concept of Brand Choreography (BC). Brand Choreography is the orchestration of all appropriate content marketing messages and tactics – across traditional, digital and social media platforms – in a way that's designed to impact critical brand touchpoints. In other words, it helps bring all of the pieces together. BC links to the consumer's basic buying process to provide solutions at each step as they seek and acquire information, make their purchase, etc. (For a more detailed discussion of the buyer's journey, see Chapter 4.) The end result is the successful achievement of a firm's business objectives. BC is a customer-focused model that aims to deliver the right message to the right person in the right place to maximize their experience and satisfy their information needs. BC takes you where your customers are. In Chapter 10, we'll take a deep dive into the concept of Brand Choreography® and what it means to the content marketing process.

THE POWER OF VIDEO

You may have heard that attention spans are getting shorter. In fact, it can seem as if attention is nearing extinction, judging from headlines such as 'Science: You Now Have a Shorter Attention Span than a Goldfish' (*Time Magazine*), 'The Eight-Second Attention Span' (*The New York Times*), 'NBA will consider shortening games due to Millennial attention spans' (*USA Today*), and other similarly scolding articles. In actuality, rumors of the death of your attention span may have been greatly exaggerated. Many of these types of articles were based on a 2015 study by Microsoft Canada commissioned to measure the attention spans of modern, digitally connected consumers. While it's true that the study claimed that in 2018 the average human had an attention span of eight seconds – supposedly the same as a goldfish – those seemingly sensational stats actually concealed quite a bit.

For one, human attention spans haven't cratered – they've adapted to our current environment of attention overload. And two, goldfish may not actually be cursed with short memories or attention spans either![22] Even the lead author of the study, Alyson Gausby, noted that the ability to focus 'hasn't changed, it's just moved online'.[23]

The larger, perhaps understated, point of this study and all of the articles both citing it and criticizing it is that there's a war for your attention. 'Rest assured, digital won't be the cause of our (at least attentional) downfall', Gausby affirmed. Any content that gets through to you must not only get to the point (very) quickly – it must be good. Very good. Fortunately, there's a powerful, and increasingly essential, tool to help you capture attention: video.

Video clips offer viewers an immersive and stimulating experience. If they're well done, they can inspire, inform, delight – and convert. It's not surprising, then, that more and more content marketing is taking the form of video.

To get a better understanding of the power of video and its role in content market-ing, let's briefly examine some companies that have garnered attention (and sales) because of their clever, attention-arresting videos. There are few better examples than the blender manufacturer Blendtec.

It's hard to think of something less sexy than a utilitarian household appliance like a blender. But through a series of clever videos tailor-made for the web era, Blendtec has racked up over 100 million views on YouTube and brought an outsized (that is, for a blender company) amount of attention to itself. In each instalment in the company's 'Will It Blend?' series, Blendtec's CEO, a greying, middle-aged, lab-coat bedecked gentleman named Tom Dickson, inserts a consumer product into a Blendtec and lets 'er rip. Said consumer products have included glowsticks, iPhones and other Apple devices, a set of golf balls, cubic zirconia, and more.

By blending (forgive us) sheer, unabashed entertainment with a demonstration of their product's raw performance muscle, Blendtec created a recipe for runaway success. In fact, 'Will It Blend?' videos are viral enough that Google offers 'Blendtec blender commercial' as an autofill suggestion after inputting the words 'Blendtec B'. (If you're autofill-able, you know you've done something right – or very wrong.) According to Dickson, the series has translated into 'a 1,000 percent improvement in our sales'.[24]

The 'Will It Blend?' series launched in 2006. It was a cheeky gambit – and it worked. As of this writing, a 'Will It Blend?' installment from 2014 investigating whether or not the iPhone 6 Plus would blend has over 6 million views,[25] and a 2010 instalment enquiring as to the blendability of an iPad has nearly 19 million views[26] – a figure greater than the population of the Netherlands.

As an important point of comparison, more straightforward Blendtec videos that simply demonstrate product features are a mere blip. A 2015 infomercial-type video for the Blendtec Stealth 875 Commercial Blender had fewer than 29,000 views as of this writing.[27] We can conclude several things from this discrepancy. One, a clever – though not completely tangential – stunt can bring a lot of attention to a product. Two, when it comes to 'boring' products – perhaps the majority of items that are sold – many potential buyers don't really care about specific technical details. *They want a story.* Namely, that Blendtecs are fun – and really, really powerful.

Dollar Shave Club offers another useful example. In 2012, the year the company was founded, it released a video announcing itself to the world. The video, titled 'Our Blades Are F***ing Great', shows company founder Michael Dubin as he gives a walk-through of the company headquarters while explaining the company's mission. The result is 1 minute and 33 seconds of video that is equal parts deadpan comedy, sales pitch and visual gag-fest. In a subversive take on the 'I'm not only the president, I'm also a client' commercials so beloved by CEOs of yore, Dubin extols the virtues of his low-cost, no-BS product and pokes fun at the tactics of the razor blade behemoths whose market share Dollar Shave Club aimed to disrupt. ('Do you think your razor needs a vibrating handle, a flashlight, a back-scratcher, and ten blades?' he asks, rhetorically and incredulously.)

To call the video a success would be like, say, calling Oscar the Grouch grumpy. As of this writing, the video has over 25 million views on YouTube and well over 8,000 comments. 'I'm quite certain this is the only Youtube [*sic*] ad I've every [*sic*] actually watched to the end',[28] explains one of the commenters, no doubt speaking for many, if not most, viewers. It'd be hard to argue that this daring coming-out video had little to do with Dollar Shave Club's meteoric rise (and eventual purchase for $1 billion).

The young, hungry upstarts and manufacturers of basic consumer products may be more predisposed to making a splash with their content because they're so new, possibly more likely to have fresh ideas, and often demonstrate a greater willingness to take risks (or fall flat on their face trying). However, they aren't the only ones who have been able to harness the power of video and good storytelling. Many larger, more established companies have also come to see video's ability to tell a good story, even if their approach is more traditional.

Take Subaru, for example. In 2017, the company released a slate of commercials to promote its newly designed Impreza. Instead of zeroing in on all of the car's no-doubt impressive technical features, the company decided to show familiar slices of middle-class American life. Short vignettes with titles such as 'Moving Out', 'More' and 'Rewind', depicted pivotal life stages, such as the bittersweet moment when a child leaves home and goes off to college. In the commercial titled 'Moving Out', the only comment that the narrator offers comes at the very end, when he explains that the Impreza is 'the longest-lasting vehicle in its class' while a young man drives away from home as his parents (and well-aged family dog) look on wistfully.

You don't need to be Sherlock Holmes to figure out Subaru's story from these ads. Through each portrayed moment, like a security blanket, Subaru was there, helping a family live well and go about their lives safely and securely. It's not the particulars that matter here – it's the feeling. It's the story.

Sidebar

The New Rules of Video Marketing Success

The Content Marketing Institute (CMI) website published a valuable article by Amir Bazrafshan, founder of Apricot, a UK-based video marketing agency. In the post, Bazrafshan drew from his years of experience to come up with a list of best practices for maximizing the impact of your video marketing operation – and a list of reasons why it could fail. The following is a brief summary of his findings.

(Continued)

Actions Likely to Result in Video Marketing Failure

1. Failing to build in regular analysis
2. Working without any strategic approach
3. Relying excessively on YouTube
4. Inadequately promoting video content
5. Neglecting to analyze performance metrics

New Rules for Video Marketing

1. Use design thinking
2. Do a video content gap analysis
3. Use correct context
4. Run a strategic promotional campaign
5. Optimize performance[29]

THE RISE OF LIVE VIDEO

One trend that has become well-established in the world of video marketing is live video (also known as live streaming). Its main benefit is that it offers a level of immediacy and intimacy that something more produced cannot. Just like a live sporting event or a play, a bit of surprise and wonder about what will happen next underlies every stream. And, perhaps most critically, it just feels real. 'With live video, it's hard to stage and curate your image. You can't apply filters, and there's no undo button. It's the real, authentic you, and anything can happen', writes content marketing consultant Dennis Shiao.[30] We also think in visuals. We dream in visuals. Have you ever had a text dream? Probably not.

If you want to start live streaming, focus first on finding a platform and figuring out your audience. Major media companies have gotten in on the trend, such as Facebook, Instagram (owned by Facebook), Periscope (owned by Twitter) and YouTube Live. 'Which one is best? The answer is pretty simple – where are your friends and followers?' writes Talking Tech columnist Jefferson Graham.[31] Each platform has pros and cons, so before you jump in, work on defining your goals. Think long and hard about what live streaming video can accomplish that prerecorded video cannot.

Just because you shoot a live video, however, doesn't mean you can leave its execution up to the hands of fate. Even if your presentation is informal and laid-back, you should still have a strong grasp of what you want to say and how you will say it – that is, the message you want viewers to walk away with. In other words, you still need a plan. Any content you put out in the world will be considered a reflection of your brand, and this applies to live videos too; it's entirely possible for your brand to be a completely authentic failure. No level of perceived realness can make up for a bumbling, uninteresting, time-wasting video moment. So always remember to ask questions first, then shoot later.

Live or prerecorded, any videos you choose to share with the world must align with your brand's story. So, if you've been wondering how effective your videos are at conveying your story, it's worth giving them an honest self-critique. To help you do so, we created an Ad Agency Competitive Analysis Template, which you can find in Appendix A.

Future Gaze

AI and Marketing

Though artificial intelligence (AI) is still in its early stages, it has significant potential when it comes to content marketing applications. In fact, many companies are already using some form of AI to personalize customer experience, micro-target potential customers, personalize their content delivery, identify optimal times to distribute marketing communications, intervene at various customer touchpoints during an online shopping experience, and interact with customers via chatbots.[32]

As this technology progresses, however, we may begin to see even smarter and more creative applications. This could include using AI to harvest more robust SEO keywords or other similar data-mining operations. CoSchedule, a marketing project management startup based in North Dakota, offers a glimpse of what may be in store. The company has developed a popular headline analyzer that rates the quality of a user-input headline based on four criteria: how common, uncommon, emotional and/or powerful the headline is. After text is entered, the analyzer, which relies on a proprietary algorithm, generates a score from 0 to 100; the better the score, the more potentially resonant the headline.[33] Talk about good content marketing – for potential marketers and CoSchedule! The company's main focus is creating scheduling solutions, not content marketing per se; but by making this tool freely accessible to marketers – and others in need of arresting headlines – it has demonstrated its competence and value.

High-tech companies such as IBM and Microsoft have been availing themselves of AI's power. The IBM Watson Tone Analyzer 'uses linguistic analysis to detect emotional and language tones in written text'. The tool, which can process up to 128KB worth of text at a time, analyses blocks of text based on the following categories: anger, fear, joy, sadness, analytical, confidence and tentativeness. The use cases IBM discusses on its website include social listening and audience monitoring,

(Continued)

personalized marketing, chatbots and customer-engagement monitoring and quality assurance.[34]

Amazon's Alexa digital assistant leads the market. This is a classic first-mover advantage in a marketplace now crowded with competitors. With literally thousands of skills available in the Alexa Skills store, new applications seem endless. And, third-party developers are aggressively creating more skills. Need help sleeping? Alexa can play calming and relaxing sounds and music. Want the latest news reports, sports, weather, control your smart home, play music, get recipes, make phone calls, and much more? The applications for consumers are of course enormous, including ease and convenience of ordering simply by using your voice. In Chapter 11, we describe a scenario where the consumer orders products like cookies or batteries from Amazon without asking for a particular brand. This results in a new challenge for every brand that spends marketing dollars to create awareness and communicate a value proposition to build a brand.

'Alexa, pay for gas at pump 4.' Now, artificial intelligence promises consumers more convenience and safety – at the gas pump. Amazon announced an arrangement with ExxonMobil and Fiserv, for a new voice experience for pumping gas that will roll out to more than 11,500 Exxon and Mobil gas stations across the US (in 2020). The ability to pay for gas via Alexa will initially be made available to customers with Alexa-enabled vehicles.[35]

Whether or not there is an AI-driven revolution remains to be seen, but at the very least it could be a promising tool for 'outsourcing' some of the more mundane, quantitative tasks critical to any marketing campaign. 'Therein lies the most powerful promise of AI: to release marketers from the mundane to focus on more creative and fulfilling efforts', writes Clare McDermott, co-founder of content marketing firm Mantis Research. 'The full vision is still out of reach, but early signs point to a machine-led period of creative efficiency.'[36]

In the end, of course, any assistance that AI provides is only as credible as the humans who execute it. AI can help you increase the breadth and depth of your message, but the message itself is still up to your – that is, human – discretion. However you decide to tell your story via content marketing, a story you must tell. In Chapter 11, 'Data In, Branding Out', we will discuss the quiet revolution in AI-generated content marketing.

CHAPTER ANALYSIS QUESTIONS

1. In what ways does content marketing differ from traditional marketing?
2. How does content marketing help drive user/consumer engagement?
3. Why does storytelling matter?
4. How can AI be used to create better content?

NOTES

1. Souza, J. (2014). 10 best quotes from Seth Godin on PR and marketing. [Blog] *Social Media Impact*. Available at: www.socialmediaimpact.com/top-10-best-quotes-seth-godin-pr-marketing/# [Accessed 31 Jan. 2020].

2. Slattery, B. (2010). Simply authentic branding. *Blue Focus Marketing*, 10 April. Available at: https://bluefocusmarketing.com/2010/10/04/simply-authentic-branding/ [Accessed 7 Jan. 2020].

3. McDermott, C. (2018). Go behind the scenes of Coca-Cola's storytelling. Content Marketing Institute, 9 February. Available at: https://contentmarketinginstitute.com/2018/02/coca-cola-storytelling/ [Accessed 7 Jan. 2020].

4. Content Marketing Institute. (2018). *Content Marketing World 2017 Keynote – Kate Santore*. [video online] Available at: www.youtube.com/watch?time_continue=311&v=8l2lpQR-f2Ug [Accessed 7 Jan. 2020].

5. Aaker, D. (2018). *Creating Signature Stories: Strategic Messaging That Energizes, Persuades, and Inspires*. Morgan James Publishing, p. 10.

6. Smith, M. (2018). Equine equity: How mid-Missouri horses boost a global beer brand. *Missouri Business Alert*. Available at: www.missouribusinessalert.com/industries/94484/2018/07/03/equine-equity-how-mid-missouri-horses-boost-a-global-beer-brand/ [Accessed 7 Jan. 2020].

7. Ibid.

8. Aaker, D. (2018). *Creating Signature Stories: Strategic Messaging that Energizes, Persuades, and Inspires*. Morgan James Publishing, p. 31.

9. Sinek, S. (2009). *How Great Leaders Inspire Action*. [video online] TED. Available at: www.ted.com/talks/simon_sinek_how_great_leaders_inspire_action [Accessed 7 Jan. 2020].

10. Ibid.

11. Stanford Graduate School of Business. (2016). *Jennifer Aaker: The Power of Story*. [video online] Available at: www.youtube.com/watch?v=CdO9a41WUss [Accessed 7 Jan. 2020].

12. Edelman. (2018). 2018 Edelman Trust Barometer reveals record-breaking drop in trust in the US. *PR Newswire*, 21 January. Available at: www.prnewswire.com/news-releases/2018-edelman-trust-barometer-reveals-record-breaking-drop-in-trust-in-the-us-300585510.html [Accessed 7 Jan. 2020].

13. Mandese, J. (2018). Havas expands 'meaningful brands,' studies role content plays – or not. *Media Daily News*, 1 August. Available at: www.mediapost.com/publications/article/323024/havas-expands-meaningful-brands-studies-role-co.html [Accessed 7 Jan. 2020].

14. Papandrea, D. (2018). Content marketing statistics 2018 for building a business case. *NewsCred Insights*, 27 March. Available at: https://insights.newscred.com/content-marketing-statistics/ [Accessed 7 Jan. 2020].

15. Aaker, D. (2018). *Creating Signature Stories: Strategic Messaging that Energizes, Persuades, and Inspires*. Morgan James Publishing, p. 7.

16. Content Marketing Institute. (2018). What is content marketing? Available at: https://contentmarketinginstitute.com/what-is-content-marketing/ [Accessed 7 Jan. 2020].

17. *MEL Magazine*. (2018). About. Available at: https://melmagazine.com/about [Accessed 7 Jan. 2020].

18. Trop, J. (2017). How Dollar Shave Club's founder built a $1 billion company that changed the industry. *Entrepreneur,* 28 March. Available at: www.entrepreneur.com/article/290539 [Accessed 7 Jan. 2020].

19. Aaker, D. and Aaker, J.L. (2016). What are your signature stories? *California Management Review*, 58(3), pp. 49–56.

20. NewsCred. (2018). The NewsCred Top 50 awards: Best content marketing brands 2018. Available at: https://info.newscred.com/rs/585-FDY-438/images/E-book_NewsCred%20Top%2050%202018_Best%20Content%20Marketing%20Brands.pdf [Accessed 7 Jan. 2020].

21. Ibid.

22. Maybin, S. (2017). Busting the attention span myth. *BBC News*, 10 March. Available at: www.bbc.com/news/health-38896790 [Accessed 7 Jan. 2020].

23. Microsoft Canada. (2015). Attention spans. Available at: www.scribd.com/document/265348695/Microsoft-Attention-Spans-Research-Report [Accessed 7 Jan. 2020].

24. *Boss Magazine*. (2018). 'Will It Blend?' star Tom Dickson shares his story. Available at: https://thebossmagazine.com/will-it-blend/ [Accessed 7 Jan. 2020].

25. Blendtec's Will It Blend? (2014). *Will It Blend? – iPhone 6 Plus.* [video online] Available at: www.youtube.com/watch?v=IBUJcD6Ws6s [Accessed 7 Jan. 2020].

26. Blendtec's Will It Blend. (2010). *Will It Blend? – iPad.* [video online] Available at: www.youtube.com/watch?v=IAI28d6tbko&t=2s [Accessed 7 Jan. 2020].

27. Blendtec Commercial. (2015). *Blendtec Stealth 875 Commercial Blender.* [video online] Available at: www.youtube.com/watch?v=XABD3t-hvkw&t=24s [Accessed 7 Jan. 2020].

28. Dollar Shave Club. (2012). *DollarShaveClub.com – Our Blades Are f***ing Great.* [video online] Available at: www.youtube.com/watch?v=ZUG9qYTJMsI [Accessed 7 Jan. 2020].

29. Bazrafshan, A. (2018). The 5 new rules of video marketing success. Content Marketing Institute, 8 October. Available at: https://contentmarketinginstitute.com/2018/10/new-rules-video-marketing/ [Accessed 7 Jan. 2020].

30. Shiao, D. (2018). Why now is the time for live video. *CMS Wire*, 14 June. Available at: www.cmswire.com/digital-marketing/why-now-is-the-time-for-live-video/ [Accessed 7 Jan. 2020].

31. Graham, J. (2017). YouTube, Facebook, Instagram, or Periscope? Rating the top live video apps. *USA Today*, 7 February. Available at: www.usatoday.com/story/tech/talkingtech/2017/02/07/youtube-facebook-instagram-periscope-rating-top-live-video-apps/97597178/ [Accessed 7 Jan. 2020].

32. McDermott, C. (2018). Are you really smart about how AI works in marketing? Content Marketing Institute, 9 August. Available at: https://contentmarketinginstitute.com/2018/08/ai-works-marketing/ [Accessed 7 Jan. 2020].

33. CoSchedule. (2018). Headline analyzer. Available at: https://coschedule.com/headline-analyzer [Accessed 7 Jan. 2020].

34. IBM Cloud. (2018). Tone Analyzer – About [7 November]. Available at: https://console.bluemix.net/docs/services/tone-analyzer/index.html#about [Accessed 7 Jan. 2020].

35. TechCrunch. (2020). 'Alexa, pay for gas' command to work at over 11,500 Exxon and Mobil stations this year [online] Available at: https://techcrunch.com/2020/01/06/alexa-pay-for-gas-command-to-work-at-over-11500-exxon-and-mobil-stations-this-year/ [Accessed 9 Jan. 2020].

36. McDermott, C. (2018). Are you really smart about AI? Content Marketing Institute, 9 August. Available at: https://contentmarketinginstitute.com/2018/08/ai-works-marketing/ [Accessed 7 Jan. 2020].

7

DISRUPTING THE CONTENT DISTRIBUTION MIX

Learning Goals

- Analyze trends in content distribution across digital, social and traditional media channels.
- Analyze the key steps for marketers to build a social media strategy for an enterprise.
- Analyze the POEM (paid, owned and earned media) model to guide media planning and selection.
- Determine the best content distribution channels to reach your target buyer personas.
- Evaluate AI's disruptive power to improve content marketing and distribution.

I would say that the days of advertising as we know it today are numbered. We need to start thinking about a world with no ads.

Chief Brand Officer Marc Pritchard, Procter & Gamble[1]

The Titanium Lion is awarded at the Cannes Lions International Festival of Creativity in the French city of Cannes to recognize 'breakthrough ideas which are provocative and point to a new direction in the industry'.[2]

In 2019, the award was presented to Microsoft in recognition of a Super Bowl commercial that featured the Xbox Adaptive Controller. While the controller itself is a cutting-edge piece of hardware, the commercial wasn't chosen because of the controller's impressive features. Rather than highlighting a technological achievement,

Microsoft's Corporate Vice President – Brand, Advertising and Research, Kathleen Hall, chose to focus on the real-life story of Owen, a young boy with special needs, who in the commercial proudly gave his age as nine and a half years old.

When Kathleen heard Owen's story, she knew that his needs lay at the heart of Microsoft's mission. As Kathleen explains, there were several reasons why people responded so well to Owen's story:

> The magic formula really was that you had a brand truth, which is that we empower people to do great things. And the great things that they do are interesting. For Microsoft, it's a brand-new product truth, one that's about social relevance in that we want to empower people of all types, shapes, and sizes to do the things that they couldn't do without our technology.

> It's part of a social movement right now. You definitely have to be part of a social movement. The trend is around inclusion. With this commercial, the secret sauce was that it had some relevance to its environment – in this case the Super Bowl. It was that line: 'When everybody plays, we all win.' The ultimate form of inclusion, which, in the context of the NFL and everything that's going on in sports, was super relevant and emotional. That was the bingo moment.[3]

The commercial's tremendous success is another sign that we have entered the emotion and sharing economy – where storytelling is the primary currency (see Chapter 6). Storytelling is one of the most important tools in a marketer's bag of tricks. It's the fuel of a culture that is centered around sharing and collaboration. Stories help to humanize a brand in the collective mind of its audience. But in order to succeed, brands must value their customers, show empathy for their pain points, and demonstrate that they understand their needs.

The right story creates an emotional connection with the customer; we trust brands when we can identify with their story. Our brains are hardwired to remember what is different, what stands out. Stories guide customers along the customer journey when they visit your website, read your blog, respond to your email, or visit one of hundreds of brand touchpoints along the Consumer Odyssey (see Chapter 4). With storytelling as our anchor, in this chapter, we will explore the ways in which modern brands are disrupting the content distribution mix.

CHOOSING YOUR PATH IN THE MODERN CONTENT DISTRIBUTION LANDSCAPE

Once upon a time, families huddled happily around their tiny 15-inch black-and-white television sets like cavemen around a fire. To get a clear (for the time) picture, they had to wiggle the antennae, or 'rabbit ears', as they were affectionately known. Back then, there was no internet, and watching TV was one of the main ways that consumers could learn about new products.

And make no mistake, advertisers *had* a captive audience. Not only was there no internet, but there were only three major television networks to choose from – and they all planned their commercial breaks around the same time. If viewers wanted to enjoy their programs, they had little choice but to endure the commercials. Determining which commercials to air, when and on what channel was a type of marketer known as the *media planner*. In any era, the media planner's role is to identify the best mix of media opportunities. The goal is to deliver an advertising message to reach the client's target buyer persona in the most effective and efficient manner. In the days of the captive television audience, the media planner's job was relatively straightforward: pay for the ad time, and the viewers would come.

Today, in the era of the 85-inch 5K ultra-high-definition smart LED television, the media planner's job is much more complicated. Not only are they competing for viewers' attention against the hundreds of other available channels, but they're also competing against an array of digital channels and social media. The question is, how do you determine where your content should be distributed, and what criteria should you use?

Brands have a lot riding on getting these answers right. Up to this point, your marketing team has worked diligently to create effective content. You have spent a lot of time refining your target buyer personas and have developed a viable content marketing strategy. Your final challenge is to reach out with your content and engage with your audience. No matter what, you'll be competing for your audience's attention with a host of other paid and unpaid options. However, if you're able to successfully match your content with the best distribution channels, you'll be able to cut through the noise and capture the attention of your audience.

To do that, start with the basics:

- Who is your audience?
- Why are you distributing this content?
- Where does brand purpose and storytelling play best, and what media choices will help the brand reach its objectives?
- What is the main message, and is it pertinent to the target persona?
- Does the content for the medium of choice fit the 80/20 rule (see Chapter 6) for delivering relevance to the persona?

As a marketer, you must carefully evaluate your distribution options and develop an appropriate channel plan. Remember, it's not always about what's new and flashy. Traditional media remain a powerful platform, but today we are seeing three ever-expanding spheres of influence comprised of digital, social and traditional media

TRIFECTA OF MEDIA POSSIBILITIES

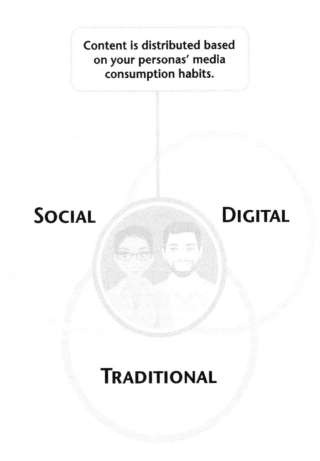

Content is distributed based on your personas' media consumption habits.

SOCIAL   DIGITAL

TRADITIONAL

Figure 7.1   Trifecta of Media Possibilities.

Source: ©2020 Blue Focus Marketing®. All Rights Reserved.

possibilities. Your job is to create a mixture of these three spheres based on what you and your team have determined will best reach your target audience – and more specifically, your buyer personas – based on their media consumption habits. For example, if your target persona watches an unusually high amount of television and little to no digital or social media, deciding where to distribute media is relatively simple. If your target persona consumes high amounts of digital and social media and little or no television, your areas of focus should reflect that. Whatever the exact mixture, your goal is to find that sweet spot where all the spheres intersect (see Figure 7.1).

In today's rapidly changing world, it's nearly impossible to perfectly predict customer preferences, let alone their behaviors. The three spheres of influence will impact one buyer persona very differently than they might impact another. For some, traditional delivery channels have become obsolete and ineffective. For others, traditional with a sprinkling of digital will rule the day. Still others are eager to follow the hot, new and unfamiliar trends, shifting their preferences every time a new distribution channel comes along.

But if different buyers all behave so radically differently, how is a marketer to know which channels to choose? According to Nis Frome, co-founder and head of experimentation at Alpha, an on-demand insights platform, the trick is to follow the leaders among your audience – and to be willing to experiment:

> Our business has had the most success when we get closer to the market, engage with the most forward-thinking customers, and place diverse bets really early. While many bets went nowhere, our marketing team was among the first in our industry to have a podcast and a *Medium* publication. Today, each generates more than 80,000 downloads and 80,000 views per month, respectively.[4]

Regardless of what channels you use, remember that your primary goal is to connect with your audience. As discussed in Chapter 6, storytelling has become a vital component of media selection. Stories allow a brand's message to rise above the noise of the marketplace and help match your content to your audience. Indeed, while today we are able to sort out our relevant media spheres into three distinct choices, there is plenty of overlap to be had. As the lines differentiating them continue to blur, a focus on good, strong brand stories allows you to create consistency in an environment filled with media fragmentation.

THE CHANGING ROLE OF TRADITIONAL MEDIA

According to writer George Simpson, 'Publicis Media's Zenith says that TV will lose its dominant share of global ad spending within the next couple of years, with internet display advertising moving into the top slot (although if you add search and classified to the mix, the internet is already the top global ad medium).'[5] This perspective isn't entirely wrong, but when you also factor in the shift of advertising to streaming platforms, it's clear that TV advertising is not going anywhere soon.

But while TV advertising isn't going away, it is changing. The game is changing for advertising, advertisers, and ad agencies in particular. Old models are eroding, and marketers are focused on the media choices that will bring ROI. There is a great old quote that says: 'Half of my advertising dollar is wasted. I just don't know which half.' It is that lack of ability to measure results that points marketers toward new, more accountable options. Specifically, digital and social channels.

Some say that advertising is becoming less essential to brand-building as consumers are proactively making use of tools like Google and Amazon to discover new products. But on the flipside of that coin there are a number of advertising success stories that cannot be ignored, such as AFLAC and the famous AFLAC duck. L'Oréal is another excellent example and one that Mark Burgess can attest to, having worked on Madison Avenue as a young account executive on the L'Oréal Preference Hair Color account. Back in the late 1970s, L'Oréal ran a campaign with the line: 'I use the most expensive hair color in the world, Preference by L'Oréal.' At the time, Preference Hair Color was priced slightly higher than the market leader. The combination of offering the most expensive hair color product, reinforced by the magical slogan, 'Because I'm worth it', rang true for millions of women who liked adding a bit of affordable luxury into their world. L'Oréal truly revolutionized the ad world with a message of recognition for women the world over. And, L'Oréal was able to grow its market share in the hair color category and move into new areas including cosmetics. Over the years, L'Oréal's well-known slogan has been tweaked a few times, but its message still resonates with women today and it remains one of the most enduring campaigns in advertising history.

As a more recent example, one of America's favorite long-running advertising efforts was the 'Get a Mac' campaign. It featured two intriguing characters: the awkward PC, and the personification of coolness that was the Mac. Simple production sets, engaging dialogue and zippy one-liners entertained viewers for years. In 2010 *Adweek* declared 'Get a Mac' to be the best advertising campaign of the first decade of the new century, kickstarting Apple's domination of the market with their next-generation phones, computers and wearables.[6]

But, as they say, the past is the past. What might the future of television be like in a digital economy? According to Geoffrey Colon, head of Brand Studio, Microsoft Advertising, we have to redefine what television is today, given the wide range and variety of channels and platforms that it's distributed on – from the traditional networks to cable, the internet and smart television. According to Colon:

> I don't like to say anything is dead. What it really is, is there's just like . . . physics. You have certain entities that have power, and when they're losing that power it's not dying, it's just ebbing and flowing into other areas. So as broadcast television starts to lose power, power is ebbing and flowing into these new entities. I think when people say, yeah television is dead, they probably [are referring to] the old broadcast models in the United States as well as other countries. [But] their power is flowing into other areas where the population is congregating.[7]

So where exactly are those 'other areas' that Colon speaks of? Here's a hint: you probably have at least a few of these apps on your phone – and you probably spend an hour or more each day checking them.

SOCIAL MEDIA: NO LONGER THE NEW KID ON THE BLOCK

In this young century, the name of the game has been *change*. And what is the root of all this change? Many would say 'social media', and in many ways they would be right. Social media have dramatically altered the way we think and interact with each other, muddling the lines between brands, employees and customers, forcing marketers to transform their approach to the marketplace.

This shift gave rise to the practice of *social media marketing*, a game-changer by any definition. In order to engage their respective audiences, modern brands began crafting powerful and relevant social media strategies.

Central to the practice of social media marketing is choice. Modern, independent consumers are increasingly in control of where they spend their money and what brands they follow. As consumers have become more empowered, marketers have come to realize that they no longer have a captive audience like in the days of the television. In order to reach and engage today's audience, they must provide deeper value – and the way to do that is through good content.

Good content is the rocket fuel of a compelling social brand. Social media requires a degree of transparency that many brands simply aren't used to, but which is essential if those brands are to build trust with their audience and win in the marketplace. Again, the key here is storytelling: brands must develop the defining stories that lie at the heart of their identity and create meaningful narratives that tell those stories in a way that audiences wish to share. This may feel intuitive to younger marketers, but to the old guard, such an approach is a far cry from the bygone days of the outbound marketing world and its one-way communications.

While components like transparency and storytelling may be essential to successful social engagement, the best social brands are able to combine these more abstract traits with a grounded, methodical approach.

Digital Marketing Blueprint

With the rise of social media, power has shifted to the consumer, traditional media has been dethroned, and content marketing is the new king. Like displaced animals forced to adapt to a new environment in order to survive, marketers must adapt to the very different world of content marketing. Compelling marketing is about engagement – not pushing out ads. Consumers are sick of marketing interruptions.

Social media provides a number of customer marketing and acquisition channels that are invaluable when it comes to creating a transparent dialogue between brands and their audiences. For instance, the American Marketing Association found that 'Investing in developing a social media community with a dedicated fan base (e.g. a Facebook page) can significantly strengthen customer–firm relationships and can lead to a definitive impact on the firm's revenues and profits.'[8] In other words, social

Figure 7.2   Digital Marketing Strategy Blueprint.

Source: ©2020 Blue Focus Marketing®. All Rights Reserved.

media isn't just about setting up a brand page and peppering your audience with content. Impactful social brands interact with their audiences, celebrate their most loyal (and vocal) fans, and participate in an authentic back-and-forth between brand and customer.

In Figure 7.2, we illustrate the seven key steps in building a digital marketing blueprint for an enterprise. Note that all of these steps are covered in depth throughout this book. This process starts with an understanding of the marketing environment and development of a SWOT analysis (see Chapter 4). Distribution of content is based on a target buyer persona's needs as well as the ability of the selected media to deliver a compelling story.

Following these seven steps, in Chapter 10, we will describe a framework called Brand Choreography, which allows for optimal integration across media platforms, empowering an organization to deliver the right message, to the right audience, at the right moment in their buyer's journey. After executing its media strategy, the brand focuses on ways to measure marketing results, manage feedback, and apply what is learned to future marketing initiatives. The key to remember is that becoming integrated into the social media marketing mix is a process, not a project.

Leading Platforms Disrupting Traditional Media

When it comes to social media engagement, the dilemma isn't deciding which platform you should use, but rather figuring out which platform your customers, prospects and other stakeholders are already using. With new options popping up every day, there are always new social channels to explore – some that might not have even existed when we wrote this book. However, the following list reflects the key players in the social world, and what makes them valuable:

- **Twitter.** Essentially a microblogging platform, Twitter is a great way for brands, thought leaders and influencers to join larger conversations and point users to valuable content – all in 280 characters or less.
- **Facebook.** The undisputed big fish in the social pond, Facebook can accommodate just about any type of content – blogs, images, messaging, memes, and even live streams.
- **TikTok.** This is a fast-growing short-form social video app that permits users to create and share videos. Users can add special effects. Each video becomes a short story. A favorite of Gen Zers, the platform presents opportunities for brands to identify new ways to reach young people.
- **LinkedIn.** LinkedIn connects the world's professionals to make them more productive and successful and transforms the way companies hire, market, sell and learn. Their vision is to create economic opportunity for every member of the global workforce through the ongoing development of the world's first Economic Graph. LinkedIn has more than 660 million members and has offices around the globe.[9]

- **YouTube.** From vlogs to product teasers, from trailers to how-to's, and from conference footage to Q&As, YouTube is a massive repository for video content – and a must for any social brand.
- **Instagram.** This image- and video-centric platform is great for visual-oriented brands. With such a basic premise, Instagram is surprisingly versatile, allowing brands to share daily deals, highlights from events, micro how-to's, and more.
- **Messaging.** Platforms like WhatsApp and WeChat allow users to send text, voice, video and other kinds of messages and media over the internet, so they don't have to eat into their phones' data plans. Some messaging platforms, like WeChat, even let users send payments and book flights and hotels.[10]

Brands Must Think Mobile-First

Steve Jobs once said, 'An iPod, a phone, an internet mobile communicator . . . these are *not* three separate devices! And we are calling it iPhone! Today Apple is going to reinvent the phone. And here it is.'[11] Indeed, in 2007, the iPhone started the smartphone revolution, introducing the world to a class of items that many now feel they can't live without.

But what makes smartphones so important to marketers? According to analyst and futurist Brian Solis:

> Customers are increasingly and overwhelmingly mobile-first. For the most part, many brands are still learning how to optimize traditional e-commerce experiences let alone mobile sites and apps. The Amazons of the world don't make it any easier to keep up. Yet every day, customers are reaching for their smartphones to learn about what to buy, what to do or where to go. But without being mobile-centric and integrating digital touchpoints, customer journeys are certain to be rife with obstacles.[12]

So, for brands today, the clear message is the need to develop a mobile strategy to reach consumers when and where they prefer to be reached. For years marketers have used segmentation to help define and organize a much larger market into clearly identifiable segments based on similar needs and wants. But, with smartphone users looking at their phones an estimated 1,500 times a week, marketers must not only practice good segmentation but also understand that cultivating a mobile-first mentality that reaches and engages consumers on their devices is imperative. A smartphone strategy becomes part of the mobile-first mentality and a new way to segment an audience. Armed with this information, brands can focus on enhancing the digital customer experience on smartphones to help the user research and purchase products.

Another reason that a mobile strategy is so important is that mobile usage is increasing. Therefore, engagement via mobile is key to gaining and maintaining the consumer's attention. *eMarketer* recently reported that 'Fewer people in the US are

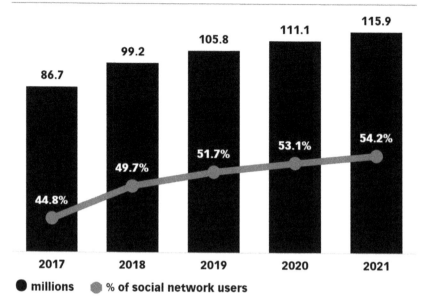

Mobile-Only Social Network Users
US, 2017-2021

Figure 7.3   Mobile-only social network users, US, 2017–2021.

Source: eMarketer, March 2019.

accessing social networking sites via computers, with the majority of users now exclusively on mobile devices. We forecast that 51.7 percent of US social network users will be mobile-only in 2019.'[13] (see Figure 7.3).

Compounding the challenges this shift presents, marketers have precious few seconds to pique a consumer's interest before they move on to something else. Smartphones are fast and will become even faster in the 5G environment of the future. On the bright side, as speed increases, so does the potential for quality and varied content. Being prepared to make the most of new mobile marketing possibilities should be a top priority for every brand.

WELCOME TO THE NEW WORLD OF DIGITAL MARKETING

According to HubSpot, 'Digital marketing encompasses all marketing efforts that use an electronic device or the internet.'[14] In other words, whether you're using a computer or a smartphone to distribute your message, you're engaged in digital marketing. Some of the specific channels that businesses can use to connect with current and prospective customers include search engines, social media, email and company websites.

The advantage of digital is that it helps marketers focus on the exact audience they want to reach to generate revenue. No longer does a marketer need to pay to run an expensive TV ad that only reaches perhaps 10% of its target audience.

Randy Frisch, co-founder of the content experience platform Uberflip, has observed how big of an adjustment it can be for marketers to acclimate to a digital landscape. According to Frisch, in the early days of digital marketing, marketers were used to dripping their messages to customers via relentless streams of emails, while working in digital only requires one good message that will get them to engage and click through onto more links. As Frisch explains, digital marketers are challenged to answer two questions: 'How do I get in front of my audience? And once I'm in front of them, the question is what am I going to show them?'[15]

The idea is to reach the right customer, with the right message, at the right time and place. Digital marketing is about making connections with the audience and zeroing in on the touchpoints that matter. Your brand lives by these connections. Think SEO, content marketing, CRM, Facebook, Instagram, social advertising, social media, Google Analytics, marketing automation, artificial intelligence and maintaining a powerful website. Focus on inbound marketing to reach and impact your audience, rather than taking an outbound approach that is loud, intrusive, annoying and outdated.

Sidebar

How Can AI Help Manage Content Across All Available Channels?

By Parry Malm, CEO, Phrasee (UK)

One of the main challenges for marketers these days is that there's sort of a million and one places to put content. You have your overarching campaign concept, creative concept, and campaign strategy, but then you need to treat that across [platforms]. It seems like every week there's a new channel cropping up. To entrust a human to write all of that copy assumes that, first of all, the human is a high-quality copywriter and, secondly, the human is not having an off day.

Phrasee is AI-powered copywriting that does something many thought only humans could do. Phrasee has developed a world-leading natural language generation system that can write marketing copy that sounds human – and fits your brand's voice.

(Continued)

For a super long time, ad men on Madison Avenue or in Golden Square, here in London, sort of sat there in their fancy ivory towers, going, 'Well, I said that this copy is going to work best. I am the expert. Believe me and pay me a bunch of money.' But we always thought that there was a better way, because language, with modern computational tools, can be deconstructed into sets of numbers. And machines can take large sets of numbers and find patterns in them, which are imperceptible to the human eye. Like, Phrasee won't think of the next 'Just do it.' But what it can do is take that 'Just do it' and extend that concept at scale, across every channel on the internet.

So, what Phrasee does instead, it takes a huge amount of inputs, some of which include human-based inputs, which we've got a whole team of linguists in house which input into the system on a client-to-client basis. And the output from that is the ability to generate huge amounts of content, which then the brand marketer can then take and distribute as they want.[16]

PAID, OWNED AND EARNED MEDIA (POEM)

The marketer's goal is to determine which channels offer the best fit with their audience. This is based on understanding the brand's voice, its value proposition, and the channel's ability to reach the target buyer personas. The goal is not to be everywhere at once, but to be where the channel affords the best opportunity to reach and engage with the persona.

In pursuit of this goal, the marketer's task is to decide among the numerous media choices available in order to distribute content in the most effective and efficient manner possible. Focusing on company-owned channels, such as websites, blogs, podcasts, and the like, offers the specific advantage of providing the marketer with greater control. Concentrating on a single owned media platform such as a blog enables marketers to build a strong base of followers before carrying them over to other channels where they can be further immersed in the brand experience. We call this the 'rolling thunder' approach to content distribution strategy – building on the success of one channel, instead of leading with a multi-channel approach that can drain marketing resources (see Figure 7.4).

Marketers realize that both short-form video (less than two minutes) and static images (photos or infographics) rule when it comes to content performance.

In the sections that follow, we'll explore the different paid, earned and owned channels that modern marketers are using to connect with their target buyers and stand out from a crowded field.

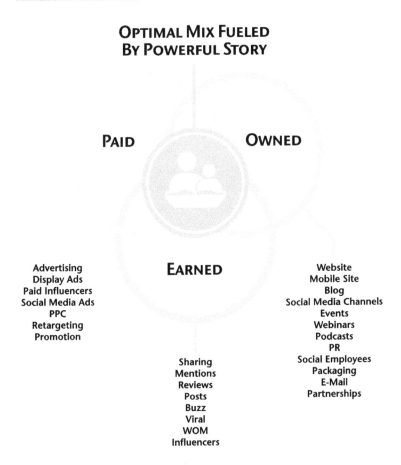

CONVERGED MEDIA STRATEGY CANVAS

OPTIMAL MIX FUELED BY POWERFUL STORY

PAID

OWNED

EARNED

Advertising
Display Ads
Paid Influencers
Social Media Ads
PPC
Retargeting
Promotion

Website
Mobile Site
Blog
Social Media Channels
Events
Webinars
Podcasts
PR
Social Employees
Packaging
E-Mail
Partnerships

Sharing
Mentions
Reviews
Posts
Buzz
Viral
WOM
Influencers

Figure 7.4 Converged Media Strategy Canvas.

Source: ©2020 Blue Focus Marketing®. All Rights Reserved.

Online to Offline

According to John Maxwell, Global Consumer Markets Leader at Pricewaterhouse Coopers (PwC):

> The key to a great end-to-end customer experience isn't just about the shopping and retail experience – it spans across industries. Consumers are looking for a seamless and easy purchasing journey, and companies can achieve this by using a blend of both physical and digital approaches. The result is a greater return on experience with the customer and more lasting results for businesses.[17]

Modern marketers understand that customers frequently switch between physical and digital worlds. This makes 'online-to-offline' or 'offline to online' (also known as O2O) marketing an effective way for businesses to reach customers across touchpoints to drive engagement and sales. There are three basic formats for the O2O process:

- Customers purchase items online and then travel to the store to pick them up – often referred to as click and collect.
- Customers take a sort of augmented approach, shopping online during a physical visit.
- Customers return items they purchased online to a physical store.[18]

Ultimately, the bottom line on O2O marketing: even though we live in an online age, it would be a mistake to disregard the value of offline marketing. The real world offers deep insight into your organization's customers and their behaviors. An effective, forward-thinking brand enables these O2O experiences to better accommodate and engage their customers.

Product Placement

Product placement is hardly a new marketing tool. Cheerios and Frosted Flakes have been a ubiquitous part of television breakfast scenes forever; Ketel One Vodka is included on the hit Showtime series *Ray Donovan*. Placing products in their natural context makes these products seem popular without any of the hard-sell overtones direct advertising engenders. For example, on an episode of *Billions*, also on Showtime, the leading character can be seen speeding around a test track in a new Mercedes before casually commenting, 'I'll buy two.' In the runaway Netflix hit *Stranger Things*, viewers are inundated with fun era-appropriate product placement, such as Coca-Cola's failed yet infamous New Coke, Eggo Waffles and 7-Eleven Slurpees. Through the power of nostalgia, viewers are transported back to a sentimental and familiar time in their lives. When viewed in the environments they were created for, these products help to reinforce the story's spell without feeling intrusive to the viewer. And it's working: according to the American Marketing Association, product visibility in *Stranger Things* was valued at $15 million.[19]

Podcasts

According to *eMarketer*, '73 million people in the United States will listen to a podcast at least monthly in 2018' – and advertisers have taken note.[20] According to the Interactive Advertising Bureau (IAB) and PwC, podcasting ad revenues in the United States were estimated at $479 million in 2018, an increase of 53% over the prior year.[21]

Numbers like that are good news for the podcasting industry, but they still pale in comparison to the ad revenue generated by some traditional channels; radio, for example, podcasting's traditional analogue is forecast to reach $14.5 billion in 2018.[22] Compared to results from other traditional media, then, podcasting still has a way to go. Nevertheless, podcasting contributes its own special qualities to digital messaging and the medium has experienced a significant rise in popularity and shows no sign of slowing down.

Sidebar

The Sharing Economy

By Behavioral Economist Ravi Dhar, George Rogers Clark Professor of Management and Marketing at Yale School of Management

There is a growing trend toward a *sharing economy* that is being fueled by millennials who prefer consuming experiences more than having possessions. Experiences are personal, unique, and memorable. Because of this, they are much more likely to be shared on social media. Those who participate in a sharing economy are more likely to have a mindset that says, 'I don't necessarily need to buy this when I could just rent it for a little while, whether it's a piece of jewelry, a watch, or a room from Airbnb.'

Millennials are also social-driven. They like to share their experiences – far more than they like to share products. For instance, if you bought a new laptop, you typically wouldn't share that to Facebook or Instagram. But if you went out for a nice dinner you might share that, or if you did something with your laptop, or used that credit card in a certain way. Either way, viral experiences are often characterized by being fast, easy, and fun. It's important, then, that brands targeting millennials focus on designing experiences in a way that are aligned with the overall brand.

Finally, brands are also able to learn about their customers by capturing such simple information as their cell phone numbers. Cell phones are ubiquitous. Everybody has them. Because of this, brands are building large first party databases in order to engage with their users – and even track them through geolocation. Through very simple data points, brands are able to learn a great deal about their customers, including what they do on the weekend, when they commute to and from work, and even when they go on vacation.

This knowledge is valuable to brands because it allows them to tailor and target messages to their customers based on what they're likely to be doing at the time. For instance, if a person is in a working mindset, the message should be framed and delivered around that. If they're commuting, the message should be framed to connect with that, and so on. By taking this approach, brands are able to build a direct-to-customer relationship to better engage their audience and increase visibility.[23]

Omnichannel

According to HubSpot:

> Omnichannel experience is a multichannel approach to marketing, selling, and serving customers in a way that creates an integrated and cohesive customer experience no matter how or where a customer reaches out.

> At its core, omnichannel is defined as a multichannel sales approach that provides the customer with an integrated customer experience. The customer can be shopping online from a desktop or mobile device, or by telephone, or in a bricks-and-mortar store and the experience would be seamless.[24]

In other words, the goal of omnichannel marketing is a seamless customer experience regardless of touchpoints. And it works. According to a survey conducted by the Chief Marketing Officer (CMO) Council in collaboration with Pitney Bowes, 'Over 85 percent of 2,000 global consumers surveyed . . . reveal that a blend of both digital and physical channel experiences is the preferred way of interfacing with brands. Yet, only 13 percent of consumers believe that brands are fully meeting and delivering on this expectation.'[25] Consumers insist on certain omnichannel communications. These include access to email, phone, web, in-person engagements, video, social media and printed mail.

Account-Based Marketing

'Account-based marketing (ABM) is a highly focused business strategy in which a marketing team treats an individual prospect or customer like its very own market. The marketing team can create content, events, and entire campaigns dedicated to the people associated with that account, rather than the industry as a whole.' Succeeding with this customized approach requires solid sales and marketing alignment.[26]

According to Braden Becker at HubSpot, here are six account-based marketing tactics for launching a campaign:

1. Identify your target
2. Research your accounts
3. Create your content
4. Choose your channels
5. Run your campaign
6. Measure your results[27]

One of your key goals in your ABM strategy is to create personalized experiences that will enhance engagement opportunities with target accounts. To ensure that key accounts see your content, focus on the right channels. For example, according to Christine Otsuka at Uberflip, here are five of the most common content distribution channels for ABM:

1. Marketing email
2. Paid ads
3. Direct mail
4. Social media
5. Sales outreach (particularly email)[28]

Focus on creating personalized content, including offers, on the optimal number of brand touchpoints. Make your brand easy to reach and stay in touch. Understanding your prospect's pain points better than your competition will show through in your content strategy.

Sidebar

Achieving Better Content Distribution with AI

Q&A with Paul Roetzer, Founder and CEO, Marketing AI Institute

Question: How does AI assist marketers in distributing content to their target audience?

Paul Roetzer: When marketers today talk about using AI, they are usually referring to *machine learning*. This is an application of AI that facilitates making predictions based on historical data. The result of its continued use is that their algorithms get smarter as new data emerges. For example, if these marketers are asked, 'How do we better distribute content?' they might use machine learning to validate or correct their own predictions.

Although machines are better than humans at the kind of analysis needed to answer such a question, most marketers don't even consider using AI because it seems very abstract, and they have difficulty understanding what it's capable of doing. However, by focusing on individual use cases, some marketers have been able to remove the abstraction of applying AI.

Among the questions that might serve as use cases are, 'What audiences should we promote to?' and 'What channels should we distribute our product through?' Applying AI tools to the creation of content is yet another way to focus on a use case. Marketers who have identified such use cases are able to use AI to predict what content, topics, and titles have the most potential for success, as well as when and where to distribute them.[29]

FROM TRADITIONAL TO NEW MEDIA – AND BEYOND

We live in an interesting time for content distribution. While new channels – driven by digital and social media – continue to grow in importance, the success of Microsoft's Xbox commercial shows that traditional messaging through traditional channels still has a place.

When considering the content distribution question, rather than ask which channel you should choose over the other, ask how each channel will complement and amplify your overall effort. After all, while Microsoft debuted their commercial on one of the biggest stages possible – the Super Bowl – they also made the content available online, sharing it to their YouTube page and distributing it through social channels to continue to grow the commercial's footprint and build brand buzz.

But will such an approach always work? If not, what might the future hold for content distribution? According to Nis Frome at Alpha, the answer is complicated, but the best thing for brands to do is to keep an open mind:

> What marketers should have learned by now is that the future is truly unpredictable. Until recently, we thought webinars and Tumblr were the next big things, while conferences and books were dead. How wrong we were! That said, social media represents a paradigm shift which demands that marketers meet consumers on their turf and on their terms. In social media, consumers are real people, not generalized personas with 2.5 kids. The sooner brands let go of the past and sprint into the future, the better they'll perform.[30]

By taking a well-integrated approach across marketing communications channels, Microsoft set an example that other modern brands would be wise to follow: keep doing what works, and pay attention to new opportunities. But above all, it's important to be flexible in your approach rather than focus all your energy on a single channel.

Future Gaze

The Content Strategist Will (Still) be King in an AI Marketing World

By Jay Baer, Hall of Fame Keynote Speaker and Founder of Convince & Convert Consultancy

There's a lot of uncertainty and, frankly, fear about AI – this idea that AI is going to take all the marketers' jobs. That fear is not entirely unfounded, because if your role in marketing is to run AB tests of email headlines, I can have a robot do that better and cheaper. If you're purely in the tactical blocking and tackling side of marketing, yeah,

AI is coming for you. But here's the way I look at it: Eventually, it might be two years, it might be five, but eventually, the price of AI marketing will come down so much, and it will be so fully embedded in all forms of marketing and communication, that it will no longer be a competitive advantage. And to me that's the best possible scenario because I am not a tactician. Obviously, we do a lot of tactical things for our clients, but I am a strategist. I have been a digital marketing strategist since domain names were free. So, I have seen many cycles of disruption.

When everybody has the same robots, when everybody has the same AI in their corner, the strategist is king because the winners in that era will be those who can tell the robots what to do best. And I'm happy to bank on myself in that environment.

When it comes to AI improving content distribution, there's already some great start-ups working on this. I would go back to my three T's (the right topic, the right type, and the right time). There's a tremendous number of AI applications now that will look at your target audiences and determine what things they are most interested in based on their search engine behavior – based on what they talk about on social media. So, this premise of, 'Well, what should we create content about?' can very much be improved using AI.

AI can look at consumption patterns of your existing customers or presumed best customers, and say, 'You know what? Yeah, video works for everybody, but it really works for *you*.' Or, 'You know what? For whatever reason, for your customer base, they don't really like video as much as other people. You ought to do more audio stuff.' So those are all knowable answers, which is pretty fantastic.

And then, also, we're seeing a lot of use of AI in content optimization. So, for example, we work with a company which will take your Facebook ads and, using a very sophisticated machine learning process, tell you, almost instantaneously, all the things you should do to increase the effectiveness of those ads by 20 percent. It's just a machine. You just press the button and it says, 'Well, you know what? You think you know what's a good headline, but actually you don't. Here's an actually good headline.' Or next best offer is another really good use of AI – so somebody opens an email and the question becomes, especially in a B2B nurturing sequence, 'Okay, what's the next email they should receive?' Well, AI can look at all the different customers you've ever had and say, 'This is the next email you should send this particular person because they match the behavioral characteristics of somebody else who's already in the funnel.' So that birds-of-a-feather premise of using the historical behaviors of a target group, and then inferring from them what you should do to the next customer, is really exciting. And, obviously, we're just scratching the surface in terms of where AI's headed.[31]

CHAPTER ANALYSIS QUESTIONS

1. What are some of the key content distribution channels beyond traditional advertising?
2. How can advertising still be effective towards influencing the target audience?
3. How can a media planner determine the best channels to recommend to his/her clients?

4.   What are some of the key steps to build a social media strategy for an enterprise?
5.   What are some of the lessons from the POEM model?
6.   How can AI be helpful in improving a brand's content distribution strategy, and why will the role of a content strategist continue to be valuable?

NOTES

1.   Lipsman, A. (2019). Why Amazon is about to upend the $70 billion TV ad market. [online] *eMarketer*. Available at: www.emarketer.com/content/why-amazon-is-about-to-upend-the-70-billion-tv-ad-market [Accessed 22 Oct. 2019].

2.   Cannes Lions. (2019). Titanium Lions | Awards | Cannes Lions 2019. [online] Available at: www.canneslions.com/enter/awards/communication/titanium-lions [Accessed 4 Nov. 2019].

3.   Hall, K. (2019). Personal communication. [23 September].

4.   Frome, N. (2018). Personal communication. [24 August].

5.   Simpson, G. (2019). TV is dying (still) (soon) (maybe). [online] Mediapost.com. Available at: www.mediapost.com/publications/article/338071/tv-is-dying-still-soon-maybe.html [Accessed 22 Oct. 2019].

6.   Academy of Art University. (2019). Mac vs PC ad campaign is a pop culture icon | Academy of Art U. [online] Available at: https://blog.academyart.edu/mac-pc-ad-campaign/ [Accessed 22 Oct. 2019].

7.   Colon, G. (2019). Personal communication. [6 Sep].

8.   Kumar, A., Bezawada, R., Rishika, R., Janakiraman, R. and Kannan, P. (2019). *From Social to Sale: The Effects of Firm-Generated Content in Social Media on Customer Behavior*. [online] Rhsmith.umd.edu. Available at: www.rhsmith.umd.edu/files/Documents/Departments/Marketing/social-to-sale-jm-2016.pdf [Accessed 22 Oct. 2019].

9.   Han, F. (2020). Personal communication. [7 Jan.].

10. Kharpal, A. (2019). Everything you need to know about WeChat — China's billion-user messaging app. [online] CNBC. Available at: www.cnbc.com/2019/02/04/what-is-wechat-china-biggest-messaging-app.html [Accessed 22 Oct. 2019].

11. Schroter, J. (2011). *Steve Jobs introduces iPhone in 2007*. [video] Available at: www.youtube.com/watch?v=MnrJzXM7a6o [Accessed 30 Oct. 2019].

12. Solis, B. (2019). Customer journeys start with smartphones, but brands still don't get mobile. [online] Available at: www.briansolis.com/2018/08/customer-journeys-start-with-smartphones-but-brands-still-dont-get-mobile/ [Accessed 22 Oct. 2019].

13. Droesch, B. (2019). More than half of US social network users will be mobile-only in 2019. [online] *eMarketer*. Available at: www.emarketer.com/content/more-than-half-of-social-network-users-will-be-mobile-only-in-2019?ecid=NL100 [Accessed 22 Oct. 2019].

14. Alexander, L. (2019). What is digital marketing? [online] Blog.hubspot.com. Available at: https://blog.hubspot.com/marketing/what-is-digital-marketing [Accessed 22 Oct. 2019].

15. Frisch, R. (2019). Personal communication. [26 Aug.].

16. Malm, P. (2018). Personal communication. [27 Dec].

17. The Financial (2019). Consumers moving away from traditional forms of entertainment and media consumption. [online] Available at: www.finchannel.com/opinion/analysis-3/77108-consumers-moving-away-from-traditional-forms-of-entertainment-and-media-consumption [Accessed 22 Oct. 2019].

18. O'Brien, C. (2019). 7 ways to optimize online-to-offline marketing. [online] Digital Marketing Institute. Available at: https://digitalmarketinginstitute.com/en-us/blog/7-ways-to-optimize-online-to-offline-marketing [Accessed 22 Oct. 2019].

19. Powers, K. (2019). Product visibility in 'Stranger Things 3' valued at $15 million. [online] American Marketing Association. Available at: www.ama.org/marketing-news/product-placement-in-stranger-things-3-valued-at-15-million/ [Accessed 22 Oct. 2019].

20. Enberg, J. and Lipsman, A. (2019). Podcast advertising 2018. [online] eMarketer. Available at: www.emarketer.com/content/podcast-advertising-2018 [Accessed 22 Oct. 2019].

21. Goldberg, L. (2019). U.S. podcast ad revenues hit historic $479 million in 2018, an increase of 53% over prior year, according to IAB & PWC research. [online] IAB. Available at: www.iab.com/news/u-s-podcast-ad-revenues-hit-historic-479-million-in-2018/ [Accessed 22 Oct. 2019].

22. Radio Ink. (2019). How much ad revenue will radio get this year? [online] Available at: https://radioink.com/2019/07/09/how-much-ad-revenue-will-radio-get-this-year/ [Accessed 22 Oct. 2019].

23. Dhar, R. (2019). Personal communication. [30 August].

24. Agius, A. (2019). 12 examples of brands with brilliant omni-channel experiences. [online] Blog.hubspot.com. Available at: https://blog.hubspot.com/service/omni-channel-experience [Accessed 4 Nov. 2019].

25. Pitney Bowes. (2019). Critical channels of choice: Customers expect Omnichannel – So why are so many brands missing them? [online] Available at: www.cmocouncil.org/thought-leadership/webcasts/critical-channels-of-choice [Accessed 22 Oct. 2019].

26. Becker, B. (2019). The ultimate guide to account-based marketing (ABM). [online] Blog.hubspot.com. Available at: https://blog.hubspot.com/marketing/account-based-marketing-guide [Accessed 1 Mar. 2020].

27. Ibid.

28. Otsuka, C. (2019). How to distribute personalized content for Your ABM program [cheat sheet]. [online] Hub.uberflip.com. Available at: https://hub.uberflip.com/blog/5-content-distribution-channels-for-your-abm-program [Accessed 22 Oct. 2019].

29. Roetzer, P. (2018). Personal communication. [28 Nov.].

30. Frome, N. (2018). Personal communication. [24 Aug.].

31. Baer, J. (2019). Personal communication. [1 Aug.].

PART 3

CONNECTING THROUGH NEW CHANNELS AND DEVELOPING YOUR PERSONAL BRAND

8

ENGAGING SOCIAL EMPLOYEES, INFLUENCERS AND GENERATION Z

Learning Goals

1. Analyze the differences between a social employee and a regular employee.
2. Illustrate why employees who represent a strategic business asset hold the key to delivering authentic communications.
3. Evaluate how social employee engagement benefits both the larger brand of the company and the personal brand of the employee to form a win-win.
4. Analyze how a company can design and deploy a pilot program to create a manageable social employee rollout plan to drive business efforts.
5. Evaluate the growth and power of influencer marketing as a disrupting force in traditional marketing approaches.
6. Evaluate the rising importance of Generation Z and Generation Alpha to marketers.

The age of the 'Social Employee' – everyone is in the 'customer contact business.' (Everyone=EVERYONE.)

Tom Peters[1]

Let's face it: digital marketing is all about reach.

Thanks to the internet and social media, brands have greater access to their target audience than ever before. But the internet is a vast space – one that's continually

growing. To connect with their audience, brands often must move in multiple directions at once, identifying the specific communities that will be most likely to engage
with them.

In terms of reach, we've found that digital brands can be divided up into two
categories: T-Rexes and octopuses. The T-Rex represents the traditional brand. They
either existed before digital marketing channels emerged or are fronted by marketing
leads who haven't changed with the times. Sure, they may have set up a perfunctory
digital presence in the form of a website or a Facebook page, but they're not using
those assets to engage their audience. Like a T-Rex, these brands may look powerful
at first glance, but closer inspection reveals that in terms of reach, they simply don't
have what it takes.

The octopus, on the other hand, represents the modern social brand. They're
intelligent problem solvers, capable of blending in with their environment and moving quickly to get where they need to be. Further, they have eight powerful arms
that can move independently to carry out orders from a central hub. And not only
are these eight arms able to engage in different directions, they're able to do so with
intelligence and care; each sucker on each arm is a sensitive data-collecting tool that
promotes deep knowledge.

Clearly, when it comes to digital marketing, it's better to be the octopus than
the T-Rex.

The question is, how? While our T-Rex and octopus analogy may be useful in understanding what makes a successful digital brand tick, what can we as marketers do to
make this vision a reality? In a word: people. In the age of social media, engagement
isn't about creating a big, monolithic brand, but rather about cultivating a community of like-minded individuals – chiefly brand ambassadors such as social employee
advocates and influencers. Each act has its own brand touchpoint, operating from a
unique perspective, with a unique voice, and on distinct channels to create a dynamic,
nuanced brand identity. In this chapter, we'll show you how it's done.

THE BASICS OF SOCIAL ADVOCACY

Before we dig into the different types of social advocates and how they can help your
brand, let's talk about what makes social advocacy so important. Put simply, it all comes
down to trust. According to Sprout Social, '61 percent of consumers said they would be
more likely to research a product or service recommended on social by a friend vs. 36
percent for influencers/celebrities'.[2] When properly empowered and deployed, brand
advocates can be exactly the trusted friends that can engage their communities and
help move the needle for your brand.

The trick, of course, is that this engagement and advocacy has to be earned. While authentic engagement can certainly help grow brand awareness, inauthentic engagement will have the opposite effect. For brand advocacy to work properly, trust can't be forced. It has to be earned. The brands that can master the following elements will be well on their way.

It Starts with Culture

Here we return to a bedrock of branding: culture. As Peter Drucker once famously said, 'Culture eats strategy for breakfast.' In other words, strategy is great, but it won't get you far if that strategy is driven by an inauthentic culture.

In modern business, where workforces are increasingly spread out across the globe, culture can be a tricky thing to pin down. How can brands establish their own identity – first internally within their own ranks and then externally across social channels – when their employees might never interact with each other face-to-face? Is it even possible to create a uniform vision for your brand in an era characterized by individuality?

The short answer is yes – but you have to work for it. Brand identity isn't created through catchy slogans or other superficial measures. To create an authentic, modern brand, let the employees lead the way. If brands are to tap one of their greatest marketing assets, they must also trust those assets to be themselves as they engage on the brand's behalf.

This is where culture becomes so important. As discussed in Chapter 3, the key here is to master the *why* – that is, your mission, vision and values. Without this clarity, any advocacy efforts risk becoming a disjointed free-for-all. However, if everyone is united around and has bought into a larger brand identity, then they will carry that identity forward with them as they engage across social channels. If your brand can do this, then you will have cleared a major hurdle toward establishing trust with your audience.

The Two-Way Street of Social Engagement

According to Ashwani Monga, Professor of Marketing and Provost and Executive Vice Chancellor at Rutgers University Newark, 'Earlier, marketing was a one-way street. Brands would advertise and signal their value; consumers would decide whether it was a good brand or a bad brand.' In other words, Monga says, trust was based only on what customers could see from a company in terms of products or messages. Outside of asking their friends and family, customers had no other real way of gauging trust.

But now, Monga says, 'A lot of that trust is external. The success of companies like Amazon and others is based on the idea that trust comes not from the seller but rather from the broader community that is rating you.' To Monga, this has meant that the power of delivering trust has shifted from the marketers to the end users.

Such a shift can be hard for brands to adjust to. Where once they had the power to control the trust conversation, now it's no longer in their hands. Nevertheless, Monga says brands need not worry. 'If I know I'm a good product or I'm a good service, I won't mind if you go and check a thousand other people's ratings of my brand. Those who hide because they don't have trust in their products or services are going to be left behind.' As Monga sees it, the more you put yourself out there and let others do the talking for you, the quicker you can build deep, lasting trust with your audience.[3]

On Leading with Humor

When it comes to social engagement, humor is no laughing matter. According to Dr. Jennifer Aaker, a renowned behavioral psychologist and General Atlantic Professor at the Stanford Graduate School of Business, who studies how meaning and purpose shape the choices individuals make and how time can be used to create meaning in unconventional ways, 'Most think humor is fun and frivolous. But it is also powerful. At the same time.' How important is humor to building community? As Aaker says, 'It is critical.'[4]

Which is why Aaker and Stanford lecturer Naomi Bagdonas teach a course, 'Humor: Serious Business', at Stanford's Graduate School of Business, where they have helped some of the world's most hard-driving, business minds build humor into their organizations and transform how they see the role of humor in their lives in business. Commenting on the course for an *Inc.* profile, Aaker said, 'Many struggle because they hold onto the false dichotomy between bringing humor and taking your work seriously.' However, she added, 'The right balance of gravity and levity gives power to both.'[5]

Often, all it takes is a moment of levity to shift a mood or interaction. And once we start looking for these moments, we start seeing them everywhere. We discover how a lighthearted line in an email can take an exchange from tense and combative to cooperative and productive. Or how sharing laughter with someone can shift how they relate to us, and us to them. And we see how humor can fuel meaningful change in our lives, relationships, and the world. Says Aaker:

> Humor isn't only useful for helping us understand our own struggles. In fact, according to some research, the appropriate use of humor is linked to perceptions of confidence, competence, and intelligence – all of which help to boost social status. But why? Simply put, because we humans often perceive people in power to be more uninhibited and comfortable expressing emotions.[6]

To Aaker and Bagdonas, humor is what makes us human – the connecting tissue throughout all human culture. As such, it should not be confined to a few hours on a Saturday night or with a room full of strangers. Shared laughter is a universal language that can tear down silos both at the office and at home.[7]

According to Ashwani Monga, humor serves as an important cultural indicator, which relates to happiness overall:

> Happiness is a way of telling people, 'I care about you. You care about me. I'm nice to you. Be nice to me.' If companies are nice in terms of all these factors – such as organizational setting, compensation, and work/life balance – then their employees will go out of their way to do things for your company, which includes what they will do for your brand, how they think, and how they take ownership.[8]

This is important. As Monga notes, happiness doesn't come simply from organizational affiliation:

> If you're trying to connect with an extended self, an organization, it's like a mythical concept. What makes an organization is us. It's the people. It's our network that forms the organization. When you make each other happy, it's like having nodes that are connecting, making you a bigger organism that can deliver more to others.[9]

As we'll see in the next section, these authentic connections lie at the core of social branding. Employees who are genuinely happy in the workplace and engage each other with affection will take that same brand spirit with them when they engage their networks of peers, friends and family on social channels.

BRANDING FROM THE INSIDE OUT

In Chapter 6, we spoke of the importance of storytelling to the modern brand. Stories help humanize your brand by focusing not on what you sell, but rather on your company's mission, vision and values. Naturally, wherever there is a story, there is a *storyteller* – and who better to tell that story than your employees?

At Blue Focus Marketing, we refer to this process as 'Branding from the Inside Out'. In our experience, a brand cannot communicate externally unless it can first communicate internally. Branding from the Inside Out can be broken down to the following core elements:

1. Testing. Do your employees know what your brand stands for? Do they care? If the answer isn't yes to both questions, your social engagement efforts will fail.
2. Understanding the *why*. Does your brand have a purpose, and are your employees aligned around your mission, vision and values? Those who are will likely be more energized and engaged.

3.   Telling your story everywhere. Social engagement thrives on good stories. When those stories aren't just fluff, but also provide real value, they can lead to increased sales and higher customer retention.

4.   Leveraging employees' voices. Social marketing is everyone's job. Right now, within your company's ranks are talented brand ambassadors. All you have to do is create the support team around them and give them a platform to engage their networks effectively.

5.   Creating impact. Don't worry about how many platforms you're on or how many posts you share. Instead, focus on being where your fans are and adding *value* with every interaction.

Approached correctly, this Branding from the Inside Out framework will align employees around your brand and position you to make the most of another key component of social marketing: employee advocacy.

EMPLOYEE ADVOCACY AND THE RISE OF THE SOCIAL EMPLOYEE

In the 2010s, the concept of employee advocacy began to take brands by storm. We were fortunate to observe and document this transformation firsthand in our 2014 book, *The Social Employee*. In *The Social Employee*, we learned of the social journeys of leading brands like IBM, Southwest Airlines and AT&T – and how they were embracing and empowering their employees to become authentic, engaged brand ambassadors.[10] Not long after, Mark had the opportunity to summarize our findings during a TEDx Navesink Talk, drawing from his own experiences from Madison Avenue to the present.

The argument went something like this: The voice of the organization has changed. Where once all communications came from a combination of the top brass and the marketing department, social tools have made individual employees more visible than ever – and more likely to be heard. While they're not the only ones doing the talking, there's no question that their voice now makes up a key piece of any brand's identity.[11]

We have seen firsthand what a social employee advocacy program can do for brands looking to leverage the power of employees. However, a word of caution: employee advocacy isn't as simple as opening a Twitter account and assigning an intern to monitor it. In current practice, employee advocacy is more of a continuum than a foregone conclusion. Some brands have successfully implemented programs and others haven't even considered trying. But most lie somewhere in the middle: they're considering the opportunity – they may have even made a few broad attempts – but they're unsure how to truly empower their social employees, or even why they're so valuable.

This may be why, in 2019, a survey conducted by Social Media Today found that only 31% of respondents reported already having an employee advocacy program in place. While it's encouraging that a further 29% of respondents planned to implement an employee advocacy program, that still leaves a whopping 40% of organizations unaccounted for.[12] But why are so many brands still on the fence about employee advocacy? As we've discovered, the root of the problem is simple: most organizations don't understand the value a workforce of social employees can bring to the table.

Why Are Social Employees Important?

The future of marketing is about activating the expertise of your entire organization, which means employee advocates are the new authentic marketing channel. The new marketing is viral and people-driven, not about push selling. The more people (customers and employees alike) you invite to celebrate your brand or champion an important cause together, the more your own brand value will grow as a result.

There is perhaps no better example of this dynamic than the Ice Bucket Challenge. In the summer of 2014, the Ice Bucket Challenge was a legitimate phenomenon, drawing brands, celebrities and everyday people to raise awareness of and donate to ALS-related research. In all, 'more than 17 million people posted videos of them participating in the challenge. It helped raise more than $220 million for ALS charities worldwide.' This is viral marketing at its best.[13]

But how can that be? It all comes down to digital footprint; the more people you have engaging, the more social chatter you generate, the more likes and shares you get, and the more amplification your brand message receives. When approached correctly, this leads to increased web traffic and sales – though perhaps not on the scale of the Ice Bucket Challenge (which was a true phenomenon).

Social employees are ideally suited for this task because they're seen as trustworthy in their community. In fact, according to the 2016 Edelman Trust Barometer, everyday employees are considered more trustworthy than CEOs.[14] The trick? Authenticity. According to marketing thought leader Simon Sinek, 'If you don't understand people, you don't understand business.'[15] At the heart of this idea is the fact that people don't want to talk to a brand; they want to talk to other people – someone they can relate to.

Unlike paid influencers (who we'll discuss later in this chapter), brands don't have to pay their social employees to say nice things about their brand – outside of their salary, that is. Most employees are happy to play brand ambassador and advocate on behalf of your brand if they know your brand has their back. The takeaway: the more you support your employees, the more they will say nice things about you, and the more public trust in your brand will grow.

To be clear, supporting your employees doesn't mean micromanaging them. Social employees succeed not because they blandly parrot their parent brand's message, but because they engage audiences from their unique perspective – in other words, their personal brand. The benefit to your brand is the cumulative impact: the more employees you have sharing and engaging in their own unique way, the more your digital footprint will grow.

All of this points to a win-win for both the social employee and your brand. By empowering your employees to engage with confidence, kindness and authenticity, they bring your company culture – its mission, vision and values – out of the cubicle and into the world for everyone to see.

Sidebar

Does Social Engagement Really Matter?

'It's interesting how much employee engagement matters, especially in a big company like ours', says Kathleen Hall, Corporate Vice President, Brand, Advertising & Research at Microsoft. 'Our employees are their own social media platform when you think about it.'

To illustrate her point, Hall referred back to Microsoft's 2019 Super Bowl commercial, which featured a child with special needs receiving a custom-fit video game controller while his friends cheered him on (see Chapter 7). 'I think I had 4,000 emails from people, saying, basically, "Thank you for representing the company I've always known I worked for."'[16]

The following are actual statements from Microsoft employees upon viewing that commercial for the first time:

Thank you, thank you, thank you. My heart can hardly stand this – as an employee, a mother of a special needs child, as a gamer, as a human.

Just need to say this is a message that will leave a lot of eyes watery on Superbowl Sunday great job on putting this together for the entire globe to see, Keep up the great work.

I'm relatively new to Microsoft, but its products and initiatives like this one that drove me to apply over and over to be a part of this organization.

This is just so beautiful, thank you for the happy tears this morning. Can't wait to share this with everyone.

What an amazing advertisement . . . brought me to tears, but in such a great way! I love what Microsoft is doing for individuals like the ones in the super bowl ad, makes me so so proud to work for this great company! Congrats on this amazing super bowl advertising launch . . . I Love it and Microsoft!!!!

Absolutely beautiful commercial that brought me to tears. Your team does a wonderful job bringing MS products and values to life – congratulations and thank you for sharing!

Thank you! That brought tears to my eyes. #SoProudToBeHere

You're killin' me. Cannot stop these tears. SO good. Thank you.

To Hall, these messages aren't just words. They're an affirmation of the company's commitment to its workforce. 'One of your best and most important constituents is your employees. With the social media tools they have today, employees can be your biggest fans. They can help perpetuate your message, as well as be personally inspired, which is nothing but good for the brand.'[17]

What Role Do Social Executives Play in Employee Advocacy?

Where there are social employees, there are also social executives. These aren't the social executives of old. Forgoing old-school 'command and control' approaches, social executives know that it's not enough to talk the talk – they have to walk the walk too.

First and foremost, this means embracing a culture of transparency. Social executives understand that in a connected era, what you *don't* say speaks just as loudly as what you do. In the case of social initiatives, this means providing internal stakeholders with regular updates, always focusing on the brand's long-term goals. To promote a culture of accountability and results, social executives also keep the focus on the valuable metrics and KPIs wherever possible.

So how do they do this? Social executives focus first on building buy-in. Again, they don't just dictate what they want done. They *explain* why it's important. Then, they take ownership of the effort, modeling the behavior or activity they want their employees to follow, and making themselves available for questions and follow-up.

Designing and Deploying a Social Employee Pilot Program

The great thing about employee advocacy is that, whether they realize it or not, brands large, small and in between likely already have informal employee advocates among their ranks. The trick for most brands is identifying them and empowering them to become full-fledged social employees. Here are three common traits to look for:

1. Engaged and passionate. Millennial and Gen Z workers are transforming the workforce. They're far more interested in working for a company that they identify with personally, and that contributes to the greater good. Look for the employees who are eager to tell your brand's story, and you've likely found a good social employee candidate.

2. Socially savvy. As the name implies, social employees have to be comfortable engaging on social media channels. This doesn't mean they need intimate knowledge of every tool and platform out there. In fact, it's more important that they have a basic understanding of social tools and engagement as a broader concept – such as how they can learn the ropes, what value it might have to the brand, how it can be deployed, and how it can be adapted into their workflow.

3. People-smart. In the term *social media*, the 'social' is just as important as the 'media'. Yes, social employees must know the tools of their craft, but they also must understand how to relate to people, how to celebrate fans of the brand, and how to leverage their relationships into positive outcomes for the brand.

There are more common traits of a social employee than this, of course. However, these three characteristics are ideal for identifying and recruiting employees to spearhead your social employee pilot program. In the following sections, we'll walk you through our five-step Social Employee Pilot Activation Plan, as illustrated in Figure 8.1.

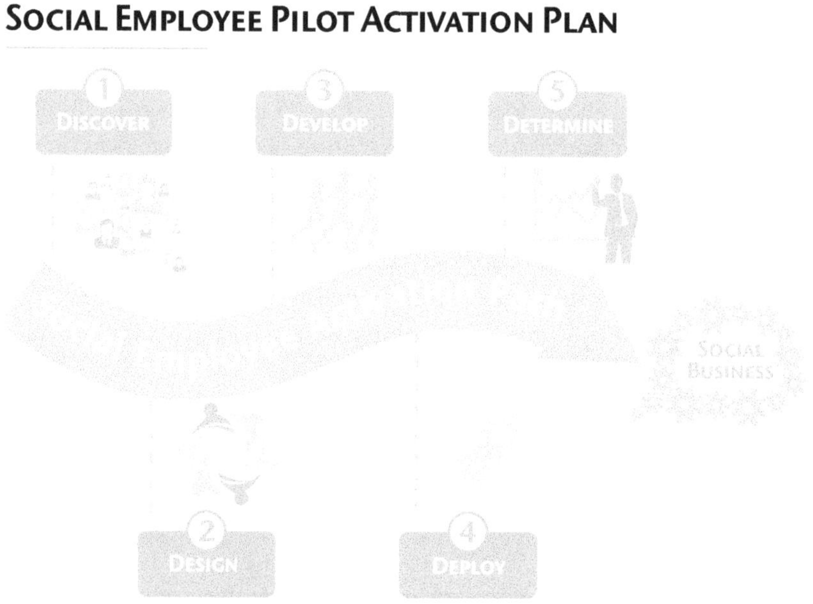

SOCIAL EMPLOYEE PILOT ACTIVATION PLAN

Figure 8.1   Social Employee Pilot Activation Plan.

Source: ©2020 Blue Focus Marketing®. All Rights Reserved.

Step 1: Discover

The discovery phase is all about selecting your pilot team, learning about their talents, and understanding what they're already doing to be successful. During this phase, many brands are surprised to learn not only what your employees already know, but what they can teach you.

The first step in the discovery phase is selecting your team. In a social business, marketing is everyone's job. Your pilot program should reflect this, with candidates drawn from all areas of your business – HR, marketing, sales, product development, accounting, and so on. New hires may also be considered for a role in your pilot program.

Once you have your pilot team, perform a skills inventory. What hidden pockets of talent do your employees have, and how can you leverage those talents in your pilot program? Some employees may be skilled early adopters, and others may be great at developing systems and procedures, while others may turn out to be excellent teachers.

Finally, perform an engagement inventory to determine your company's baseline. How are your employees already engaging communities online? Who has the strongest and most robust personal brand, and how did they earn it? Is anyone from the marketing or sales team already using employee advocacy to move the needle for your organization?

Step 2: Design

Throughout your pilot program, your goal is to let your burgeoning social employees take the lead and to learn from their example. As such, during the design phase, it's important that your social media policy mixes reasonable boundaries with the freedom to maneuver and engage independently. Here are five common components:

1. **Employee identification.** No matter the social platform, if your employee is engaging on behalf of your brand, this should be clear to anyone who views their posts or content. For example, bios should clearly state their employer affiliation.
2. **Confidentiality.** This may sound obvious, but mistakes happen. Employees should be acutely aware of what they shouldn't disclose to outside parties.
3. **Engaging in good faith.** Social employees should represent the best of your brand. As such, they must remember to engage with integrity, give others the benefit of the doubt, and avoid being drawn into arguments.
4. **Respecting copyrights.** Social engagement means social sharing – both of your own branded content and of other content that aligns with your mission, vision and values. Be careful though: if you post someone else's content, make sure to give credit where it's due.
5. **Accountability.** If you post something popular, own it. If you slip up, own that too. It's better to admit you were wrong than to double down on an obvious error.

With guardrails like these in place, your social employees will feel empowered to put their best foot forward.

Step 3: Develop

After you've designed the rules for engagement, it's time to train up your employees. Here are five considerations:

1. **Follow the 70:20:10 learning model.** When it comes to learning, 70% should be performed independently, 20% should come through informal training through managers and co-workers, and the final 10% should come through formal training programs.
2. **Focus on the *how*.** Social engagement is constantly evolving, which means the concepts your social employees learn should be too. Design training materials and programs to help employees find the answers they *need*. And encourage knowledge-sharing: if an employee learns something valuable, empower them to share what they've learned in the form of a video or blog post.
3. **Encourage outside training.** No business wants to create an echo chamber. Outside knowledge builds your company's overall business intelligence while also boosting your employees' resumes through verifiable training and certifications.
4. **Keep it social.** Help social employees take ownership of the learning process by allowing them to design their own knowledge gaps and learning goals. Then, whenever your employee has levelled up within your social program, help them show off their progress with badges, certificates, or employee leaderboards.
5. **Make training for everyone.** Scaling from a pilot program to an organizational initiative can be tricky. Therefore, to build a social culture in the workplace, it's important to develop social learning resources that everyone can access and understand – from the C-suite down to the mailroom.

As you continue to develop your social employee pilot program, it's important not to forget your senior-level employees too. Consider a reverse-mentorship program where lower-level employees help guide managers and executives through their own skills acquisition process.

Step 4: Deploy

At long last, it's time to turn your social employees loose so they can begin engaging their social networks and expanding your brand's digital footprint. When it comes to social engagement, the conversation begins and ends with content. Here's how it works:

1. **Start by building a Brand Choreography Team (see Chapter 10).** Through creating, commissioning, or curating, the Brand Choreography Team will provide social employees with a steady stream of brand-approved content.
2. **Decide what types of content to share.** Every brand will have their own answer to this question, but the general guideline is this: if it's valuable, then it's worth sharing.

And remember, variety matters – infographics, news, retweets, blogs, and more are all fair game.

Use the 80/20 rule. Social employee advocacy is about engagement, not one-way advertising. As a general rule, make 80% of your posts about valuable content, and 20% about your brand.

Make sharing easy. Your content should be able to pass through your Brand Choreography Team to your social employees in as few steps as possible. The easier it is to share, the more likely that your employees actually will.

Many platforms have emerged in recent years to help enable the employee advocacy process. One such platform is LinkedIn Elevate. According to Warren Quach, principal product manager for LinkedIn Elevate, the platform is a way for companies to provide their employees with tools to build their brand on social media. 'What's special about Elevate is that we are members-first – meaning that we are thinking about what a member wants and needs out of this product in addition to what a customer or a company might want', says Quach. 'We believe that if we solve a member or employee's need, ultimately, that will lead to a better product and better outcomes for the company itself.'

To Quach, this means creating a platform that allows employees to share to whatever social network they choose. It also means encouraging employees to take ownership of the process by allowing them to track and measure the impact of their sharing – and even aggregating those numbers in terms of marketing dollars.

No matter what the specific features, Quach believes that the true value of an employee advocacy platform comes down to one word: ownership. 'We believe that as a member, *you* decide what is most important, the most interesting for you', Quach says. 'We want you to understand the company's mission and vision and forward that stuff that you bought into, and you believe in. It's not a company that's forcing you to do this.' [18]

Step 5: Determine

Now that you've deployed your social employee pilot program, it's time to measure what you did, study the results, and prepare for the next iteration. Here are some things to keep in mind:

Measure what matters. Especially in the pilot phase, your goal is to understand (1) who is talking about you, (2) what they are saying, and (3) how these conversations are affecting web activity.

Measure your employees. Not every employee will behave the same way during the deploy phase. Here, your goal is to determine (1) which employees are most active,

(2) which platforms are the most effective for your brand, and (3) who has generated the most engagement relative to their online activity.

3   **Identify your biggest fans.** Engagement is a two-way street. Who is engaging with *you*? Most importantly, how can you leverage that engagement to boost your brand's signal even more?

Once you've learned these things, your job is to refocus, reapply and redeploy. Eventually, you will have built the kind of employee advocacy program that other brands will be jealous of.

As you set out on your pilot program, just remember: nothing matters more than the human component. Successful social employee advocacy combines storytelling with authentic engagement to help create a sort of 'brand soul'. In a world where brand identity is a living collaboration between brands, employees and customers, the value of having your employees out on the front lines cannot be overstated.

Sidebar

Social employees are the gateway to brand awareness. In our book *The Social Employee*, we interviewed Julie Kehoe, chief communications officer at Domo, a cloud-based software company based in American Fork, Utah. Domo was one of the pioneering companies in humanizing the brand by starting with its employees. We asked Julie to provide an updated case for *The New Marketing*. The following case study is a firsthand account provided by Julie Kehoe and her team.

Case Study: Domo by Julie Kehoe, chief communications officer and team at Domo

Scaling a Social Employee Program

Since launching the Domosocial experiment, we've leveraged employee-led social media as part of our ongoing marketing mix.

In the early stages of the program, onboarding and training of new employees was conducted via a monthly meeting in our Silicon Slopes offices with a web-based conference option for remote employees. This monthly in-person session ensured that questions could be answered personally and that employees had a group of peers who would be in the same 'class' working towards their Domosocial badges, designations for employees who successfully completed each step of the program.

During each monthly training, employees were given a deadline to hit milestones in the Domosocial project, but as we grew, the process became difficult to scale. Tracking employee progress and making sure everyone was able to attend an orientation program became challenging. If an employee couldn't make the first monthly meeting, it sometimes took months to get them through an orientation, and tracking, and follow-up became more and more difficult and time-consuming for our team. As a result, Domosocial project completion rates began to slip.

How to Keep Up

The Domosocial project had grown because it was a partnership between Domo's marketing and HR teams. HR would introduce the Domosocial project in its weekly new hire orientation meetings and collect the social media handles employees wanted to use for this program, so that marketing could set up the right tracking systems. However, a few years into the program, with our rapid employee growth both in the US and international, program management started to become too time consuming.

We knew we had to redesign the program to become more scalable.

Redesign: Automation through Domo's Learning Management System

In partnership with Domo's HR team, we decided to create a self-guided orientation program for the Domosocial project in our learning management system [LMS]. One of the benefits of putting orientation in the LMS was that employees could begin the program anytime during their first week at Domo. The LMS also provided an automated mechanism to keep track of where employees were in the program.

Update and Simplify the Program Requirements

Before setting up the LMS-based training, our team updated the social media tasks that we were asking employees to complete and the program design. Social media platforms/tools and programs had changed significantly in just a few short years, and we really were aiming to provide relevant social experiences so employees could become more effective advocates for Domo, while also understanding how to better build and sell a product that was social in nature.

Once we updated the tasks and program design, our team worked with our HR partners to build the self-guided program.

Carrot, Not the Stick, to Increase Engagement

As the company grew, new employees joining Domo were more socially savvy than many peers in the years prior. As a result, we shifted focus to reward employees for participation in the program, rather than putting pressure on people just to check off the boxes. One of the ways we did this was to tie the new hire tech benefit (a $500 bonus that could be applied to the purchase of personal technology such as a tablet) to completion of the Domosocial project in the LMS.

We also used contests at strategic times during the year to increase engagement. For example, before and during Domopalooza, our big annual customer event, we

(Continued)

create a friendly competition where employees and departments can win prizes and bragging rights for their participation as brand advocates. We limit these contests to two to three per year, so we don't create contest fatigue. And we typically time them to other marketing events to help drive more value from those marketing investments. Example contest prizes include:

- MVP – Most social employee: Apple Watch (Up to $500)
- Fan Favorite: Best event-related post/most engagement: $250 gift card
- All-Stars: Top 10 most social employees: $25 gift card
- Champions: Best overall department: Bragging rights and a team trophy (judging will heavily factor the percentage of each department active in the contest)

It's interesting to note that while our engineering department typically doesn't lead in social participation during normal times, when we run contests the engineers really come to life and have taken the team trophy away from the naturally competitive sales team on several occasions.

Providing Regular Content and a Social Employee Platform

To realize our goal of employees becoming regular brand advocates for Domo (beyond the completion of the Domosocial project) required the adoption of a social employee platform and a regular supply of relevant content.

The platform, which includes a mobile app, makes it super easy for our employees to share curated content about Domo and related thought leadership topics with their social networks across numerous social platforms.

To ensure our global teams would use the tool, we set up administrators in each region who can approve regional content that is submitted into the tool and submit content for global sharing. We also created 'divisions' so that people within region or departments could easily find content that was relevant to their interests and social followers.

Having one global platform for social employees ensures we are consistently leveraging the power of our employees as brand advocates and make[s] it easy for employees to share relevant content. (Employees are also now active contributors of content to the platform.)

We put all Domo news and significant media coverage about our company product and customers into the social platform, almost immediately after it hits the wire so employees can share it quickly with their networks. For content that is more significant in nature (like a great product or customer story), we hit a broadcast/alert feature in the mobile app and also send a company-wide email, so employees know there is something noteworthy to share.

We also require employees to sign up for a third-party marketing platform and download the mobile app during their LMS training.[19]

MARKETING TO MILLENNIALS AND GENERATION Z

As we move into the 2020s and beyond, brands will become increasingly focused on marketing to two prominent generations. First is the Millennial generation, which includes anyone born between roughly 1980 and 1995. Second is Generation Z, which includes those born between 1995 and approximately 2010. (Here, we should note that different groups define the beginning and end points of each generation differently. The ranges we have chosen reflect the general consensus.)

During the 2010s, much was written about the challenges marketers faced trying to reach Millennials. However, as the decade progressed and the oldest members of the Millennial generation began to approach middle age, many found those challenges to be overstated. According to Cheryl Conner in a 2019 article for *Entrepreneur*:

> Marketing to Millennials used to be tricky. Their youthfulness and tech-savvy ways kept us on our toes as we redefined authenticity and sought new and fresher ways to bring brand identity to life. While these needs still apply, adults under forty are revealing themselves to be regular adults after all, with grounded and sensible needs.[20]

So, while Millennials have turned out not to be quite as enigmatic as many marketers originally feared, brands have learned that reaching them requires a new approach to the idea of authenticity. And as Gen Z continues to mature and occupy a growing segment of the market, the need for real, authentic engagement is only likely to continue. According to Adam Grant in an article for *Forbes*, 'Gen Zers desire even more transparency from companies and distrust obvious forms of traditional advertisements.'[21]

If Millennials – and Gen Zers especially – don't trust traditional advertising, what's the solution? According to Tim Calkins, Clinical Professor of Marketing, Kellogg School of Management, Northwestern University, the answer begins with word of mouth:

> Word of mouth is incredibly important because it tends to be fairly trustworthy advice. People tend to trust and listen to what other people say. So, if you think about what shapes a brand, very often it's the word of mouth around a brand that will shape it. Sometimes it will do so much more powerfully than what the brand can say. In that way, I guess you could say that what somebody says about you is much more impactful than what you say about yourself.[22]

As we'll see in the next section, a word-of-mouth approach to branding doesn't have to be random. Through an approach known as influencer marketing, brands can create the conditions for authentic, person-to-person interactions focused on their brand.

But while these approaches may work for Millennials and Gen Zers in the short-term, we must always remember that each new generation brings unique marketing challenges. Already marketers have begun turning their attention to the *next* generation – Generation Alpha, the children of Millennials – who will be growing up in a digital environment much different than that of their parents.

Imagine a young child listening to her parents talk to inanimate objects and telling them what to do. Order a six-pack of batteries. Remind me to leave for a haircut appoint-ment by 7:00 pm on Tuesday. Turn on the lights. What's the weather for tomorrow? Did the Steelers win? The list is endless. This newest generation is not only born digital but has been hearing voice commands from humans to machines since birth. There has never been a generation that has experienced the power of the human voice to this extent.

What will this mean for marketers? How can brands capture the attention and interest of a generation raised on voice command, AI and automation? The marketers able to answer this question will have a head start on winning the future.

THE RISE OF INFLUENCER MARKETING

During the 2010s, as social media became a mainstay of mass culture, another new marketing channel emerged: influencers. By carefully crafting online personas and engaging communities around a topic of interest – be it online gaming, fashion, pop culture, and so on – influencers have built massive followings on their platforms of choice. Day in and day out, they share useful content and engage with their followers, and in so doing, become trusted hubs within their chosen communities.

As these influencers rose to prominence, marketers took notice and began to partner with these influencers to share their brand message. The result was power-ful. According to Chris Detert, chief communications officer at Influential, it's not hard to see why:

> Social media takes word of mouth and puts it at scale. The people you follow on social media are like your friends. They might be people that you don't know, and they might be people with elevated status, but because you followed them, they're a trusted source for you. When they speak to their audience, it's like they're speaking to you – and what they say to you, you take with greater trust levels. This means you're much more likely to take action, whether to go see a movie or go buy a product, based on their recommendation.[23]

The question is, why has influencer marketing been so successful? What is it about it that is able to cut through the noise and reach younger generations so well? According to Geoffrey Colon, head of Microsoft Advertising Brand Studio, the answer may actually be multigenerational:

> There is definitely a difference between monetary influence and cultural influence. Cultural influence is definitely held by Generation Z now, but you have to look at how Generation Z is being influenced by Generation X, or by parents who basically are saying, 'Don't trust the system, don't trust any of this.'

In other words, the fact that Generation Z largely comes from a generation who *also* didn't trust traditional advertising means they aren't likely to either. This is why the need for authentic, word-of-mouth branding is so important. However, for Gen Z, this need runs far deeper. 'Generation Z is very communal. They're very interested in the communal effect in terms of how they behave', says Colon. The result is that Gen Z is deeply interested in shared experiences and in activities they can enjoy with their friends and community.[24] Connecting with influencers – and the communities they attract – is just one way they do that.

When it comes to identifying and collaborating with influencers, brands don't necessarily have to go out looking for celebrities. In fact, often they shouldn't. According to Chris Detert, influencers can be subdivided into different categories:

- Nano-influencers: fewer than 10,000 followers
- Micro-influencers: 20,000 to 50,000 followers
- Macro-influencers: 50,000 to 1 million followers
- Mega-influencers: 1 million or more followers

It would be easy for marketers to assume that targeting mega-influencers is the best approach. After all, more followers mean more engagement, right? According to Detert, the opposite is often the case. 'With mega-influencers, typically you see a sharp drop-off in the amount of engagement', he says. 'They may see these people as trusted voices, but as it gets to celebrity level, they feel out of touch with them. If they try to engage with the influencer, they figure their comment is just going to fall into a hole, and no one's ever going to respond to them.'[25]

Micro-influencers, however, tend to be far more responsive, actively working to respond to at least 20 or 30 of their fans per interaction. 'That way', says Detert, 'when the fans make a comment, they actually believe that there's a decent chance, especially if they say something laudatory or creative, that they're going to hear back from their influencer.'[26]

But what about return on investment? Does influencer marketing actually lead to positive outcomes for brands? To Detert, the answer is a resounding yes – especially if brands approach the process with a sound, tech-enabled methodology:

1. **Determine your demographics.** Detert and his team use IBM-powered tools to search for social users who align with target demographics such as age, gender, household income, and so on.
2. **Find your fans.** Who is talking about your product – or at the very least, your product category? For instance, if you're Taco Bell, you'll be most interested in users speaking highly of your brand. However, users interested in similar foods (i.e. burritos, tacos, nachos, etc.) are likely valuable to you as well.
3. **Psychographics.** With the help of IBM Watson, Detert and his team have identified 47 different personality characteristics that they consider unique to all human beings. Watson then scans potential influencers' posts to find people whose personality profiles most align with the brand.

From there, it's a simple matter of outreach – and eventually, collaboration. To measure the success of those collaborations, marketers have come a long way. 'In the early days, it was just an impression count', Detert says.

> As time went on, we have found that we're able to drive the whole sales journey – to drive people into stores so they buy products, to drive people into car dealerships so they buy cars, to drive people into movie theaters so they watch movies. The KPIs have changed over the years, and because of technology and rapid advancements in the industry, we've been able to continue to up the stakes and make influencer marketing much more valuable.[27]

As advanced as influencer marketing has become, however, the key is still authenticity. Here, Detert acknowledges somewhat of a catch-22. 'It's funny, because sometimes it's still contrived', he says, alluding to the fact that influencer marketing is driven by extensive research, AI-powered matching efforts and branding efforts. 'But coming from a trusted source, a word-of-mouth type of source, these influencers that are born and bred on social, influencer marketing feels more real. People recognize that and gravitate to it.'

However, the rules of social media engagement are always changing, and both brands and influencers alike must understand the potential legal stakes of their collaborations. Measures such as the General Data Protection Regulation (GDPR) and the California Consumer Privacy Act not only place significant restrictions on the collection of third-party data, but also on disclosure and transparency. According to *eMarketer*, while 52% of influencers label sponsored content, 41% only do so when asked – and 7% don't disclose those relationships at all.[28] Suffice to say, if authenticity *is* the name of the game when it comes to *any* form of brand ambassadorship – be it social employee advocacy or influencer marketing – keeping secrets from your audience may not be the safest way to go.

Future Gaze

Jane Cheung, IBM Institute for Business Value (IBV), Consumer Industry Research Leader[29]

In 2017, the IBM Institute for Business Value, in collaboration with Oxford Economics, set out to understand Generation Z – specifically, what drives them to choose a brand. The results of that study, which surveyed 15,600 consumers between the ages of thirteen and twenty-one in sixteen countries across six continents, were published in a report titled *Uniquely Generation Z*.[30]

Of those surveyed, researchers generally found the participants fell into one of three categories based on their media consumption habits (see Figure 8.2):

1. **Devotees.** Those most willing and happy to engage with brands.
2. **Connectors.** This takes more into consideration. They may have a favorite brand, but they haven't made a stand to stay, they're going to follow that brand.
3. **Pragmatists.** Generally more neutral, members of this group haven't declared a favorite brand. They are still trying to make up their mind.

No matter which category they might fall into, Gen Z is the first generation born in the digital age. They weren't alive to see the transition from an analog to a digital world, as Millennials were. The result is that Gen Z is very digital savvy. They're comfortable with technology, they know social media, and they understand how the digital world works.

From this viewpoint, one of Gen Z's greatest shared values is authenticity. Because they grew up immersed in social media, Gen Z is very smart. They can tell whether something is fake, real, genuine, or authentic. From a marketing standpoint, this means that anything you publish *has* to be genuine and authentic. Otherwise, you will lose them.

It's also important for marketers to understand that while Gen Z may engage extensively online, they still live in the real world. In fact, our study results found that 98 percent of respondents said that they typically make purchases in brick-and-mortar stores sometimes or most of the time.

So, while Gen Zers are very high-tech and more advanced, they still have to go to the store – particularly when it's more convenient to do so. Often, the decision of when to go to the store comes down to category. If they're buying a small electronic gadget or a gift, most likely, they will order it from Amazon. If they need something to wear that evening, however, they can't wait for delivery; they have to go to the store. The takeaway is that, as fast as digital technology might be developing, people of any generation are still creatures of habit. Generation Z still goes to the store, and they don't think much of it.

(Continued)

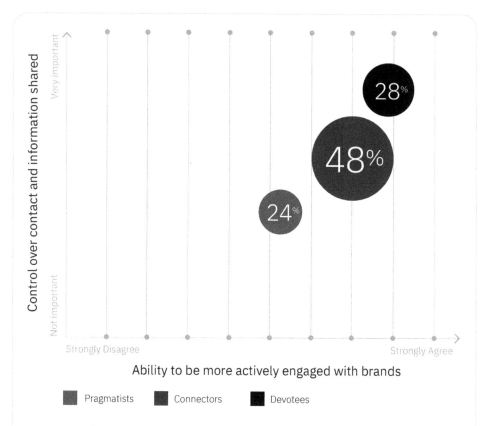

Figure 8.2 Degree of Gen Z's desire to control the information for brand engagement.

Source: IBM.

There's a lesson here for retailers: make it easy. Deliver on the fundamentals. Have the right assortment of products, keep everything stocked, and make the checkout process convenient.

But above all else, make sure that your product or service lives up to its hype. According to our research, *quality* is the number-one consideration guiding Gen Z's choices on where to shop or what to buy – and it's also the number-one reason why they switch brands.

These findings were somewhat surprising to our team. Given their relatively young age, Gen Zers aren't seen as having much disposable income, so our assumption was that they would be thrifty, price-driven shoppers. However, take this with their other top criteria – *value* – and the picture starts getting clearer. Generation Z literally has the world at their fingertips. As such, they want the best of what the world has to offer. It's not enough for a brand to be authentic. If a product or service is of inferior quality, if it doesn't offer value, and if it doesn't somehow connect with the Gen Zer's sense of individuality, then they will take their business somewhere else.

This isn't just an idle threat. Generation Z may not have much buying power, but our research found they have tremendous influence when it comes to purchase decisions within the household. They are the key researchers and drivers of family decisions large and small – where to eat, where to take a vacation, what furniture to buy, and so on.

For Generation Z's influence on family alone, marketers shouldn't sleep on them. But the truth is that their influence extends far beyond the household. Our survey found that 25 percent of Gen Z – some as young as thirteen years old – make their own money. How? By engaging online communities, writing product reviews, editing online magazines, and so on. To Generation Z, the practice of influencer marketing is as natural as breathing.

Beyond that, the keyword with Generation Z is 'trust'. In order for a brand to build a relationship with its buyers, it needs to know *how* to build that relationship. This means a brand has to collect data. For members of any generation, data collection can be an uncomfortable subject. So, in our study, we asked respondents how comfortable they were sharing data and information with the brands they interact with. Many were okay with sharing their purchasing data. However, the more personal the nature of the data became, from location information to credit score and beyond, the more uncomfortable the respondents grew.

Such information is naturally more sensitive, but it's also invaluable to brands interested in building lasting relationships with their customers. So, we asked respondents what brands could do to make them more comfortable with sharing their data. We found that the core issue came down to control. Members of Gen Z wanted to know how their data was being used, why the brand needed it, and even how it was being stored. But most importantly, they wanted the freedom to opt in or out of sharing. Again, this comes down to transparency and authenticity. Be clear about what you're doing with customer data, give them some say in their participation, and maybe even sweeten the deal with some added incentives – even something simple, like a coupon or a discount.

CHAPTER ANALYSIS QUESTIONS

1. What is social employee advocacy, and why is it so important?
2. What are the key steps for starting a social employee pilot program?
3. What is influencer marketing, and what should brands considering this approach do to ensure success?
4. What do Millennials and Generation Z value and look for in a brand more than anything else?
5. What are some of the benefits of social employee engagement to the brand, and to the employee that makes it a win-win?

NOTES

1. Peters, T. (2015). 32 customer entanglement strategies. [blog] tompeters! Available at: https://tompeters.com/2015/11/32-customer-entanglement-strategies/ [Accessed 28 Jan. 2020].

2. Sprout Social. (2019). The Sprout Social index, edition XIV: Realign & redefine. [online] Available at: https://sproutsocial.com/insights/data/2018-index/#key-findings [Accessed 19 Nov. 2019].

3. Monga. A. (2019). Personal communication. [10 July].

4. Aaker, J. (2019). Personal communication. [4 Dec.].

5. Buchanan, L. (n.d.). Why funny leaders are better leaders, according to 2 Stanford professors. [online] Inc.com. Available at: www.inc.com/leigh-buchanan/everyone-loves-a-funny-leader.html [Accessed 20 Nov. 2019].

6. Aaker, J. (2019). Personal communication. [4 Dec.].

7. Ibid.

8. Monga. A. (2019). Personal communication. [10 July].

9. Ibid.

10. For more information, see: Burgess, C. and Burgess, M. (2014). *The Social Employee: How Great Companies Make Social Media Work*. McGraw-Hill Education.

11. Burgess, M. (2014). *The Rise of the Social Employee: Mark Burgess at TEDx Navesink*. [video] Available at: www.youtube.com/watch?v=FZUlp0ybaec [Accessed 26 Nov. 2019].

12. Hutchinson, A. (2019). SMT Employee Advocacy Survey 2019 – Part 1: The current state of employee advocacy. [online] Social Media Today. Available at: www.socialmediatoday.com/news/smt-employee-advocacy-survey-2019-part-1-the-current-state-of-employee-a/563018/ [Accessed 1 Dec. 2019].

13. Niezgoda, A. (2019). With a big splash, Ice Bucket Challenge celebrates 5 years. [online] NBC Boston. Available at: www.nbcboston.com/news/local/Ice-Bucket-Challenge-5th-Anniversary-512751831.html [Accessed 13 Dec. 2019].

14. Dishman, L. (2016). Why employees don't trust their leadership. [online] Fast Company. Available at: www.fastcompany.com/3058630/why-employees-dont-trust-their-leadership?utm_content=buffer311d6&utm_medium=social&utm_source=twitter.com&utm_campaign=buffer [Accessed 13 Dec. 2019].

15. Sinek, S. (2019). *If You Don't Understand People, You Don't Understand Business*. [video] Available at: https://simonsinek.com/discover/if-you-dont-understand-people-you-dont-understand-business/ [Accessed 13 Dec. 2019].

16. Hall, K. (2019). Personal communication. [23 Sept.].

17. Hall, K. (2019). Personal communication [30 Sept.].

18. Quach, W. (2019). Personal communication. [28 Jan.].

19. Kehoe, J. (2020). Personal communication. [6 Jan.].

20. Conner, C. (2019). How to market to Millennials in 2019. [online] *Entrepreneur.* Available at: www.entrepreneur.com/article/339563 [Accessed 3 Dec. 2019].

21. Grant, A. (2019). Council post: The difference between marketing to Millennials and Generation Z. [online] Forbes.com. Available at: www.forbes.com/sites/theyec/2019/03/26/the-difference-between-marketing-to-millennials-and-generation-z/#986553b58c9b [Accessed 3 Dec. 2019].

22. Calkins, T. (2019). Personal communication. [3 December].

23. Detert. C. (2019). Personal communication. [5 June].

24. Colon, G. (2019). Personal communication. [6 Sept.].

25. Detert. C. (2019). Personal communication. [5 June].

26. Ibid.

27. Ibid.

28. *eMarketer.* (2018). Why disclosure is essential when it comes to influencer marketing. [online] Available at: www.emarketer.com/content/why-disclosure-is-essential-when-it-comes-to-influencer-marketing [Accessed 3 Dec. 2019].

29. Cheung, J. (2019). Personal communication. [25 October].

30. Cheung, J., Glass, S., McCarty, D. and Wong, C. (2017). Uniquely Generation Z. [online] IBM Institute for Business Value. Available at: www.ibm.com/downloads/cas/9PPL5YOX [Accessed 4 Dec. 2019].

9

UNLOCKING THE
POWER OF YOU

Learning Goals

1. Understand what a personal brand is and why it is important.
2. Analyze the essential branding concepts – value proposition, positioning and brand purpose – to create your personal branding story.
3. Create a content strategy to engage your target audience and tell your story.
4. Demonstrate how to develop a personal branding marketing plan.
5. Analyze how to measure your plan's success.

We are CEOs of our own companies: Me Inc. To be in business today, our most important job is to be head marketer for the brand called You.

Tom Peters[1]

Dorie Clark wasn't sure what came next. Fresh out of Harvard Divinity School, she had taken a job at *The Boston Phoenix* to be a political reporter at the iconic alternative weekly newspaper. It would be a start, she assumed, to a long career in journalism. The following fall, though, she was laid off. The day after that, the September 11 attacks occurred. Life hadn't gone as planned.

Unable to find work in journalism, Clark took on a hodgepodge of jobs. She parlayed her knowledge of politics into a stint as a campaign spokesperson and then became a non-profit executive. She eventually realized that she had a knack for communications and branding, and in 2006 she launched her marketing strategy consultancy.

The problem was, the country was already saturated with marketing strategy consultants. If she was going to succeed, she would have to stand out from the pack – and quickly. 'I realized that unless I was going to make a career at the bottom of the barrel, charging the lowest prices, I needed to establish a brand for myself', says Clark. 'Because it is only by having a strong brand and a strong reputation that people will be willing to pay fair prices and even premium prices to work with you.'[2] In order to build that strong brand and reputation, she would have to tell the world exactly who Dorie Clark was and why they should work with her over her competitors.

Clark's hunch turned out to be right. Her dedication to strengthening her personal brand has helped her become an in-demand, nationally known marketing strategist and keynote speaker, an adjunct professor at Duke University's Fuqua School of Business, and an author of the highly regarded personal branding and entrepreneurship books the *Entrepreneurial You, Reinventing You, Stand Out* and *Stand Out Networking*, a frequent contributor to the *Harvard Business Review*, and an in-demand consultant to companies such as Google and Microsoft.

According to Clark, even as the economy waxes and wanes, if your reputation in your field is sturdy enough, you should be able to weather any storm. Regardless of your accomplishments, she says, 'The only thing that you can count on is developing a strong brand. It makes you resilient in the marketplace irrespective of what's going on in the broader economy.' A strong brand, she maintains, is 'a form of personal career insurance'.[3]

SOFT SKILLS + HARD SKILLS = CONCRETE RESULTS

Clark embodies the importance of a personal brand and the doors that open once you successfully cultivate one. But her story also illustrates the value of so-called 'soft skills'. These are traits that are less tangible, but no less essential to success in any area: charisma, openness, empathy, adaptability, grit, oral and written proficiency, the ability to communicate.

The opposite are 'hard skills'. These are talents that are measurable, such as the ability to program or analyze earnings reports, or graduating top of the class in your MBA program. They reveal a lot about what you can do, but not who you are. All of us have both hard and soft skills, and we need both to succeed in our careers. Why? Because while hard skills – what we look like on paper – can help us get our foot in the door, it's our soft skills that embody how we function in the real world. To create a premier personal brand, then, you must tap into your arsenal of soft skills.

The hard/soft skills dichotomy is discussed in Tom Peters' 2018 book, *The Excellence Dividend*. 'Hard is soft. Soft is hard', Peters says. Too much is made of hard skills, he argues, although, he notes, 'Plans are often fantasies, and numbers are readily manipulated.'

On the other hand, 'Soft (people/relationships/culture) is hard (difficult to achieve and enduring only if incessantly worked at). While I hardly dismiss the traditionally empha-sized "hard stuff," I do insist that the "soft stuff" is the key to long-term success and the bedrock of excellence.'[4]

Peters speaks from decades of experience as a business management consultant, but his perspective is no less relevant today, especially when applied to newer, tech-oriented companies. In a talk at *WIRED*'s 25th Anniversary Festival in 2018, the CEO of LinkedIn, Jeff Weiner, echoed Peters' hard line on soft skills. 'The biggest skills gap in the United States is soft skills', Weiner lamented to *WIRED* editor Nicholas Thompson during a discussion. 'Written communication, oral communication, team building, people leadership, collaboration. For jobs like sales, sales development, business devel-opment, customer service. This is the biggest gap, and it's counterintuitive.'[5]

Driving every authentic personal brand is a perfectly balanced mix of both hard and soft skills. This makes sense. First, people with rock-solid personal brands have the experience, expertise and/or accomplishments (hard skills) to back up their claims. They also have a knack for getting people to respond positively to them (soft skills). Like yin and yang, the two types of skill sets complement each other perfectly. If you have wondrous technical skills but no soft skills, you're much less likely to succeed – either professionally or in brand-building. We all know people who are geeky, gifted, or brilliant within their field, but just never seem to advance. Most likely, they lack the touch of soft skills.

WHAT IS A BRAND?

Such a question may seem a bit silly – or obvious – but before we dive into the ins and outs of personal brand-building, it's important that we start on the same page.

Branding is typically associated with marketing elements like advertising, logos, slo-gans and trademarks. But a *brand* is much more. It's a promise and a reason to choose one company's product or service over their competitors' offerings. It's what comes to mind when you think about a company. It's the culmination of years of product history – for both good and bad – provoking a feeling of either delight or disgust (and often something in between). It's the widely accepted perception of an organization, whether justified or not.

A brand is all this and more. And for that reason, marketers often find it difficult to agree on a precise definition. For simplicity's sake, here's our definition: A brand is the sum total of the entire customer experience, the collection of perceptions in the mind of the consumer. Think of well-known international brands that you've interacted with, such as Apple, Ford, Netflix, or Microsoft. What comes to mind – Excellence? Value? Competence? Dependability? Frustration?

Whatever the case may be, when it comes to brands, perception is reality. A company may have the best product in the world, but if their brand turns people off in some way, then no amount of technical features can save it. A bad brand equals a bad product, no matter its virtues.

THINK LIKE A BRAND

Adding more nuance to our discussion of brands and branding is the concept of the *personal brand*. Tom Peters first introduced marketers to the idea of the personal brand in a 1997 *Fast Company* article titled 'The brand called You'. In the article, Peters argues that people should apply the logic of business brand-building to their own professional lives. In application, this means differentiating yourself in the marketplace, getting your name (and possibly face) out into the world, and providing value. Do all this and watch your professional stock soar. That's what happened to Dorie Clark.

The difference between a brand and a personal brand is in the end result. You're not selling a product – you're selling yourself. And the rewards for this are the increased level of influence and opportunity you'll accrue. This cuts across all professional fields and career levels. 'Regardless of age, regardless of position, regardless of the business we happen to be in, all of us need to understand the importance of branding', Peters writes. 'We are CEOs of our own companies: Me Inc. To be in business today, our most important job is to be head marketer for the brand called You.'[6]

In a world of instantly shared media, viral tweets and viewer engagement metrics, Peters' view feels prescient. The brand called You challenged readers to figure out how to stand out in a competitive world – all this before the twenty-first century ushered in the social media era!

Peters' take is echoed by personal branding guru William Arruda. 'There are a myriad others who share your job title and ambitions. To succeed in our ultra-competitive, global marketplace, you need to stand out from the pack and attract the attention of decision makers', explains Arruda, the author of *Digital YOU* and co-founder of CareerBlast.TV. 'Personal branding gives you the opportunity to increase your influence, turn fans into promoters and ultimately achieve your goals.'[7]

If this message isn't taught, people will be forced to learn it the hard way, as Clark did early on in her career. Business schools that focus on teaching personal branding skills, particularly when it comes to social media, will be ahead of the curve. In a 2017 paper in the *Journal of Advertising Education*, Monfort College of Business professors Denny McCorkle and Janice Payan observed that 'there is a marketing curriculum problem in that students are not entering the workforce with adequate preparation in using social media for marketing/business or for personal branding to support their job search and career'.[8]

SEVEN STEPS TO BUILDING YOUR PERSONAL BRAND

The Seven Steps

1. Do an environmental scan
2. Create a brand value proposition (BVP)
3. Position your brand
4. Figure out your brand story
5. Develop a content strategy
6. Develop a content distribution strategy (a.k.a. media plan)
7. Measure results

Now that you have a good sense of what a personal brand is and why it's so important, let's talk about how you go about creating a personal brand that stands the test of time. To help you work through the personal branding process, we've created a proven seven-step blueprint. As you proceed through these steps, use the Personal Branding Workbook in Appendix B to evaluate the strengths and weaknesses of your personal brand. These steps will help you fire up your personal brand and help you figure out ways to differentiate yourself.

Before we dive in, however, one quick word of caution. When you build a personal brand, you're essentially identifying and assuming a 'personal brand persona'. Just don't confuse *persona* for *character*. The brand that you construct must be authentic and tethered to a real person – that is, the *real* you. We live in an age of widespread distrust and cynicism, and potential customers will happily reject any product – or any person – that they believe is fake.

Step 1: Do an Environmental Scan

By 'environmental scan', we don't mean you need to get out your work boots and shovel; we're talking about taking stock of the marketplace and your position in it. To begin the process, ask yourself questions like, 'What's out there that I need to be aware of? What are the major trends in the market? What skills will be highly valued in the future – and do I have them? How do I compare to my competitors?'

Be honest with yourself. You can't improve your brand until you candidly evaluate where you currently stand. It's okay if you're not where you want to be, or even where you think you *should* be. The purpose of the environmental scan is to glean a truthful assessment. To paraphrase Sherlock Holmes, you need high-quality data. Only then can you progress – and create a killer personal brand.

Step 2: Create a Brand Value Proposition (BVP)

To think like a brand, you need to start by defining your personal brand value proposition. A value proposition explains the benefits of a product or service and what makes it different. It answers the question 'Why should I care?' A brand value proposition, or BVP, is similar – but for a brand. For example, Honda's brand value proposition is reliability. Consumers know that they can buy a new Honda car or truck anywhere in the country and it will be dependable for many years to come. They don't need to know much about cars, or even the workings of the Honda corporation. The Honda brand is synonymous with high quality, which is enough to satisfy most consumers.

Your goal is to build a personal brand persona that resonates in the marketplace. A BVP answers questions like:

- Who are you?
- What do you stand for?
- What are your beliefs and values?
- What are your personal traits?
- What makes you unique?
- What is your passion?

Your BVP should be a simple but powerful distillation of the answers to these questions. Ideally, it's a short sentence that sums up who you are, what you offer, and why you're different than your competitors.

To help you define your BVP, start by brainstorming with people who know you well. Conduct your own focus group with trustworthy friends and/or close professional connections and ask them to list five things that come to mind when they think about you. What are you all about?

If their feedback is surprising or, in your opinion, less than flattering, try not to take it too personally. It's all a part of the fact-finding mission. As you cultivate your BVP, your mission will be to maximize your strengths and minimize your weaknesses.

A good brand value proposition doesn't just tell prospective customers what you do – it tells them why you do it better than anyone else. Once you refine your BVP to a concise but powerful statement, it will be your North Star – guiding your marketing and brand-building efforts and driving your messaging in social media channels (and elsewhere).

Step 3: Position Your Brand

To figure out the optimal position for your brand, tie together your brand value proposition to your environmental scan. Think long and hard about where your BVP fits – and where it doesn't. To help you with this process, think about well-known products and where they fit within their market. To offer one example, BMW positions itself as makers of 'the ultimate driving machine'. With this slogan, they are signaling their value to consumers who prioritize performance in their cars. Compare this to our previous example, Honda. Though most Hondas drive just fine, most people who purchase them may not value ride quality, quick acceleration, and other performance metrics as much as they value dependability and safety. While BMW drivers also value dependability and safety, they're looking for a more complete driving experience. Love driving? Then you'll probably enjoy 'the ultimate driving machine'.

The same logic applies to your personal brand. Think about how you want your target audience (prospective customers/employers/recruiters) to think about you. Since positioning is about creating a space in the minds of the people you want to influence, what space can you own? What makes you stand out from your competition?

The following formula is a good starting point for drafting a personal brand positioning statement and helping you figure out your place in the world:

For [target market], the [brand] provides [point-of-difference] because [reason to believe].

Take a moment to jot down a few personal brand positioning statements based on this template. Most likely, it will take at least a few tries until your statement starts to click. Keep at it until you're fully satisfied with the result. (For more in-depth exercises, see the Personal Branding Workbook in Appendix B).

Step 4: Figure out Your Brand Story

As you'll recall from Chapter 6, when people look to purchase a good or service, most of them don't remember – or don't necessarily care about – data and figures. They want a *story*. Disney bills itself as 'the most magical place on earth'. Apple dares its users (and itself) to 'think different'. It's clear that for millions of people, these simple but compelling taglines say enough.

Similarly, Blendtec blenders offer various speed settings and a vented latching lid. Is that why they have become one of the country's most popular blenders? No. Thanks to the enduring popularity of their 'Will It Blend?' videos, Blendtec has helped customers understand that they will get an extremely powerful, well-built machine – whatever its specs may be.

You want to develop a story you can live by. It should be effortless and authentic, and perhaps a touch aspirational. You should be able to wear it like a favorite pair of pants. But remember, performance matters. Your story shouldn't be a myth. You must have the goods to back up your story. If you don't, you will find yourself stuck with a low-value brand. The real art is in translating your technical specs and performance (hard skills) into a compelling brand story (soft skills).

Figuring out your purpose will lead you to the story you want to tell the world. So take some time and ask yourself: What's your purpose, and how can it become part of your personal branding story? Why should someone choose you over your competitors? When it comes to personal branding, Simon Sinek's famous statement well applies: 'People don't buy what you do. They buy why you do it.'[9] Trying to define your true purpose is hard, because it's almost like trying to read the label from inside the bottle. Nevertheless, it must be done.

Sidebar

Unlocking the Power of You with AI (Artificial Intelligence)

To help people figure out your story, IBM is ready to lend a hand. Its Watson Personality Insights analyzer 'use[s] linguistic analytics to infer individuals' personality characteristics'.[10] Users submit written content to the program, including email, blog posts, tweets and forum posts, and it analyzes what their writing reveals about their needs, values, and the 'Big 5' personality traits: extraversion, openness, conscientiousness, emotion range, and agreeableness. The analyzer sorts the user into even smaller categories, pointing out how much they evoke 'excitement', 'harmony', 'establishment-challenging', and much more. For instance, according to an analysis of Mark's writing (see Figure 9.1), 99% of his writing indicates 'trust', 88% 'practicality' and 2% 'melancholy'.

For its part, LinkedIn provides each user with a Social Selling Dashboard. This handy chart, which is updated daily, 'measures how effective you are at establishing your professional brand, finding the right people, engaging with insights, and building relationships'.[11] It displays an easy-to-use graphic that helps you quickly assess your impact on the platform, just like it does in Figure 9.2 with Cheryl Burgess.

One growing trend among apparel startups is the idea of giving back. This illustrates how a socially useful purpose has become a valuable point of difference for brands beyond what they sell. Apparel companies that have embraced the buy-one, give-one model include TOMS shoes, Warby Parker glasses, Make a Difference Intimates (MADI), and New York-based sock startup Bombas, who donates a pair of socks to the homeless for every pair that's purchased by a customer. All of these companies have added a fifth P to the traditional marketing mix: purpose.

(Continued)

Sunburst Chart Visualization

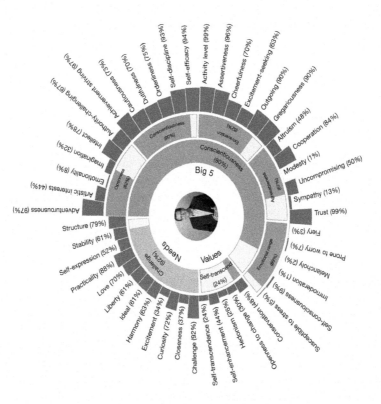

Figure 9.1   IBM Sunburst Chart Visualization Personality Insights for Mark Burgess.

Source: IBM: Personality Insights; https://personality-insights-demo.ng.bluemix.net/ [Accessed 28 April 2019].

Figure 9.2   LinkedIn Social Selling Dashboard for Cheryl Burgess.

Source: LinkedIn.com Social Selling Index; www.linkedin.com/sales/ssi/ [Accessed 28 April 2019].

Step 5: Develop a Content Strategy

Once you establish an authentic story with a purpose, the next step is to tell the world about it. As we discussed in Chapter 6, one of the most effective ways to do this is through high-quality content. It's not enough, however, to just create fantastic content. If nobody sees it, it can't help you or your business. This means that you must have a content strategy.

As you consider your strategy, here are some basic questions to ask yourself:

- Where are my customers? How do I reach them?
- What type of content is best suited for my product and audience – articles, videos, newsletters, a combination?
- What content topics will generate an enthusiastic (positive) response from my audience?

Remember that your personal branding story is the fuel for your content strategy, which should include both original content and curated content relevant to your target audience. Brainstorm the types of content that would be most relevant and bring the most benefits to your target audience. Remember, you are marketing your interests, knowledge, passions and skills to your target audience and trying to create new and meaningful connections in the process. As you develop new skills, they become important pillars in your content strategy as well. Whatever content you settle on, it should reinforce your brand story – and vice versa.

The goal of your content is to provide value to your audience while affirming your brand story. If you do this, your brand will have a better chance of becoming 'sticky'. The concept of stickiness was developed by Chip and Dan Heath in their influential 2007 book *Made to Stick*. In the book, the Heath brothers provide six essential principles for creating sticky marketing using the SUCCESs acronym: Your message should be **S**imple, **U**nexpected, **C**oncrete, **C**redible, **E**motional, and tell a **S**tory.[12] All of the content marketing you create to bolster your brand should satisfy at least a few of these principles.

Devising an effective strategy may feel less sexy than coming up with compelling content, and it may very well be challenging. But if you want to help your personal brand grow, setting aside time to strategize is essential. As the old saying goes, 'Those who fail to plan, plan to fail.' This is true both in life and in personal branding.

Step 6: Develop a Content Distribution Strategy (a.k.a. Media Plan)

Once you develop a solid content strategy, it's time to tell your personal branding story by leveraging relevant social media channels. Call this your personal media plan. Much like a company must decide whether to promote itself on radio, TV, print, or the web (or in all of them), you must decide which channels offer you the best opportunities to find your audience. Your plan should be holistic and tailored to your specific industry and goals.

Begin by asking yourself what distribution channel(s) will go farthest in reaching potential customers. SEO-optimized webpage? A LinkedIn blog? A Facebook page? An Instagram video? Guest-blogging on established blogs? Focusing on the social media channels that you already know and use to tell your story is a worthwhile place to start, but – as with every other step in the personal brand-building process – your brand story should lead the way here. If you want to be known as, say, the best leader of cycling adventures through Greenland, LinkedIn probably isn't the best platform, even if you're an old pro at it. A product or service whose attraction is visual likely fits best on Instagram or Facebook, platforms that are commonly used for photo- and video-sharing.

The following is a brief rundown of the most important social media channels and how they can help you build your personal brand:

LinkedIn

A LinkedIn profile is the new resume. According to a 2016 survey conducted by Jobvite, a developer of recruiting software, '87 percent of recruiters use LinkedIn, but only 55 percent use Facebook'.[13] So put the paper version of your resume away until you get the interview – right now, your top priority is to land one.

The key to utilizing LinkedIn is to become active on it. This is no place to be a passive bystander, waiting to be discovered and scooped up. Your LinkedIn strategy should include regular updates on your profile, which LinkedIn makes easy. Take advantage of their blogging platform to write short blog posts on topics of interest or your personal passion, and share relevant content within your network.

To get the most out of LinkedIn, first, it's helpful to ask yourself what your goals are. Are they to expand your network, get a new job, build thought leadership, or something else? This should help focus your media strategy. From there, here are a few tips and tricks to consider:

- For blog posts, 200–300 words is a good bet.
- Be sure to include a photo and/or video of yourself. Without a picture, you will make it harder for people to care about or connect with you.
- For the LinkedIn Summary at the top of your profile, write a clear, concise description. This tells viewers who you are, so make sure you tell your brand story right.

Again, whatever else you do, be active. Liking, commenting and sharing posts from others shows that you're an engaged community member while providing a signal boost for others. The more you engage with others' content, the more they'll engage with yours – and the greater visibility you'll achieve.

Twitter

Twitter is a global information network that connects you to the latest news, stories, ideas and opinions. When it started in 2006, users only had 140 characters to express themselves with, but in late 2017, the company doubled that character count to a larger, but still minimalistic, 280.

Some personal branding tips for Twitter:

- Don't follow more people than are following you.
- Your photo is critical, and you should always include one. A good photo can be a deciding factor for people considering connecting with you.
- Pay close attention to your bio. Be creative how you use the allotted 160 characters to tell your story, which will attract leads and Twitter followers.
- Focus on tweeting quality content so people will be inspired to visit your page and share your tweets.

- Use your Twitter page to show off your skills and talents in creative ways. But remember the 80/20 rule we discussed in Chapter 6. You shouldn't use your platform to just promote your own brand; this will make your page grow old, fast.
- Share photos and videos to increase visibility and engagement. According to Twitter, posts with images or video are three times more likely to be engaged with than posts without either.

Once you've been active for a while, use their analytics tool to track your impact and influence. In your dashboard at analytics.twitter.com, you can view a list of your followers, your most engaging tweets, and trends over the last 28 days.

Facebook

On the strength of sheer numbers, it's hard to top Facebook. More than two-thirds of all Americans are on the platform, and three-quarters of adults use it at least once a day.[14] On top of that, Facebook boasts 2.5 billion monthly active users around the world.[15] Despite the numerous scandals involving the company since the 2016 United States presidential election, Facebook is still a media behemoth and a platform that may be worth your time.

Facebook makes it easy to share text updates, images and video content. You can write posts as short or as long as you want, connect with your content from other channels (i.e. your blog, YouTube), and distribute your offerings to your friends. If you're so inclined, you can even set up a separate page for your business that people can like (as opposed to setting up a personal page connecting you to friends and family). The more that people like your business page, the more your search ranking on Google will improve, and the more potential users will be exposed to your brand.

Instagram

Instagram is a photo-sharing and video site that can help you really express yourself – and your brand – to the world. In some ways, it offers more of a look into your personality and interests than Twitter, which is primarily text-based, or LinkedIn, which can feel more buttoned-up. 'Instagram and Facebook show a living, breathing person', Carly Johnson, a project manager at Simply Hired, told *Fast Company* in a 2018 article on social media and recruiting. 'It's great to have a second level of information.'[16]

Instagram is particularly essential if your work has a heavy visual component. Artists, musicians, photographers, builders, fitness buffs, product manufacturers, and others who create things that people want to see or hear will benefit the most from developing an Instagram following.

Sidebar

Use #Hashtags in Social Media

If you participate in social media, you are well aware that hashtags have become somewhat of a sensation since their introduction. A well-known example comes from retailer REI, who became relatively famous with their use of the daring #OptOutside hashtag. Instead of requiring their employees to work grueling retail shifts on Black Friday, REI encourages them and others to go outside and share their adventures using the #OptOutside hashtag on their social media accounts. These efforts have created a community around #OptOutside. So, what does this mean to you? Hashtags can literally reach millions of people around the world. Think of hashtags as a key component in your personal branding toolbox to gain visibility, expand your audience, and increase awareness of brand YOU. Try to include hashtags on your Facebook, Instagram, Twitter or LinkedIn posts to make them more discoverable. To help you identify hashtags to align with your personal brand story, Hashtagify.me offers a useful (and free) tool for helping you find just the right hashtag.[17]

Step 7: Measure Results

The last step is to come up with ways to measure success. Your metrics should be aspirational but realistic; if you only have 100 LinkedIn followers to start, it's unlikely that you'll get to 10,000 within the year. Be conscious of setting yourself up for failure, which can lead to discouragement and disengagement.

Some of your goals can be medium-specific (e.g. '500 more LinkedIn followers'), some not ('20% increase in traffic to my website', '20% increase in sales revenue', etc.). Just make sure they're quantifiable. Try to avoid measuring your progress in fuzzy, abstract terms like 'raise awareness' or 'increase my brand exposure'. Google Analytics and similar influence-tracking tools can be very helpful here.

Your assessment should be ongoing. Check in regularly to see how you are faring and whether your strategies for standing out in a crowded marketplace are bearing fruit. If they aren't, don't be afraid to tweak your positioning, your purpose, or some other aspect of your BVP. Be open to feedback, and try to gather as much of it as possible so you can apply its lessons to your brand. (To help you keep track of your progress, don't forget to check out the Personal Branding Workbook in Appendix B).

SAVOR THE SMALL VICTORIES

When it comes to personal branding, you should always relish the small victories. Someone emailing you to tell you how much they liked or learned from a blog post you wrote, a comment on Periscope offering encouragement – these are worth celebrating, even if their impact can't be strictly measured. They offer a much-appreciated confidence boost and an indication that you're moving the dial on the brand called You.

From the small victories will come larger ones, and the stronger your personal brand, the more robust your 'personal career insurance' will be.

Future Gaze

Tom Peters' 'The Everything Paper'

In this chapter, we have encouraged students and marketers alike to 'think like a brand', a concept invented by Tom Peters, known as the Red Bull of Management, in *Fast Company's* most popular article, The brand called You.[18] Below, we offer more insights from Tom Peters in what he calls 'The Everything Paper'.[19] Tom captures his main themes to work on for years to come – based on 30+ years with his finger on the pulse of business. Tom shared the initial draft with Cheryl Burgess on 1 February 2019,[20] from his winter home in Golden Bay, New Zealand. This is an agenda for excellence from the bestselling author of *In Search of Excellence* (no less than the bestselling management book of all time).

Per Tom, 'Excellence . . . it's an even more important idea/state-of-mind/action item in 2019.'[21]

Here is Tom's final draft of 'The Everything Paper' (as of this writing) and what you need to know now.

And, as you come away from reading this chapter, remember to think like a brand as you start to craft *your* personal brand using our Personal Branding Workbook (Appendix B).

EEE/EXTREME EMPLOYEE ENGAGEMENT
VISIBLE MORAL LEADERSHIP/A FULLTIME RESPONSIBILITY, NOT AN OPTION
HARD (NUMBERS/PLANS) IS SOFT. SOFT (RELATIONSHIPS/CULTURE) IS HARD.
EXTREME HUMANIZATION/PRODUCT-SERVICE DIFFERENTIATOR #1
EXCELLENCE IS THE NEXT FIVE MINUTES

"[Business has the] responsibility to increase the sum total of human well-being."
—Mihaly Csikszentmihalyi

"Business has to give people enriching, rewarding lives ... or it's simply not worth doing."
—Richard Branson

*"The role of the director is to create a space where actors and actresses can be more than they
have ever been before, more than they have ever dreamed of being."*
—Robert Altman

"Your customers will never be any happier than your employees."
—John DiJulius

*"He said for him the craft of building a boat was like a religion. You had to surrender yourself to it spiritually.
When you were done, you had to feel that you had left a piece of yourself behind in it forever, a bit of your heart."*
—The Boys in the Boat, on George Yoeman Pocock, racing shell designer-builder extraordinaire

AGENDA/ENTERPRISE EXCELLENCE 2019:
*EEE/EXTREME EMPLOYEE ENGAGEMENT. The sine qua non for all that follows. "Double down" on employee investment—play offense, not defense, to respond to tech-mad-job-obliterators. Note: This employee engagement axiom applies to 100% of job slots, including part-timers. (*And*: In the spirit of the above, *ban* the term "HR." My colleagues are *not* "human resources," [*not* "assets"]; they are Ruth, Dick ...) (*And: "People First" is Strategy #1 for long-term success.*)

*MBWA/MANAGING BY WANDERING AROUND. "MBWA" is code for managers/leaders in touch with—communion with—those who do the work. *Leaders/managers literally desperate for their team members to succeed and make a small "dent in the universe"; managers/leaders who avidly live "people first." (Helping others succeed = Human Aspiration #1.)*

*CULTURAL DIFFERENTIATORS: Bedrock: RESPECT. Leader Trait #1: "FIERCE" LISTENING. Hiring/E.g.: "EMPATHY"/"GOOD PEOPLE"/"NO JERKS." Investment #1: TRAINING. Asset #1: OUR 1ST-LINE MANAGERS.

*PRINCIPLE #1/40 YEARS/6-WORDS: "HARD IS SOFT. SOFT IS HARD." Hard (plans, numbers) is soft (abstractions). Soft (relationships/culture) is hard (embedded). (E.g., Google gets a "soft" surprise: BigData re top employees/most innovative teams: "Soft stuff" reigns. Top eight traits: Interpersonal/"soft" skills/#1-7; STEM last/#8. Message: EQ>IQ.)

*INVEST FOR THE LONG-TERM/SHARE THE WEALTH/END 50 YEARS OF ECONOMIC/ SOCIAL DEVASTATION WROUGHT BY SLAVISH DEVOTION TO SHAREHOLDER VALUE

MAXIMIZATION. 94% of big public-company earnings (50%/1970) go to share repurchase/dividends enriching the rich—leaving a puny 6% for R&D/employee growth and well-being. FYI: *Analyses show companies investing for the long-term dramatically outperform quarterly profit maximizers.*

*UNFLINCHING MORAL RESPONSIBILITY AS A FRONT, CENTER, AND VISIBLE OBSESSION—ONE DAY AND ONE DECISION AT A TIME. The benefits of an always visible moral touchstone accrue to oneself, our mates, our clientele, vendors, our communities. (And: *you can look in a mirror and tell yourself you have tried to make the world a little bit better.*)

*"*I (TP) WILL NOT SERVE ON BOARDS WITH <50% WOMEN*." Board gender balance pays (McKinsey: +56% operating profit). More/Unassailable research: Women are more effective leaders/negotiators/investors than men. (*And*: Women = Market #1/principal purchasers of *everything*.) (*And*/U.S.A.: $22 trillion wealth transfer to women 2015–2020.)

*EXTREME HUMANIZATION OF PRODUCTS/SERVICES VIA INJECTION OF "ARTS THINKING"/SPIRITUALITY INTO ALL WE DO. Emotionally connective design *is* the enterprise. Cases/Laurene Jobs: *"Steve and Jony [Ives] would discuss corners for hours and hours"*; review/MINI Cooper S, *"No car has provoked more smiles"*; Thomas Merton on the "peculiar grace of a Shaker chair": *"made by someone capable of believing an angel might come and sit on it."* Humanization/ Small>>Big/Henry Clay: "Courtesies of a small and trivial character are the ones which strike deepest in the grateful and appreciating heart." Axiom: *Distinction by Extreme Humanization is Core Competence #1, least likely to be matched by AI.*

*SMEs ROCK & RULE. The hell with the job-destroying-tech-gaga-short-term-obsessed giants. *Small- and Medium-size Enterprises create virtually all the new jobs and are architects of almost all innovation.* In terms of citizens' vocations and community and national health, we *are* our SMEs. Action: Encourage/support SME s every way imaginable. (SME Excellence Mantra/courtesy George Whalin, *Retail Superstars*: "Be the best. It's the only market that's not crowded.")

*PROFESSIONAL EDUCATION (BUSINESS, LAW, ENGINEERING, MEDICINE, ETC.) RADICALLY RE-TOOLED TO REFLECT THE ABOVE. Professional education must acknowledge the primacy of developing people and moral leadership as a daily preoccupation. (Step #1/MBAs: The Master of Business Administration becomes the Master of Business *Arts*.)

*EXCELLENCE. PERIOD. *In the end, EXCELLENCE is the only acceptable standard—for our products and services, for our relationships and the care and development of our employees, for our role in our community and in society at large.*
TTD Now: *Excellence is not an "aspiration" or a "mountain to be climbed." Excellence is the next five minutes. (Or not.)*

Tom Peters/Golden Bay New Zealand 0307.19/South Dartmouth MA 0425.19

CHAPTER ANALYSIS QUESTIONS

1. What are the strengths and weaknesses of your personal brand value proposition (BVP)?
2. What do you admire in people with strong personal brands?
3. What content marketing channels are most likely to reach your target audience?
4. How can you create a 'sticky' personal brand?

NOTES

1. Peters, T. (1997). The brand called You. [online] *Fast Company*. Available at: www.fastcompany.com/28905/brand-called-you [Accessed 28 Jan. 2020].
2. Clark, D. (2018). Personal communication. [29 Oct.].
3. Clark, D. (2018). Personal communication. [16 Nov.].
4. Peters, T. (2018). *The Excellence Dividend: Meeting the Tech Tide with Work that Wows and Jobs that Last*. Vintage.
5. Thompson, N. (2018). *Jeff Weiner Explains the Most Important Challenge for Tech in the Next 25 Years. LinkedIn*, 12 October. Available at: www.linkedin.com/pulse/jeff-weiner-explains-how-linkedin-diversify-global-nicholas-thompson/ [Accessed 6 Dec. 2018].
6. Peters, T. (1997). The brand called you. [online] *Fast Company*. Available at: www.fastcompany.com/28905/brand-called-you [Accessed 6 Dec. 2018].
7. Arruda, W. (2018). Personal communication. [3 Oct.].
8. McCorkle, D. and Payan, J. (2017). Using Twitter in the marketing and advertising classroom to develop skills for social media marketing and personal branding. *Journal of Advertising Education,* 21(1), pp. 33–43.
9. Sinek, S. (2009). *How Great Leaders Inspire Action*. [Video online] TED. Available at: www.ted.com/talks/simon_sinek_how_great_leaders_inspire_action/ [Accessed 6 Dec. 2018].
10. IBM Watson Developer Cloud. (2018). Personality insights. Available at: https://personality-insights-demo.ng.bluemix.net/ [Accessed 6 Dec. 2018].
11. LinkedIn Social Selling Dashboard. (2018). Available at: www.linkedin.com/sales/ssi/ [Accessed 17 Dec. 2018].
12. Heath, C. and Heath, D. (2008). Made to Stick SUCCESs Model. Available at: www.heathbrothers.com/download/mts-made-to-stick-model.pdf [Accessed 6 Dec. 2018].
13. Jobvite. (2016). *Job Seeker Nation Study: Where Job Seekers Stand on the Economy, Job Security, and the Future of Work*. Available at: www.jobvite.com/wp-content/uploads/2016/03/Jobvite_Jobseeker_Nation_2016.pdf [Accessed 6 Dec. 2018].
14. Gramlich, J. (2018). 10 facts about Americans and Facebook. Pew Research Center, 24 October. Available at: www.pewresearch.org/fact-tank/2018/10/24/facts-about-americans-and-facebook/ [Accessed 6 Dec. 2018].

15. Tech Crunch. (2020). Facebook hits 2.5B users in Q4 but shares sink from slow profits [29 January]. Available at: https://techcrunch.com/2020/01/29/facebook-earnings-q4-2019/ [Accessed 2 March 2020].

16. Vozza, S. (2018). Recruiters look at this more than your LinkedIn [20 April]. Available at: www.fastcompany.com/40558075/recruiters-look-at-this-more-than-your-linkedin [Accessed 6 Dec. 2018].

17. Hashtagify. (2018). Available at: https://hashtagify.me/hashtag/tbt [Accessed 6 Dec. 2018].

18. Peters, T. (1997). The brand called You. [online] *Fast Company*. Available at: www.fastcompany.com/28905/brand-called-you [Accessed 28 Jan. 2020].

19. The Everything Paper | The EEE/Extreme Employee Engagement | Visible Moral Leadership/A Fulltime Responsibility, Not an Option | Hard (Numbers/Plans) Is Soft. Soft (Relationships/Culture) Is Hard. Extreme Humanization/Product-Service Differentiator #1 | Excellence is the Next Five Minutes. Available at: https://tompeters.com/2019/04/tep-the-everything-paper/ [Accessed 19 May 2019] Tom Peters/Golden Bay New Zealand 0307.19/South Dartmouth MA 0425.19.

20. Peters, T. (2019). Personal communication. [1 Feb.].

21. TEP/The Everything Paper +. (2019). Available at: https://tompeters.com/2019/04/tep-the-everything-paper/ [Accessed 19 May 2019].

PART 4

BRINGING THE FUTURE INTO FOCUS

10

THE NEW INTEGRATED MARKETING STRATEGY: BRAND CHOREOGRAPHY®

Give me six hours to chop down a tree and I will spend the first four sharpening the axe.

Abraham Lincoln (c. 1860)[1]

In her 2002 hit 'Soak up the Sun', singer-songwriter Sheryl Crow sings, 'It's not having what you want. It's wanting what you've got.' Increasingly, brands still following a traditional marketing approach are finding these words to be all too true. Where once it was enough to slap your logo on all your marketing materials, sprinkle in the same well-worn branding slogans, and perhaps even create a hashtag or two, such an approach is no longer enough. Brands have the logos – and they have the slogans – but no one wants what they've got. Simply put, modern brands are struggling to connect with their audiences.

A brand's number-one goal is to build lasting, profitable relationships with its customers. The more they're able to do this, the more they are able to generate brand equity – and therefore a competitive advantage in the marketplace. First proposed in the late 1980s, integrated marketing communication (IMC) offers marketers a framework for integrating traditional and inbound marketing approaches, enabling them to deliver clear, consistent and compelling messages across a variety of platforms and communication channels. At the time, crafting an effective IMC strategy was fairly straightforward. The early view of integrated marketing stressed the importance of creating TV and print ads that looked alike. That was about it.

A lot has changed since the 1980s. Executing a successful IMC strategy has become increasingly complex. Media options – and the devices used to consume them – continue to proliferate. Social media has rewritten the rules of engagement, shifting power from the brand to the connected consumer, and giving way to newer tactics such as inbound and omnichannel marketing. An inbound marketing approach uses strategies like search engine optimization (SEO), email campaigns and content marketing to encourage their audience to engage with and share content related to their brand. Omnichannel marketing focuses on creating an integrated shopping experience. For instance, a typical modern buyer journey often stretches across desktop, mobile, and in brick-and-mortar touchpoints. Omnichannel marketing works to create a seamless experience across touchpoints.[2]

Inbound and omnichannel marketing have evolved from buzzwords to best practices. Advanced metrics for proving campaign effectiveness and ROI are commonplace. With all these advances, one would think brands would have an *easier* time connecting with audiences than ever before – and yet, in an era marked by the decline of brand equity and trust, the opposite is true. According to *Marketing Week*, 'Almost 70 percent of consumers don't trust advertising, and 42 percent distrust brands, seeing them as part of the establishment and therefore "remote, unreachable, abstract, and self-serving".'[3]

Today's marketers face a monumental task. There remains little doubt that integrated marketing leads to better outcomes for brands. But, many brands are struggling to adapt integrated marketing for the new digital era.

While traditional methods – such as advertising, sales promotion, public relations and direct marketing – still have a place, they must now contend with web-based methods such as search, social media and content marketing. Such an environment is both complex and full of opportunity.

According to researchers Rajeev Batra and Kevin Lane Keller, 'Integrated marketing communications are the coordinated, consistent means by which firms attempt to inform, incent, persuade, and remind consumers – directly or indirectly – about the products and brands they sell. Technological advances and other factors have transformed the marketing communications environment and present new challenges and opportunities to marketers. Digital media, in particular, offers tremendous potential through their greater versatility and precision, but they also create greater integration challenges.'[4]

In other words, while marketers have much to gain through an effective integrated marketing strategy, they also have their work cut out for them. Enter Brand Choreography. This customer-centric, adaptive framework helps marketers to deliver the right message to the right person at the right time. In this new age of declining trust, brands must learn to deliver relevant and consistent messages to multiple touchpoints and across every stage of the customer decision journey. Brand Choreography offers a much-needed update to the traditional IMC methodology, allowing brands to meet audiences on their channel of choice – be it blogs, social channels like Facebook and Twitter, streaming video, and much more.

In this chapter, we will take you through our Seven-Step Brand Choreography process, giving you a dynamic, adaptive IMC methodology to help your brand thrive in a digital ecosystem that is in perpetual evolution. Then, we will teach you how to leverage synergies across a range of disciplines, including digital marketing and analytics, storytelling, content marketing, social media, digital anthropology, consumer insights, mobile-driven experience marketing, advertising, PR and live video. Finally, we will offer a new internal and external communication model to help your brand leverage both customer experience (CX) and employee experience (EX) throughout your organization.

INTRODUCING THE SEVEN-STEP BRAND CHOREOGRAPHY PROCESS

Brand Choreography (BC) follows a *holistic marketing* methodology. In holistic marketing, marketers work to make their brand's mission, vision and values a unified element of all organizational communication, whether internally or externally.

Internally, the marketing department makes a conscious effort to infuse the organization's mission throughout the organization. This mission serves as a sort of catalyst, driving the customer spirit throughout the organization and encouraging department leaders to identify and leverage interdependencies across departments. Ultimately, the job of every employee is to serve customers, and employees must understand their role in the process.

Externally, a holistic marketing approach recognizes that every touchpoint is an opportunity to win (or lose) prospective buyers. A brand touchpoint is any place where your customers or prospects come into contact with your brand.

- A call to customer service
- A website visit
- Social media channels (e.g. Facebook, Twitter, Instagram, or LinkedIn)
- Visiting a storefront (physical or digital)
- Reviewing a billing statement
- Reading and watching ads and other marketing materials

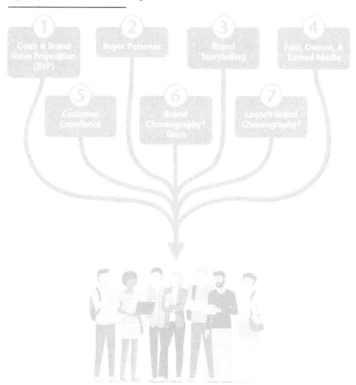

Figure 10.1 Brand Choreography® Seven-Step Roadmap.

Anywhere your brand is present, however a prospective buyer might find you, that is a touchpoint. As we discussed in Chapter 3, your brand could be succeeding on multiple fronts – good products, an appealing storefront and strong prices – but even a single breakdown or pain point anywhere along the way can result in a lost sale.

This is the core understanding at the heart of holistic marketing – and therefore of Brand Choreography. The following seven-step process will help your brand manage its presentation across every touchpoint along the buyer journey, resulting in a higher net impression of the brand, improved customer loyalty and more impassioned brand advocacy (see Figure 10.1).

STEP 1: GOALS AND BRAND VALUE PROPOSITION (BVP)

To properly execute the Brand Choreography framework, you must first have a clear understanding of your brand – its strengths and weaknesses, what sets it apart in the marketplace, and how your buyers perceive it. To do that, you will need to perform the following three exercises.

Start with a SWOT Analysis

As the old saying goes, 'If you don't know where you're going, any road will take you there.' In other words, if you don't have clearly defined marketing objectives, then you won't understand your role in the marketplace. Before determining your BVP, you must first determine your objectives as a brand. To do that, you will need to perform a SWOT analysis.

The SWOT analysis, which stands for *strengths, weaknesses, opportunities* and *threats*, is a time-tested process for developing and refining your marketing objectives. While you should formally reassess your SWOT on a regular basis, an agile marketing team always has an eye on the following considerations.

Strengths

Apple innovates. Disney creates immersive family experiences. McDonald's are masters of managing a global supply chain. Much like these branding powerhouses, your brand's strengths should be on display with every piece of messaging – and yet many brands struggle to define what those strengths are. To whatever extent you can, answer this question with data: study customer and employee surveys, analyze your capabilities, determine your resources, and study your processes.

Weaknesses

To protect against your weaknesses, you must first understand them – but whatever you do, don't ignore them. Here, external perception is critical. Use social listening to learn what your fans (and detractors) are saying about you. For instance, in 2003, when a struggling Lego faced possible bankruptcy, they engaged fan communities to find out how they could improve their products and brand (see Chapter 3), a move that may have single-handedly saved the company.

Opportunities

The best brands aren't threatened by changes in the business, tech, or cultural landscape; they're invigorated. For instance, when Apple saw the market moving away from physical media and toward streaming content, they seized the opportunity and created a new revenue stream for the company. Identifying new opportunities is the new oxygen for your firm.

Threats

Even the most powerful brands aren't immune to threats to their business model – just ask Kodak, Blockbuster, or Toys R Us. Nothing stays the same forever. Brands that actively seek out threats, rather than ignore them, are often the first to embrace opportunity and innovate.

Determining Your BVP

In marketing, a brand value proposition (BVP) is a way of answering essential marketing questions:

- What value do we deliver to the customer?
- What customer needs are we satisfying?
- Why do customers buy from us?
- Why should they care about our brand?

A winning BVP isn't just an empty statement designed to make a company's shareholders happy. As discussed in Chapter 6, effective content marketing aligns your content to your brand vision, and an effective integration strategy links your brand value proposition to the brand story. Therefore, it is critical to the planning process and affects decision-making at all levels of the company. Behind every great brand – be it Apple, Verizon, McDonald's, or Google – is a winning BVP that has enduring value. Each of these organizations understands that to win in highly competitive categories, they must be clear on who they are, what they stand for, and what differentiates them from their competitors. Using their BVP as a north star, these companies then focused both internal and external resources in order to manifest their vision in the marketplace.

The brand value proposition, then, is the foundation upon which all successful integrated marketing efforts are built. Without a strong BVP, customers are unlikely to trust or connect with your brand – and are therefore unlikely to value your products or services. Further, brands with rich BVPs avoid being sucked into the commodification trap. In other words, rather than compete on price, they compete on their reputation and the emotional bond they've formed with their customers.

So how do you develop a winning brand value proposition? Because you took the time to conduct a SWOT analysis first, most of the hard work is already done. Thanks to your SWOT, you now have a good sense of what makes your brand unique in the marketplace. From there, to determine your BVP, simply take the most valuable insights from each step of your SWOT and refine them until you have a concise, powerful statement that reflects who you are as a brand.

Take your time on this. The best BVPs are the result of multiple iterations as you slowly peel away the layers to get to the essence of your brand. Remember: don't focus on what you sell. Focus on the problem you solve.

Done correctly, your BVP will guide every marketing decision you make about your brand. For instance, when Audi re-launched the A4 in 2017, they were careful about how they positioned this new vehicle both within their own product line and within the marketplace. The A4 represented a leap for Audi, incorporating intelligent systems into the vehicle's machinery to improve the driving experience. They wanted to communicate this exciting point of departure to both Audi loyalists and those who might be new to the brand. To do that, they came up with the slogan 'Intelligence is the New Rock and Roll' (see Figure 10.2).

According to Loren Angelo, Vice President of Marketing at Audi of America, the decision to adapt in-car technology into the A4 may have surprised some, but it fit perfectly within its brand value proposition. For years, Audi has defined its brand by challenging industry standards in order to drive progress in the industry while creating a better overall driver experience. This BVP drove the development of their all-wheel drive technology for the Quattro, or their switch to LED lighting in all their cars. The A4's in-car technology was simply the latest example of Audi's BVP in action – and of their leadership in the marketplace.

Audi was excited to share the new technological leaps it had made with the A4, but they had to be careful how they positioned it. As Angelo explains, 'We didn't

Figure 10.2   2017 Audi A4 print ad.

Source: Audi USA.

want to be like every other brand who talks about their latest gadget in their vehicle.' Audi wanted to present these new innovations in a way that was relevant and exciting to their target buyers. They wanted to give their customers something to celebrate and idealize.

'If you go back thirty years, rock and roll stars were the epitome of the person you wanted to meet, the person you idealized', Angelo says. However, since then, a new kind of rock star has also emerged in the popular consciousness: celebrity intellectuals like Steve Jobs or Jeff Bezos. 'So many people across the world, whether they're working in the business sector, the technology sector, or even in other industries, idolize these individuals for the innovations that they bring', Angelo says.

Audi knew that if they could relate the innovations in the A4 to this new kind of rock star intellectual, they could tap the cultural zeitgeist and rally people around their brand. The result was a slogan that was elegant and to-the-point. Most of all, the slogan was free from any technical jargon or labored discussion of the A4's many eye-catching features. It was, in a word, accessible.[5]

Brand Positioning

The final step to creating a winning BVP is brand positioning. Essentially, while your BVP states your value as a brand, brand positioning is the process that allows you to communicate that value to your audience – which therefore determines how they perceive your brand. Suffice to say, this perception is everything, often determining whether you buy from one brand or the other.

It's no surprise, then, that brands like Audi take brand positioning very seriously. 'Consumers in today's world are expected to have to go through a variety of different brands each and every day', says Loren Angelo. To stand out in a crowded field, Audi has staked out their own territory in the automobile market. If Audi simply positioned their brand as one luxury option among many, they wouldn't do much to stand out. Instead, Audi positioned themselves as the *progressive* luxury choice.

But what's the difference between a luxury carmaker and a progressive luxury carmaker? As Angelo explains, 'A progressive brand has an opinion. A progressive brand is memorable. A progressive brand has a level of wit in the intelligent point they want to land.' More than anything, Angelo says, a progressive brand uses storytelling to bring their message to life.[6]

The bottom line is that, no matter what your product or service, you're not the only brand in your market. Brand positioning allows you to tell your customers what sets your brand apart – what makes you special. To get the most out of your brand positioning efforts, use the following steps.

Develop a Strategic Positioning Document

Using existing market data, answer the following questions:

- What is your market?
- Are any similar products or services available? How is yours different?
- How would you describe your competitors' brands?
- Who is your target buyer?

When considering your answers, be as specific as possible. The more specific you are, the greater the likelihood that you will differentiate your brand from your competitors.

Write Your Positioning Statement

Once you have your positioning document, the next step is to condense all that information into a simple, effective statement. Many statements use the following pattern:

> To [target market], [brand X] is the brand of [competitive framework] that provides [meaningful point of difference].

Using this positioning statement format, here is an example we have crafted for a well-known, quality airline that operates in a highly competitive industry.

> To [target market] business and consumer airline travelers, [brand] ABC Airlines, is the brand of [competitive framework] airline that [meaningful point of difference] is dedicated to delivering the best customer experience at affordable prices.

Your positioning statement has several applications. A good positioning statement will help you develop a blueprint for marketing and product development, focus all marketing and development and activities, and guide the creation of sub-strategies like trademark selection, copy, media, naming, promotion and distribution.

Test Your Statement

No matter how much time you spent crafting your brand positioning statement, and no matter how proud you and your team are of it, be sure to test it with your target buyers. Traditionally, focus groups made a great testing ground for positioning statements (see Chapter 2). However, social listening and other testing methods can help you here as well.

Wherever and however you decide to test your positioning statement, your goal is to answer the following questions:

- Does your audience relate to your stated point of difference?
- Does your audience see value in your stated consumer or business benefit?
- Does your audience find your positioning statement persuasive?
- Does your audience find your positioning statement unique, or does it remind them of other brands? If so, who?

You may find your positioning statement undergoing several rounds of testing and refining before both your marketing team and your audience are happy. If that's the case, don't panic; most brands don't get their positioning statement right on the first try. As long as you commit to the process and continue to seek feedback, you will eventually find a statement that lands with your target buyers.

STEP 2: BUYER PERSONAS

Now that you've completed step 1, you have a good sense of your brand's strengths and weaknesses through your SWOT, its point of difference through your BVP, and a sense of where you belong in the marketplace through your brand positioning statement. Knowing all that, the next question is, who do you sell to? What type of person, or people, would be interested in purchasing from a brand with your particular profile? To answer that question, you'll need to develop a series of buyer personas.

If you read Chapter 3, you're already familiar with this process. However, here is a brief overview of our seven-step process to develop your buyer persona.

1. **Gather buyer data.** Using a combination of demographics, psychographics, purchase behavior and social listening, learn as much as you can about your target buyer – both their own likes and interests, and what they like and enjoy about your brand.
2. **Assemble your team.** With the rest of your marketing team, it's time to create your different personas. During the brainstorming process, keep the environment loose and open. The point here is ideation. You'll have plenty of time to eliminate and refine profiles later.
3. **Get to know your buyer.** Now that you've brainstormed the basics, it's time to fill in the specifics. Give your buyer a name, a job, an appearance, hobbies, etc. Here is where all the data collected in step 1 come into play.
4. **Evaluate pain points.** When your buyer interacts with your brand, what pain points prevent them from making a purchase? The more diligent you are in this step, the more effective your persona will be.
5. **Craft your persona.** Using the data you've collected and the persona sketches you've developed in the previous steps, it's time to finalize your persona. Don't be surprised to discover that your target persona is far different from the persona you had in mind.

6. **Revisit and revise your persona.** We live in a world where the only constant is change. Your personas are no exception. The target buyers you sell to for one year may not be the same people you sell to the next year. Continue to collect and analyze data on your customers – and get ready to adapt.

7. **Validate your persona.** The best way to know whether you created the right persona is to begin marketing to them and start measuring results. Did you see a boost in engagement or sales? Did you see a drop? Again, study the data; it's dying to tell you a story.

Remember, when crafting your buyer personas, prioritize segmentation. It's far better to have multiple, narrow personas than a single, catch-all persona.

STEP 3: BRAND STORYTELLING

When considering your integrated marketing efforts, what you do you think is going to be more compelling across channels – facts and logic or good old-fashioned stories? If you guessed the latter, you are correct. In fact, Stanford professor Jennifer Aaker has found that stories are as much as 22 times more memorable than facts.[7] As it turns out, the media that connect with us emotionally leave a more lasting impact than do media that rely simply on logic.

The following is a summary of the most essential elements of brand storytelling. For a full discussion, see Chapter 6.

When it comes to storytelling, your number-one job is to communicate your *why*. As noted marketing thought leader Simon Sinek famously said, 'People don't buy what you do. They buy *why* you do it.'[8] While Sinek has helped revitalize this idea for modern marketers, the best brands have long been masters of the *why*. Just look at the emotionally resonant ideas leading brands have associated themselves with:

- Apple: 'Think different'
- IBM: 'Smarter planet'
- Mastercard: 'Priceless'

Make your *why* the center of what Sinek calls 'the Golden Circle'.[9] From there, expand out to the *how* and finally the *what*. By leading with the *why*, your audiences will be more receptive to concepts like the *how* and the *what*. Further, the *why* helps you forge an emotional connection with your audience.

Why is the *why* so powerful? Perhaps because stories are far more persuasive than facts and statistics, and far more likely to be shared.[10] Stories, in other words, are viral-ready. Stories can be delivered via word-of-mouth and stories resonate with people. 'The most credible form of advertising comes straight from the people we know and trust. Eighty-three percent of online respondents in 60 countries say they trust the recommendations of friends and family, according to a Nielsen Global Trust in Advertising Report.'[11]

Unsure whether you're telling good stories? Here's another chance to put your social listening skills to use. Monitor conversations about your brand to determine who's talking about you, what they're saying, and which of your content assets – if any – that they're sharing.

STEP 4: PAID, OWNED AND EARNED MEDIA (POEM)

In football, the best quarterbacks exhibit a combination of preparation and adaptability in their pursuit of excellence. They arrive on the field with a game plan, but they're prepared to switch that plan at a moment's notice to keep their opponents off-balance. The best marketers operate in a similar way when deploying their paid, owned and earned media (POEM) strategy. Let's take a closer look at each of these media channels to get a better understanding of how they work.

Paid media include advertisements, commercials and sponsorships – or any other outlet in which your brand has to 'pay to play', as the saying goes. Brands use paid media to gain visibility in high-traffic areas, such as popular TV shows, websites, or events. Paid media is perhaps the most traditional approach to attracting brand attention. However, in the changing digital landscape, paid channels aren't yielding the same returns they used to. The modern marketer would be wise not to blow their budget on paid media alone. Studies show that a growing number of customers are willing to pay premium prices to avoid ads, Netflix, Sirius XM, HBO, Showtime and others.

Owned media refer to content on any channel owned by your brand, most commonly your brand website. Pages on social channels such as LinkedIn and Facebook also constitute owned channels of sorts, since that space is yours to do with as you please. However, a word of caution: while you have a considerable latitude on what you can do with your page, the social platform hosting your content ultimately has final say.

Earned media include reviews, feature articles and interviews. Any time your brand has organically attracted attention and others want to talk about you, that's earned media. Think of earned media as word-of-mouth on steroids, ideally suited for a world marked by shareable content and peer recommendations.

Just as there is no uniform way to compose a good poem, there are no hard and fast rules for managing your POEM mix. For instance, while modern marketers rely less on paid media than in previous eras, paid nevertheless has a place. Here's our advice: spend less time worrying about creating the perfect media mix and more time asking how you can use different channels in service of a broader branding effort. Again, it is important to understand your target buyer persona's media consumption behavior.

Sidebar

Social Media Advertising

By Stacy Smollin Schwartz, Assistant Professor of Professional Practice, Department of Marketing, Rutgers Business School[12]

Marketers follow eyeballs. And with so many of their customers' eyes on social media, it is no wonder that brands hold their collective breath every time Facebook announces even a minor update to the way it determines the content you see in your feed.

Facebook's algorithm prioritizes person-to-person posts, pushing content created by business pages further and further to the back of the line. With their organic reach dropping close to what some have apocalyptically dubbed 'Facebook Zero', marketers are compelled to buy ads to ensure their content will be seen. Other social media platforms have followed suit, making social media marketing a largely pay-to-play game.

And paying to play they are! Social media advertising revenue in the US comprised over one-quarter of the almost $108 billion spent on all digital advertising in 2018.[13]

This investment affords marketers more than just a reserved spot on your news feed. Other benefits include:

- Enhanced reach. Even before the algorithm apocalypse, organic reach only allowed marketers to show their content to their existing followers. Paid media gives brands the ability to get their posts in front of new people beyond their social media base.
- Enhanced targeting. Consider all of the rich demographic data you share with social networks – your age, gender, location, education, occupation, etc. Layer on the psychographic information you knowingly and unknowingly indicate based on your stated interests, pages you follow, groups you belong to, posts you like, and comments you make. Advertisers can target users based on all of these nuanced parameters. Further, they can assess the profiles of their current customers, and use lookalike audience targeting to reach new people likely to be interested in the same products or services.

- Enhanced creative capabilities. Paid posts in our social media feeds often appear 'native' to their environment, making them subtler and less intrusive than other forms of digital advertising. They can also be beefed up with increased functionality, including larger scrolling canvases, custom calls-to-action tied directly to campaign objectives, and ecommerce checkout right inside the ad.
- Enhanced measurement. Paid media unlocks access to important analytics that aren't offered with unpaid posts. Both options allow brands to see how many people viewed, liked, commented, and shared. Advertising reports provide deeper insight, such as how many people completed those actions by device, time of day, and location.

STEP 5: CUSTOMER EXPERIENCE (CX)

'Welcome to the new era of business, in which your brand is defined by those who experience it.'[14] These are the words of prominent business thought leader Brian Solis. While they perfectly define the current marketing area, implicit in them is a warning: ignore the customer experience (CX) at your own peril.

When it comes to managing the CX, the modern marketer must be able to answer two questions:

- How do you want your customers to experience your brand?
- How do your customers *actually* experience your brand?

Whether they set out to or not, every brand creates a customer experience. A bad CX results from indifference and lack of planning. A good CX arises when a brand has clearly established its BVP and buyer personas and has infused that vision into every branded touchpoint.

To help you become a master of the CX, your first step is to assemble a Brand Choreography taskforce. The best brands understand that marketing is everybody's job. Your Brand Choreography taskforce should reflect that. To understand how your brand can best serve your customers and create a unified experience across departments, you must bring in voices from every area of your company – such as product design, IT and customer service.

With your team assembled, you will work together to map out both your current customer experience and your ideal customer experience (see the following steps). This is a lot of work. Plan for two to three days to map it out. To keep your team engaged, make an event out of it by setting up shop somewhere fun. The following is a summary of what that mapping session might look like. For a full discussion, see Chapter 5.

- **Establish goals.** By the end of your session, your team should be able to answer the following questions: What are your customers' most common buying strategies? Is your brand set up to accommodate those strategies? Does your brand support customers through every phase of the buying cycle – research, purchase and post-purchase? If the answer to any of these questions is, 'It's complicated', don't be surprised – that's why you're doing this exercise!
- **Assess the current state experience.** While many brands are sincere in their CX efforts, they often see a discrepancy between how they think their customers experience their brand versus how their customers actually do experience their brand. Spend some time on this discussion and use whatever available data you have.
- **Create the ideal state experience.** Most likely, you will discover a clear gap between your current and your ideal state experience. It is about satisfying your target buyer personas' needs. The good news, however, is that now you know the problem, you can address it. Brainstorm solutions with your team, approaching the problem from multiple angles.

Finally, once you've completed the Brand Choreography Mapping process, be sure to implement your changes and monitor results. You may not be able to implement all the discussed changes at once, so use a cost-benefit analysis to prioritize your initiatives. From there, use both employee and customer feedback to test and validate your ideas. After a designated period, perhaps quarterly or bi-annually, reconvene your team and repeat the process.

STEP 6: BRAND CHOREOGRAPHY TEAM

Now that your Brand Choreography Mapping taskforce has done its job, it's time to expand your Brand Choreography efforts beyond the customer experience and begin crafting your integrated marketing communications strategy. To do that, the first question you need to answer is, 'Who's in charge?'

The answer may appear obvious. However, according to brand strategist Dr. David Aaker, one of the main ways that siloed organizations inhibit brand-building is that 'There is no person or team with any authority that is in charge of the brand.'[15] Without clearly delineated roles and responsibilities, your Brand Choreography efforts could end up siloed within your organization – resulting in an inconsistent brand message and marketplace confusion.

To avoid this, outcome, Aaker says,

[T]he goal should be to foster a culture of communication and cooperation rather than isolation and competition. What works is to use nonthreatening roles for the CMO team, teams and networks, common processes and systems, ways to adapt the brand vision, silos as a source of ideas, and CEOs to enable difficult organizational compromises. The functional silo problem has become acute with the advent of digital. IMC teams are needed, and the ongoing challenge is to learn to make them work.[16]

To create the culture of communication around IMC that Aaker promotes, brands must create what we call a Social Ecosystem. First proposed by Blue Focus Marketing president Mark Burgess in a 2016 article for the *Rutgers Business Review*, the social ecosystem model provides an effective organizational blueprint for social media adoption and offers organizations the cross-silo infrastructure and oversight necessary to deliver a powerful, unified brand message across platforms.[17] To achieve that, the social ecosystem is built on three pillars: the social governance council (SGC), the employee experience (EX) and the customer experience (CX), as Figure 10.3 illustrates.

In the following sections, we will walk you through each of them.

The Social Governance Council (SGC)

Today's marketers operate in a world of increasingly prolific – and always growing – marketing and media channels. On the one hand, this abundance of options represents an incredible opportunity for brands to share their message and connect with their target audience. On the other hand, if not managed as part of a unified effort, these channels also pose a barrier to effective messaging.

Much like the Brand Choreography Mapping taskforce, the SGC is composed of employees across the organization, representing a range of departments and ranks. Such diversity allows those most familiar with the inner workings of the company to create a unified front for their brand, regardless of platform, channel, or content type. To accomplish this, the SGC works together to establish objectives, determine key metrics and monitor progress. While the needs of every organization are different, members of the SGC should plan to meet regularly, whether monthly, quarterly, or bi-annually, to assess progress and adapt to changing needs.

The Employee Experience (EX)

Often overlooked in most IMC strategies is the role of the brand's messengers – specifically, their employees.

- People also trust your employees far more than they trust your CEO and media representatives. The 2014 Edelman Trust Barometer found that the credibility of employees increased 20% since 2009, shooting far ahead of trust in CEOs.[18]
- Employee advocacy done right benefits the consumer, the employee and the brand.[19]
- Those that start employee advocacy programs learn that simply sharing content about the brand with employees will make the individual contributor feel more connected and engaged.[20]

THREE PILLARS OF THE SOCIAL ECOSYSTEM

SOCIAL GOVERNANCE COUNCIL (SGC)	EMPLOYEE EXPERIENCE (EX)	CUSTOMER EXPERIENCE (CX)
• Executive leadership: C-Suite	• Focus on culture, communication, and collaboration	• Focus on two-way exchanges through social advocacy and earned media
• Department representatives: Marketing, Sales, HR, Customer Support, Product, IT, Legal, and Communications	• Reflects organization's mission, vision, and values	• Produce enduring brand relationships through marketing insights and excellent customer support
• Internal Evangelists: Early adopters and high-performers	• Empowered through social computing guidelines	• Use customer feedback to improve the experience throughout product/marketing cycle
• Business mission, objectives, strategy, and metrics	• Engage as authentic brand ambassadors	• Objectives, strategy, and metrics
	• Objectives, strategy, and metrics	

Figure 10.3   Three Pillars of the Social Ecosystem.

Source: An earlier version appeared in *Rutgers Business Review* 'Shaping the future: The New Social Ecosystem', by Mark Burgess (2016), 1(1), pp. 107–122.

In order to function properly, Brand Choreography depends on social employee advocacy. Whether designing marketing materials, engaging with digital communities, or even sending off an email, who better to communicate who your brand is and what it stands for than an organization's employees?

Creating a compelling, unifying employee experience (EX) extends beyond the reach of the marketing department alone. In fact, it impacts how organizations interact with employees at a fundamental level. However, the marketing team plays a vital role in this effort, using both internal and external channels to engage with employees, share relevant content, and encourage them to amplify the brand's message by sharing branded content through their own social networks.

The Customer Experience (CX)

By this point, your brand is already well on its way to creating an excellent CX. In step 5, we showed how a Brand Choreography Mapping taskforce could help you identify and solve problems in your CX. Here in step 6, you have learned how creating a social governance council and strong EX can help create a unified brand persona. Here, you will bring all these skills to bear to create a full, healthy social ecosystem.

Ultimately, the goal of a good CX is not simply to create satisfied customers, but to create satisfied *repeat* customers. To create a strong customer experience:

- Provide helpful content at every stage of the buyer journey (see Chapter 4).
- Provide opportunities for feedback.
- Create a community that engages your fans.
- Consider ways to create co-branded content that celebrates your customers (and shows potential customers why buying from you is so much fun).

However you go about creating a thriving CX, never forget the prime directive: stand for something. Whatever you stand for is entirely up to you. Starbucks, for instance, literally stands for the customer experience. Over the past several decades, Starbucks has forced marketers in every brand and in every category to ask how they could create a customer experience that rivals that of Starbucks. We know that in our jobs as consultants, when we're in the middle of a busy day in Manhattan, moving from the east to the west side without an office to drop into, we often find ourselves looking for that familiar green and white Starbucks logo. As soon as we see it, we know we'll have a quiet place to find a comfortable chair, open our laptops, connect to the free WiFi, say hello to a friendly barista, and, of course, enjoy a quality cup of coffee. This public commitment to not just serving a product, but also creating an *environment*, has helped Starbucks continue to stand out in an increasingly competitive market.

As another example, up-and-coming brands like Warby Parker have mastered the customer experience in two ways: (1) making it incredibly convenient to pick a stylish pair of glasses through their direct mail service, and (2) partnering with their customers in service of a humanitarian cause. At Warby Parker, for every pair of glasses a customer purchases, the company donates a pair to communities in need.

However you approach the situation, remember that what your brand stands for is increasingly your most compelling point of difference. Today's buyers have a variety of options to choose from. When you represent a cause or ideal that extends beyond your brand and into your community, you give your customers a powerful reason to choose you over your competitors.

Step 7: Launch Brand Choreography

Just like any well-choreographed dance, the purpose of the performance isn't simply to execute the motions, but to create something special – to dazzle your audience. Management guru Tom Peters calls this 'the pursuit of Wow!' In his book of the same name, Peters says:

> For great actors and actresses, each performance is a fresh opportunity to experiment with a new approach – in fact, to experiment with nothing less than a new persona. Who are you going to be today? How are you going to connect? Every day the play begins anew. On this day, how will you perform it?[21]

The best *wow* moments may feel fresh and spontaneous, but in reality, they are the result of countless hours of work behind the scenes – hours spent crafting brand value propositions, buyer personas, customer experiences, and so on. Only through such careful practice can we truly bring life and character to our performances. Dr. Philip Kotler agrees. 'Winning companies and brands are those that do not leave *wow* moments to chance', Kotler says. 'They create *wow* by design. They productively guide customers from awareness to advocacy.'[22]

Ultimately, Brand Choreography is an ongoing process of reinvention. Just as a dancer is right back in the practice hall after wowing their audience the night before, so too is the marketer – analyzing more data, practicing social listening, and refining their content delivery across channels. As you refine the steps in your own Brand Choreography performance, remember that the best leaders are also the best listeners. Engage with your audience. Learn from them. Be curious. Then, bring that back to your organization, lay out the steps to an unforgettable performance, and then deliver a performance they will never forget.

Future Gaze

Mobile Strategy within an IMC Roadmap

When crafting a comprehensive IMC strategy, the modern marketer must not only be aware of the many channels available to them, but the portal through which their audience receives this content – specifically, mobile devices. According to *eMarketer*, 'Among the 3.75 billion internet users worldwide in 2019, 86.2 percent will use a mobile phone to go online.'[23]

With so much riding on mobile, it's important for marketers to consider how to account for mobile browsing in their overall IMC strategy. Chuck Martin, author of *Digital Transformation 3.0* and CEO of Net Future Institute, offers the following 10 pieces of advice.[24]

#1: Be Everywhere

Location matters. In the new mobile environment, the consumer controls when and where they engage with a brand. Shoppers can make digital purchases from any-where – at home, on the bus, even inside a brick-and-mortar store. In fact, many use their mobile devices to research products and compare prices even when they're out shopping. Consumers take their mobile devices everywhere they go, giving brands the opportunity to go along with them. But to do that, brands must work to become omnipresent across channels and touchpoints.

#2: Make It Easy

It's easy to make things hard on mobile – and it's hard to make things easy. Companies invest tremendous resources into creating a mobile experience that they think is smart and intuitive only to discover that their users are confounded by it. Every function of the mobile experience must be designed to be as easy as possible to the mobile user. If you're not sure, test it.

#3: It Pays to Be Flexible

Things change, especially the dynamic in this marketplace. People, companies, brands, and providers all must be ready to adapt to these changes on a moment's notice.

#4: Determine Range

Customers are different. Some are early adopters, some are laggards. Some are young, some are old. Some have grown up with technology, some haven't. Some have adopted, some haven't. Some like mobile, some don't. Whatever the case, brands must determine what range – or ranges – of customers they have. Most likely, they serve

(Continued)

multiple segments, affording them the opportunity to customize what they provide, how they provide it, and who they provide it to.

#5: Follow the Standards of Market Leaders

If you sell books, follow the standards of how Amazon sells books. If you sell enterprise software, follow the standards set by other enterprise software providers. You don't want to frustrate your customers by foiling their expectations. Make sure you fit within the standards of your market.

#6: Make It Easy to Buy

Again, mobile allows people to purchase goods and services from anywhere at any time. Your job is to make it so they can do exactly that – buying what they want, when they want, and how they want. If prospective customers routinely abandon their carts or put off their purchases for later, you've likely introduced an unintended barrier.

#7: Adapt to Platform

As of this writing, most mobile users own either Apple- or Android-based devices. These users operate from different platforms, which in turn lead to differences in their behaviors. Be aware of these differences and develop your marketing approach to accommodate users on both platforms.

#8: Tap the Latest Technology

Whether it's facial identification, fingerprint scanning, or even eye scanning, mobile devices are constantly rolling out new features. Look to the examples of other market leaders to see how you might incorporate these features. For instance, American Express has embraced both facial identification and thumbprint scanning as means of opening their app. This makes it incredibly easy – and secure – for users to access potentially sensitive information. If you're in a similar business, you should be doing the same.

#9: Build in Memory

In the coming Internet of Things (IoT), users will often begin their buyer journey on one device, such as their computer, and finish on another, such as their mobile device (or even their car). Your platforms must have the memory and capacity to track and recognize users from device to device to provide a seamless integrated experience.

#10: Measure Your Steps

The best systems are the least complex. Create the fewest steps to action – no matter what the action is. Whatever process you've designed, measure out the steps, and then look for ways to combine or eliminate certain steps to create an easier, more fluid experience.

Finally, after practicing all these 10 steps, be prepared to change.

CHAPTER ANALYSIS QUESTIONS

1. What are some of the major integration challenges facing marketers?
2. Choose three of the steps in the Brand Choreograph roadmap you believe are the most important and why.
3. Discuss Audi's positioning strategy for the Audi A4. What makes it stand out?
4. Choose three of the most relevant trends in mobile marketing and discuss why they are relevant.

NOTES

1. Goodreads.com. (n.d.). A quote by Abraham Lincoln. [online] Available at: www.goodreads.com/quotes/83633-give-me-six-hours-to-chop-down-a-tree-and [Accessed 28 Jan. 2020].
2. Manthei, L. (n.d.). The differences between multichannel & omnichannel marketing. [online] Emarsys. Available at: www.emarsys.com/en/resources/blog/multi-channel-marketing-omnichannel/ [Accessed 15 Apr. 2019].
3. Roderick, L. (2017). 'Arrogance' around brand purpose making consumers distrust ads. [online] Marketing Week. Available at: www.marketingweek.com/2017/06/29/arrogance-brand-purpose-distrust-ads/ [Accessed 31 Dec. 2019].
4. Batra, R. and Keller, K. (2016). Integrating marketing communications: New findings, new lessons, and new ideas. Journal of Marketing, 80(6), p. 137.
5. Angelo, L. (2019). Personal communication. [10 Jan.].
6. Ibid.
7. Stanford Graduate School of Business. (2013). Jennifer Aaker: Harnessing the Power of Stories. [video] Available at: www.youtube.com/watch?v=9X0weDMh9C4 [Accessed 10 Apr. 2019].
8. Sinek, S. (2019). How Great Leaders Inspire Action. [online] Ted.com. Available at: www.ted.com/talks/simon_sinek_how_great_leaders_inspire_action [Accessed 1 Jul. 2019].
9. Ibid.
10. Sudakow, J. (2017). A good story is always far more persuasive than facts and figures. [online] Inc.com. Available at: www.inc.com/james-sudakow/why-a-good-story-is-far-more-persuasive-than-facts.html [Accessed 10 Apr. 2019].
11. Nielsen. (2015). Nielsen Press Room: Recommendations from friends remain the most credible form of advertising among consumers; branded websites are the second-highest rated form. [online] Nielsen.com. Available at: www.nielsen.com/us/en/press-releases/2015/recommendations-from-friends-remain-most-credible-form-of-advertising/ [Accessed 6 Jan. 2020].
12. Schwartz, S. (2020). Personal communication. [6 January].
13. IAB. (2019). U.S. digital ad revenues surpass $100 billion mark for the first time, hitting landmark $107.5 billion in 2018, according to IAB internet advertising revenue report.

Available at: www.iab.com/news/u-s-digital-ad-revenues-surpass-100-billion-mark/ [Accessed 6 Jan. 2020].

14. Solis. B. (2015). *X: The Experience When Business Meets Design*. John Wiley & Sons, inner flap.

15. Aaker, D. (2014). *Aaker on Branding: 20 Principles That Drive Success*. Morgan James Publishing, p. 183.

16. Ibid., p. 191.

17. Burgess, M. (2016). Shaping the future: The new social ecosystem. [online] *Rutgers Business Review*. Available at: http://rbr.business.rutgers.edu/article/shaping-future-new-social-ecosystem [Accessed 10 Apr. 2019].

18. Hawley, D. (2014). Your biggest social media risk: Not doing anything about social employees. [online] *WIRED*. Available at: www.wired.com/insights/2014/11/social-employees/ [Accessed 31 Dec. 2019].

19. Terpening, E. (2016). Tapping into the power of an engaged social workforce. [online] Prophet.com. Available at: www.prophet.com/2016/03/social-media-employee-advocacy-tapping-into-the-power-of-an-engaged-social-workforce/ [Accessed 31 Dec. 2019].

20. Ibid.

21. Peters, T. (1995). *The Pursuit of Wow!* Macmillan, pp. 13–14.

22. Kotler, P. (2017). *Marketing 4*. Wiley, p. 169.

23. eMarketer. (2018). Global digital users update 2018. Available at: www.emarketer.com/content/global-digital-users-update-2018 [Accessed 31 Dec. 2019].

24. Martin, C. (2019). Personal communication. [19 February].

11
DATA IN, BRANDING OUT

Learning Goals

- Illustrate how customer journeys can be optimized based on computer-generated algorithms and AI.
- Learn how companies can use (Big) Data and AI to analyze and predict ROI and marketing outcomes.
- Analyze the role of data in optimizing and informing future integrated marketing initiatives and branding.
- Critique the importance of trust and integrity when it comes to data-driven and AI-driven marketing.

> Without big data analytics, companies are blind and deaf, wandering out onto the Web like deer on a freeway.
>
> Geoffrey Moore, author of *Crossing the Chasm*[1]

Imagine a world in which you know what your customers like, what they don't like (or possibly even hate), and what they *could* like. Well, that world exists – it just lives in the rectangular screen in your living room. Or, possibly, the one in your pocket or purse. There's actually a term for such a place: Netflix.

Netflix is one of the world's best examples of micro-segmentation. The company's success is well-known to most, but only after seeing some numbers can you really grasp the scale of their accomplishment. In 2018, for example, they spent $12 *billion* on original content, a figure that was estimated to rise to $15 billion by the end of 2019.[2]

This is a staggering sum to spend on creative development. (To put it in different terms, it's roughly equivalent to the GDP of Albania.) That said, the company hasn't grown from scrappy startup to supplier of 10% of Americans' screen time just because of its programming quality, however.[3] Netflix also pays meticulous attention to customer data. Because the vast majority of Netflix customers subscribe to their streaming (as opposed to its mail-in) service, Netflix is able to collect invaluable information about every user – including their likes and dislikes – with every visit to the app. In turn, Netflix is able to use this data to present each customer with well-informed predictions about other shows or movies they may like. The result is an irresistible – or addictive, depending on your view – path to even more high-quality content.

And, of course, paid subscriptions. The company's subscription model is arguably the key to its incredible growth since 2007, when it first introduced its streaming service. Movie studios, TV networks and cable channels have multiple ways of reaching their target audience, but none can compare to targeting those audience members directly where they are, at the precise moment they are about to make a decision.

Indeed, Netflix's obsessive, data-driven focus on the customer journey has helped differentiate the company from its rivals on both the small and big screen, creating a new model for the customer journey in the process. 'Netflix is a twenty-first century analytical model, while Hollywood is still stuck in the twentieth century', writes business professor and consultant Enrique Dans.[4] It's hard to disagree. Like Netflix, countless other brands are embracing a twenty-first century, data-centric approach to marketing. In this chapter, we'll explore the ways brands are unlocking the world of Big Data and analytics to deliver great customer experiences.

DATA-DRIVEN CUSTOMER EXPERIENCE

Having access to good data can do more than just help guide your marketing efforts. It can improve your customer experience too. Chatbots and virtual assistants offer a good example of this kind of real-world application. In 2017, the Australian online bank UBank launched a 'virtual agent' dubbed 'Mia' to assist customers seeking information on home loans. Developed with the help of IBM Watson, the AI-powered agent is outfitted with natural language processing (NLP) capabilities, enabling 'her' to speak with customers through their computer or cell phone. While the scope of Mia's assistance is limited to one topic, she has proven her value. By providing immediate answers to routine but crucial questions, Mia frees up UBank customer service staff to deal with more complicated inquiries. As the company grows, this will make it easier to scale its customer service operations without degrading service.[5]

Mia's promise lies in a modern, streamlined customer experience. Using Mia, customers can be helped more quickly and, in most cases, satisfactorily. 'Having AI as your eyes and ears across your digital channels will ensure that your customer experience is seamless and that you haven't got challenges or hurdles that you're putting in place for somebody when they're trying to go through a process', says Jodie Sangster, chief marketing officer, IBM Singapore. Because the store of data powering Mia is so robust, she – or any other AI-powered customer service app – will be armed with useful, tailored information that can be provided instantly. 'When a customer phones up and says, "I'd like to know about this transaction on this specific date and how much it was", the call center assistance, rather than wading through all of that data, can actually ask the AI: "Can you find this information for me?" And it can be brought up in literally a matter of seconds', says Sangster.[6] The result is a win-win for both customers and UBank.

IBM Watson has become something of an industry leader in developing AI innovations for financial services firms. In addition to creating an assistant named Cora for the Royal Bank of Scotland, the Watson team has also developed assistants for Bradesco Bank (Brazil), Banco do Brasil, and similar organizations.[7] You can almost imagine Cora, Mia and all of the other bots getting together for a drink after a long workday. Almost.

That said, as chatbots adoption has increased over recent years, there have been some setbacks. In 2017, for example, the clothing retailer Everlane decided to discontinue their use of chatbots because of high failure rates; ultimately, user requests were too complicated for the company's bots to handle. Similarly, in 2018, Facebook announced it would be discontinuing M, the virtual assistant it made available to a select group of users. In a 2017 *Digiday* article taking stock of the chatbot scene, Joe Corr, executive creative tech director at CP+B, said for some companies, bots simply couldn't live up to expectations. Firms that used chatbots to respond to limited requests often found them worth the cost, but those who expected a more wide-ranging functionality were usually disappointed. 'Brands that created bots with a structured request or utility like Domino's or in retail were easy," he said.[8]

Despite their limitations, chatbots may still be a good option for companies who find themselves spending a lot of time addressing the same types of customer service issues. And, if you're able to invest in more robust functionality, chatbots may very well prove their worth as sophisticated, data-driven AI tools, as Mia and Cora are. The best approach is to weigh the costs and benefits of an out-of-the-box solution vs. working with a company that develops custom bots, and then decide what works best for you.

THE HANDS-FREE VIRTUAL ASSISTANT

Voice search is another virtual assistant trend that has established itself as part of everyday life. Over the past few years, Siri, Alexa and Cortana have been trailing the likes of Cher, Prince and Madonna in the battle for most recognizable single-word names. These virtual assistants can add events to a calendar, order products, schedule reminders, play songs on request, provide updates on weather and Amazon package delivery status, make phone calls, adjust your thermostat, offer a question of the day, retrieve information, and more. Their capabilities are limited mostly to mundane tasks but are still appreciated by the millions of people who use them to save valuable time in their day.

Paul Roetzer, founder and CEO, Marketing AI Institute, predicts that we're just scratching the surface of what these kinds of virtual assistants can do. In fact, Roetzer predicts that voice search will be 'unrecognizable' by the mid-to-late 2020s:

> We look back to today, in ten years we'll just laugh at how 'preschool' level everything we were doing seems. The movement is obviously towards voice. Amazon has Alexa. Microsoft has Cortana. Apple has Siri. The biggest tech companies in the world have set the futures of their companies in part on voice. More and more we will get answers to questions and we won't be looking at a screen with links to click on – we'll be getting what they predict is the best answer for us. And so, voice will have a massive impact on every industry.[9]

Roetzer also believes marketers should pay special attention to where this tech is headed, since it will have far-reaching effects on how people seek out and then purchase things:

> Marketers will need to be able to understand it, understand how it works, start looking at the trends of users and how they're applying it, and start realizing that it's going to change the way they have to build their websites and run their marketing. The way someone may make a buying decision is asking Alexa while they're sitting in their living room, you know, 'Order me this.' And it just orders it. You might not even tell them a brand. It just knows what you want or predicts what's best for you. So, yeah. It's gonna completely change the buyer journey. It'll change everything for marketing.[10]

These changes, though, won't be without their risks. As marketing guru and entrepreneur Gary Vaynerchuk warned at VoiceCon 2018, if voice search becomes a preferred way for millions of people to order products, then differentiating yourself in the minds of your target market will take on a new urgency. 'If you do not start the process right now of branding Chips Ahoy over "cookies," what's going to happen is we are going to say, "Alexa or Google, send me some chocolate chip cookies."'[11] This means the brand loses. As Fred Burt, former managing director at Siegel+Gale, London, says, 'A brand is a reason to choose.'[12] If you want voice search users to choose you, you have to make sure you're on their mind.

Daniel Binns, CEO of the brand consultancy Interbrand, imagines a future where AI-powered assistants usher in an 'Age of You' where personalization becomes the

Age of Identity 1950s-1960s	Age of Value 1970s-1980s	Age of Experience 1990s-2000s	Age of You Present
Brands acted as a tool to identify and differentiate offering	Brands leveraged to command a premium and establish loyalty	Brands become the higher purpose that inspires a lifestyle	Brands are becoming the consumer's personal partner

Figure 11.1 Building brands has become more complex.

Source: ©2018 Interbrand. All Rights Reserved.

norm. Assistants will be able to identify brands consumers are most interested in interacting – or *may* be interested in interacting with – and will tailor their assistance accordingly. 'Age of You is all about brands being built around the needs of the individual, and AI is the center of that in many ways, to be able to offer increasingly personalized experiences', says Binns. Through micro-targeting, AI will 'be the source of learning and the data and ability to respond and create things that are more relevant to people'. In this new world, Binns believes, there will be a 'huge change to how brands and marketers have to operate'.[13]

Put differently: data in, branding out.

Figure 11.1 illustrates the evolution of brand-building, from the Age of Identity to the Age of You.

BIG DATA = BIG ROI

The bedrock of chatbots, voice search and other assistant-type programs is raw data. On their own, siloed and untouched, data is useless. But meticulously sorted and analyzed, data is a powerful tool for marketers, helping them learn even more about their customers' preferences.

For most companies, it all begins with machine learning. This term refers to conducting data analysis via automated programs that trawl through raw data to identify patterns. In turn, these patterns yield insights that can predict, to varying degrees of certainty, future behavior. Netflix's recommendation feature offers an easy-to-grasp example of this. Before it's offered to subscribers, every movie or show it makes available is classified. *Sleepless in Seattle*, for example, may be designated as a romantic comedy, quirky 1990s movie, and/or a film under two hours long. In fact, it would even be searchable by the film's prominent actors and its director – in this case, Tom Hanks, Meg Ryan and Nora Ephron. If you're a Netflix user and you spend the next few weeks watching a lot of quirky 1990s movies, Netflix's data analysis system will make a note of this. Whenever you log in to Netflix in the future, that system will present you with even more varieties of quirky 1990s movies. Through data analysis in scenarios just like this, Netflix identifies preferences (patterns) in your viewing and uses this information to serve you up more of what you've shown a preference for. (Admittedly, this is a simplistic explanation of how machine learning works, but it's easy to grasp.)

Netflix is just one player in the enormous world of data-driven marketing. For obvious reasons, tech companies are most likely (and best-positioned) to take advantage of this practice, but they are by no means the only companies harnessing data to guide decision-making.

Natural language processing, as we briefly touched on earlier, is a subset of AI that can also offer important benefits to marketers. It involves analyzing and cataloging language – oral or written – to identify speech patterns. It then uses this data to create programs that can interact with humans. This is a very complicated process, since speech is rarely direct and clear. In the course of an interaction, someone may be vague or sarcastic, say something that is open to interpretation, or simply become difficult to understand. The more sophisticated NLP programs, however, can go beyond mere recognition of simple speech. After going through and analyzing hundreds of thousands to possibly billions of language patterns, these programs are able to predict with an impressive degree of certainty what certain phrases or expressions *mean*, even if they're indirect or unclear. As a result, NLP can help companies direct customers and potential customers to the right information and make their journey quicker and more efficient. Amazon and Google's autopredict features are good examples of NLP in action, as are virtual assistants.

One approach to NLP, known as *sentiment analysis*, gauges user responses to a given stimulus, such as a brand or a news story. For sentiments to register accurately, the program must be smart enough to distinguish positive responses from negative ones (or whatever metric is intended to be measured). Accurate sentiment measuring can give marketers invaluable feedback, since it offers a quick, large-scale analysis of consumer feelings. According to Katrina Troughton, managing director IBM Australia/New Zealand, this sort of natural language processing application is an important part of what data and analytics can do to assist marketers.

> Because we all get attached to what we think and the experiences that we've had and without even realizing it, we can create some bias. There is no question that one of the ways you can eliminate more bias is by having a much broader spread of opinion and data to draw from, and that's really what this can do.[14]

The examples we've discussed so far highlight just some of the capabilities of AI. Many of the world's biggest and most respected brands rely on machine learning to improve their customers' experience in innovative and unforeseen ways. For instance, in the summer of 2019, Nike released 'Nike Fit', an app that allows users to scan their feet through their smartphone to get an accurate fit. The app relies on 'a proprietary combination of computer vision, data science, machine learning, artificial intelligence, and recommendation algorithms' to ensure that each fit is accurate within less than two millimeters.[15] Given how common bad shoe fit is, especially as more and more people forgo trips to the store to order online, this has the potential to be a game-changing differentiator for Nike.

Other examples abound. Disney World's MagicBand has revolutionized the visitor experience at the famous theme park. A plastic RFID-equipped bracelet preloaded with payment information, wearer details and preferences, and other crucial data points, it functions as an all-in-one key that helps wearers navigate the park with minimal 'friction'. With the MagicBand strapped to a visitor's wrist, restaurant and ride wait times, credit card payment exchanges, hotel check-ins, and the like are either eliminated or minimized. As visitors make their way through the park, real-time data is transmitted via radio to Disney staff: where the visitors are, where they're headed and what they want.[16]

Finally, while the Starbucks app's functionality is more modest, its goal is the same: to anticipate a customer's needs and fulfill them. The app makes recommendations based on a customer's previous orders, a useful feature for many regular customers. It's well-designed and makes navigating orders a simple process. It also saves time, as it allows users to easily customize drink orders in the app, bringing the in-store experience online. The experience repeats itself every time – without fail. But its goals are more ambitious: in 2019 the company announced it was collaborating with Microsoft to upgrade the app's capabilities. One innovation involves offering drive-thru customers on-screen recommendations based on their purchase history.[17]

Using data to gain a marketing edge isn't the prerogative of huge companies. Advances in AI have the potential to take marketing tools that were long available only to a select few and share them with the masses, relatively speaking. Call it a democratization of data. According to Scott Brinker, VP, Platform Ecosystems, at HubSpot, 'nonspecialists', or 'regular business users in marketing' are increasingly able to apply creative, data-driven marketing solutions on their own. 'Citizen developers can build their own apps. Citizen data scientists can analyze their own data sets. Citizen designers can use tools like Canva to produce amazing creative. Citizen integrators can use tools like Zapier to connect different cloud services together', Brinker says.[18]

METRICS-BASED CONTENT MARKETING

The examples we've explored so far show just how powerful data and the savvy use of metrics – measurable data points – can be when it comes to customer experience. This is no less relevant when it comes to content marketing. In our burgeoning, digital-first media landscape, there are all sorts of metrics available for harnessing data, which is good to know for companies who are much smaller and have significantly fewer

Table 11.1

Marketing Objectives	Suggested Metrics
Increase brand awareness.	Volume of conversations, reach, brand sentiment, website traffic, video views, etc.
Increase engagement.	Interactions with content, likes, retweets, shares, mentions, use of campaign hashtags, time on site, page views, click-through rates, etc.
Lead generation.	Cost per lead (by channel), qualified sales leads, form completion, whitepaper downloads, blog subscriptions, conversion rate, etc.
Increase sales.	Online and offline (O2O) sales; revenue influenced by content.
Improve customer retention.	Retention rates, churn rates, content consumption, followers, etc.
Increase customer advocacy.	Number of advocates, conversations driven by advocates, revenue generated by advocates, word-of-mouth, etc.
Increase cross-sell/upsell.	Measure shopping cart and landing page conversions, sales of new products, etc.

resources than Netflix. With a little effort, marketers at companies of all sizes can gain insight into where they should best direct their attention and resources.

To begin this process, marketers need to decide what their objectives are. These could include a higher open rate on emails, a higher click-through rate, or something else. Your objectives should be SMART:[19] specific, measurable, achievable, realistic and timebound. When setting SMART goals, make sure that the *measurable* component is quantitative. It's not enough to say, get more revenue in 2021. Such goals are too hazy to be helpful. Instead, a much better measurable goal would be, increase the leads generated each month from our blog to 200. Based on our history, we know that blog leads are converting to paying customers at four times the rate of leads generated from whitepaper downloads. This goal is timebound to achieve 200 blog leads per month in six months.

Key performance indicators (KPIs) will help you determine your progress in achieving your objectives. They can help keep your strategy on track because they offer evidence that your marketing strategy is working – or isn't. Once you figure out appropriate KPIs, it's important that you map them to your objectives, as Table 11.1 demonstrates.

Metrics like these are particularly useful when it comes to content marketing, since they can provide real-time updates on how your efforts are received. Did a blog post land with a bang – or a thud? Can certain content reliably drive traffic to your site? Well, spending some time with the data can help you figure this out. Well-paired metrics and KPIs can also help answer critical questions, such as:

- Who are your consumers?
- What do they want?
- What don't they want?

- When are they abandoning their customer journey?
- What are they looking for from your company or website?
- What are you doing right – and wrong?

This list goes on and on. The bottom line is that the more data you have on customer behavior, the stronger your positioning will be.

For Jay Baer, founder of Convince & Convert consulting and a content marketing expert, the simplest and most important KPI when it comes to content marketing is ultimately sales. 'We have to remember that the goal is not to be good at content. The goal is to be good at business because of content. So the real metric that matters is money. Are people buying stuff? And are they generating leads and raising their hand?'[20] That said, Baer says, there are technical ways you can measure the impact of your content as well.

Baer also cautions that when it comes to gauging impact, context is key: you can only measure improvement based on where you started. To illustrate this, he uses the example of a webinar:

> Let's say you've done fifteen webinars. If we look at your fifteen webinars, going backwards, we can very easily identify a baseline performance level of your typical webinars. Well, then if you do the sixteenth one and the sixteenth one has far more attendance, show-up rate, re-watch rate, etc., then we're looking at the effectiveness of your content versus your content [itself].[21]

Keeping proper perspective will help you stay on track. Aiming to make a big splash or go for broke is less effective long-term than strategizing ways to steadily increase your impact. 'I think the key is to really look deeply at what you have done in the past as an organization and then try to incrementally improve versus that baseline', says Baer.[22]

Sidebar

Calculating Brand Strength

The following section includes Interbrand's Brand Strength Score Chart, which is calculated by weighing 10 brand dimensions. This is a statistical model, based on the 10 Brand Strength dimensions (those used in the Interbrand Best Global Brands methodology to measure the performance of a brand), which identifies the exact perceptual, behavioral and transactional data sources underpinning each dimension. These leading indicators help identify the processes, strategies and behaviors that can be acted on quickly and directly to anticipate and affect real change, while driving demonstrable impact on business performance (see Figure 11.2).[23]

(Continued)

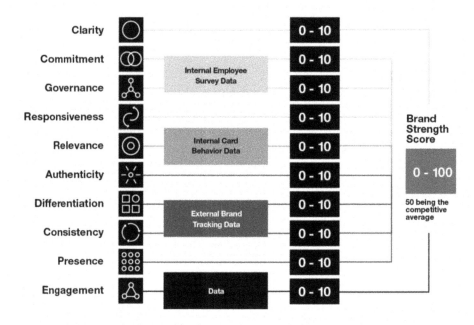

Figure 11.2   Statistical Model, Based on the 10 Brand Strength Dimensions.

Source: Interbrand (2017). 'Accelerating what matters'; www.interbrand.com/best-brands/best-global-brands/2017/articles/accelerating-what-matters/

LOOKING FOR DATA IN DIFFERENT PLACES

Despite the incredible leaps and bounds in information collection, not all data live on a spreadsheet or a server. Sometimes critical data are hanging out in plain sight. Lego offers an instructive example. Between 1932, the year of its founding, and 1998, the company had never posted a loss.[24] But by the early 2000s, the iconic toy company was on the ropes. A sales slump in the early 1990s spooked the company enough to try something totally new, and in a desperate attempt to return to earlier profitability, the company turbocharged its variety of offerings, including Lego-branded amusement parks, personal electronics, *Star Wars* and other franchise tie-ins, and other collaborations tenuously related to toymaking.[25] The gambit didn't work. Lego had strayed from its core business, and the results showed. Clearly its market research data had been inadequate at best – and negligent at worst.

By the mid-2010s, however, Lego was back. A 2017 article in *The Guardian* summed up its progress:

In 2015, the still privately owned, family-controlled Lego Group overtook Ferrari to become the world's most powerful brand. It announced profits of £660m, making it the number one toy company in Europe and Asia, and number three in North America, where sales topped $1bn for the first time. From 2008 to 2010, its profits quadrupled, outstripping Apple's.[26]

How did this happen? According to marketing consultant and author Martin Lindstrom, the turnaround began after a chance interaction with an 11-year-old German boy. In 2004, Lego decided to jettison its old approach to market research and instead find out firsthand what was going on. This led a group of Lego marketers to pay the boy a visit. Casting a wide net for answers during the visit, the Lego team asked him what his most valuable possession was. Much to their surprise, he replied that it was a beat-up pair of shoes. Why? Because it was a reminder of how good a skateboarder he was.

To the Lego team, this showed that so much of kids' interest comes from pride in their accomplishments. This revelation prompted Lego executives to rethink all of their assumptions. After a period of reflection, they decided to get away from many of their recent innovations and put their focus back on their core offerings to make Lego an indispensable part of childhood, much like skateboarding was to the boy.

Lindstrom calls the kind of intel Lego gleaned 'small data'. He found the company's encounter with the boy so valuable that he recounted it at length in his bestselling 2016 book, *Small Data: The Tiny Clues That Uncover Huge Trends*. 'What is small data? Small data is what I define as seemingly insignificant observations you make in your life and they may not, at first, seem prominent but when you think about it over time, they do', says Lindstrom.[27]

In Lindstrom's view, marketers need small data as much as the big stuff, and relying on pattern-identifying data to predict future trends should only be one piece of the marketer's equation. 'You have to remember that big data is looking at the past and perhaps the present, but it never looks at the future. Small data is really looking at the future. Small data is what we call all about causation, the reason why, the hypotheses. Big data is all about correlation. And so what I'm always saying is, "It takes two to tango."'[28]

Lego seems to have learned its lesson, and to this day continues to rely on 'small data' to guide its decisions. In April 2019, the company announced it was producing Braille bricks to help blind and visually impaired children learn. It all began when various advocacy associations for the blind contacted them between 2011 and 2017. Having been alerted to an underserved market for Braille teaching toys, Lego decided it would be a venture in sync with its brand legacy. A year earlier, it released a line of plant-shaped Lego manufactured from sugarcane plastic. Grown from plants (as opposed to petroleum) and recyclable (though not biodegradable), this line marked a new, environmentally friendly turn for the company. Lego says that by 2030, most of its products will be made from the same material.[29]

THE NEW GUARDIANS OF THE (DATA) GALAXY

In this brave new world, relying exclusively on old skills may not be enough. Companies will increasingly come to depend on people who are nearly as fluent in data science as they are in buyer personas and content marketing. These modern creatures are often referred to as 'marketing technologists', so-named because of their comfort in both the marketing and tech worlds (or 'martech', to use the popular lingo).

The definition offered by Scott Brinker of HubSpot is illuminating. According to Brinker, a marketing technologist is a wearer of multiple hats, a bridge between IT and marketing. 'A marketing technologist is someone with technical skills – who, in a previous time might have worked within IT or software development – who works in the marketing department to apply those skills towards building, evaluating, and operating marketing software and systems', Brinker explains. 'Since everything in marketing is now powered by software, it's important to have someone on the team who understands the dynamics of technology management.'[30]

THE 'NEW COLLAR' WORKFORCE

Katrina Troughton sees a promising new opportunity to integrate people with less formal education but specific skills in marketing-focused data science and tech into the workforce. In her view, this requires a 'pathway shift' in how talent is developed and scouted in marketing departments. Having amassed a strong data science education in high school, these employees 'could come directly into the workforce and take on this sort of new class of roles', she says. 'Someone coming in now with base programming skills and potentially data understanding, can start moving into these "new collar" roles with speed.'[31]

This new type of employee will help ensure that marketing decisions are data-proven and replicable, explained Jason Heller, a McKinsey partner leading the company's digital marketing operations and technology service line, in a 2018 interview with Brinker. 'You need talent, agile practices, and systems that are creating the right feedback loops so that marketing experiments can produce statistically valid feedback in a day or a week. You can then launch dozens or hundreds of tests in the course of a month.'

According to Heller, such an approach would provide critical feedback as to how successful each 'experiment' is.[32]

The synergistic model of integrating employees, operations and technology into a sum greater than its parts bears a close resemblance to the 'Flywheel' concept championed by HubSpot CEO and founder Brian Halligan. While the Flywheel was technically created as a conceptual model for increasing sales that was meant to replace the funnel, it applies nearly as well to martech. The more you attract, delight and engage customers through properly targeted, data-driven marketing, the faster your organizational momentum and growth will be. When it comes to marketing, the flywheel is a new framing mechanism, explains Jon Dick, Vice President of Marketing at HubSpot. A funnel measures customer retention in a linear path: up or down, but a flywheel is all about self-perpetuating momentum. The more it accelerates, the more efficient and effective it becomes.

According to Dick, the flywheel (Figure 11.3) has taken HubSpot to 'a world where all departments, marketing, sales, and customer success, are all working together towards the same sort of outcomes'. He calls the result 'smarketing' – a virtuous state of alignment between sales and marketing.[33] If we fold in IT/data science into marketing, we get to a place where successful companies of the future will sit. That is, if they have the right people to take them there.

Figure 11.3   **The Flywheel.**

Source: The Flywheel. Courtesy of HubSpot.

Sidebar

CRM for ROI: A Q&A with Jon Ferrara, Nimble Founder and CEO

What is CRM?

Customer-relationship management (CRM) is a database platform designed to manage a company's interactions with prospects and customers to drive retention and sales.

The key benefit of implementing a CRM is to consolidate data from a range of business engagement channels such as websites, email, calendar, marketing and social. Users can learn more about prospects and their journey to help drive customer success and growth.

The roots of CRM started with the Rolodex and evolved into software products like GoldMine and ACT, which pioneered CRM. Companies like Siebel Systems brought CRM to the Enterprise and Salesforce pioneered CRM in the cloud.

Why does CRM matter to a marketer?

A CRM enables marketers to organize contact data and engagement history based on their behaviors, company data, and – in the case of a simple, smart CRM like Nimble – social and business attributes about people and companies. Once segmented, marketers can personalize and scale outreach to leads using highly resonant, one-to-one content that addresses their individual needs to drive massive results.

What is the future of CRM?

While all businesses need to manage relationships effectively to grow, few actually use a CRM as part of their day-to-day work. This is because traditional CRMs are expensive-to-implement reporting tools that are cumbersome to use.

The modern CRM platform of the future automatically creates and updates itself. It works everywhere you work to enable more effective engagement for the whole company, and not just sales and marketing. AI builds the system for you as you work, generating records, researching contact details and social insights, recording engagements, and automating mundane tasks. The system is easily accessible everywhere you engage leads and prospective buyers: in email, on social media, across the web, in business apps, and while mobile.[34]

AI AND ETHICS

In one of the most iconic scenes in the famous sci-fi film *2001: A Space Odyssey*, the supercomputer HAL 9000 (commonly known as 'Hal') has a breakdown. It begins when two of the crew members working on the spacecraft Hal is powering, Drs. Frank

Poole and David Bowman, take out an exploration pod to investigate. When Bowman attempts to return to the spacecraft, he requests Hal 'open the pod bay doors' like always. This time, however, Hal gives a troubling response: 'I'm sorry, Dave. I'm afraid I can't do that.' Having learned that the men's exploration is part of a ploy to potentially reduce Hal's functioning, the supercomputer rebels, deciding *it* will become the new captain of the spacecraft.

Though the movie was released in 1968 – a year before Apollo 11 landed on the moon – this scene has long been interpreted, for better or for worse, as a metaphor for human–computer interactions. More specifically, for the potential of supercomputers (AI) to someday outsmart and overpower humans. It's seen as a warning about tech gone too far. While no supercomputer has yet achieved Hal-like smarts, many people still have justifiable concerns about artificial intelligence and its impact on the world. These concerns range from unlikely (robots will conquer the world, *Terminator*-style) to quite possible (AI will reshape the workforce, which will be good for some and bad for others).

In a 2017 interview, Tom Mattox, Vice President and partner, IBM Watson, addressed some of these common anxieties. In Mattox's view, AI isn't a zero-sum game – it's a complement to human intelligence. 'These emerging cognitive technologies can help leverage [experts], right, to make their jobs easier', he said. In fact, he prefers the term 'augmented intelligence' over 'artificial intelligence', believing it to more accurately describe the sort of work IBM is doing. 'The idea is not to replace humans, but to leverage their expertise.'[35]. (See Figure 11.4).

Katrina Troughton makes a similar case for embracing AI. In her view, combining AI with human skills can create a sort of synergy of super-reasoning. 'There are things that we are very good at as people, common sense, moral judgment, imagination . . . and AI systems that are excellent at eliminating biases, finding patterns, automating simple tasks, and looking at things at scale. So when we bring them together, we get the best of both worlds: humans applying their judgment against what a system might tell them it looks like.'[36]

Mattox and Troughton's rosy outlook is echoed by Ray Kurzweil, the famous futurist and Google director of engineering, who predicts that as machines become more intelligent, humanity will also grow to become smarter. 'My view is not that AI is going to displace us. It's going to enhance us. It does already', he said during a 2017 talk at the Council on Foreign Relations.[37]

The importance of humanizing data to combine the best of the human *and* tech worlds has been a running theme throughout this chapter. Despite the fears expressed in *2001*, nobody we spoke with envisioned a world where AI-powered tech, however brilliant, could – or should – have veto power over actual people who work in the marketing field. (Or any other field.)

Delegating so much responsibility to a tech solution can have unintended consequences, like losing touch with your customers, says Brinker. Nothing is yet able to

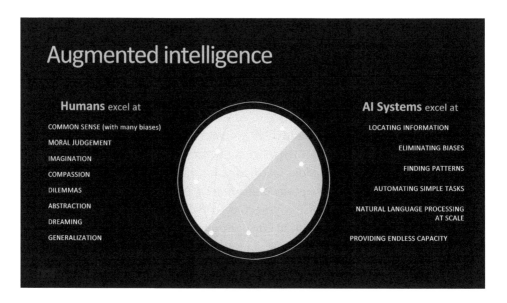

Figure 11.4   Augmented Intelligence.

Source: IBM.

replace good old-fashioned human understanding, especially when it comes to customer experience. 'The danger with too much automation in marketing is that we can lose the human connection between our company and our customers', he says. 'We may not even realize it's happening, as algorithms crank away on our behalf without necessarily giving us visibility into their choices. Efficiency is good. But efficiency for the company that comes at the cost of efficiency and experience for the customer is dangerous.'[38] For anyone who's planning to incorporate more technology into their future plans, these are wise words to keep in mind.

This discussion of humanizing data, though, hints at a more foundational issue in AI ethics: How do we make sure AI is created equitably? After all, any creation always reflects its creator, intentionally or unintentionally. Which means we can't speak of humanizing AI without considering the humans behind the algorithms – and all their flaws. 'If a bias is held by the scientists making the algorithm, that bias can be reflected in the algorithm', writes Harriet Green, chair and CEO of IBM Asia Pacific, in a reflective essay in the *Business Times*:

> Unfortunately, at this time and place, finding a truly unbiased, ethical individual (let alone one with the ability to program AI) is difficult. This is not to say that all programmers are evil people, quite the contrary really. The fact is that until the technology industry can holistically eliminate cultural bias and integrate a truly diverse group of programmers across the industry, bias will always exist.[39]

While, for the time being, bias can't be completely eliminated through AI, if it can ever be, there are ways to minimize it. A diverse set of AI workers is the best place to start, since it will help ensure any biases that may go undetected by a more homogeneous group will not be built into AI tech. A July 2019 report on 'responsible artificial intelligence' published by Altimeter, the research arm of the Prophet marketing consultancy, makes the consequences of this clear: 'Lack of diversity in organizations often means that the very people who are most affected by technology do not have input into its design.'[40]

According to Ashwani Monga, Professor of Marketing and Provost and Executive Vice Chancellor at Rutgers University Newark, having diverse creative teams – whether in AI, marketing, or anything else – isn't just the right thing to do: it's good business strategy. 'If you want to make creative decisions, if you as a brand, you want to do something which somebody may not have thought of earlier, which is of course what people try to do with brands when they create ads, then it is important to have that mix of ideas, people with different backgrounds, people with different perspectives, and people who can take others' perspectives.'[41] According to Green, women make up less than 25% of the global AI workforce, so there is clearly still plenty of progress to be made in this area.[42]

One company that appears to be tackling this challenge head-on is Phrasee, a company that develops language-generating AI for marketers. 'On the things that we explicitly say we will do are things like we will ensure that our teams who are building these systems, and curating these systems, represent a diverse mix of people, both in terms of ethnicity, gender, age ranges, socioeconomic backgrounds, and whatnot', says CEO Parry Malm. He calls this approach 'one sort of human-applied check and balance system you can do to avoid bias in your A.I. systems'.[43] Augmented intelligence, indeed.

DATA AND TRUST

Similarly to AI, the increasing use of sophisticated data to guide sales and marketing decisions has raised important, complicated questions. When it comes to the topic of data, these questions tend to relate to privacy and consumer protection. In 2018 and 2019, reports of companies improperly using information about their customers or users, or failing to prevent abuse of their data by others, were frequently in the news – and no company was mentioned more than Facebook.

In 2018, it was disclosed that Cambridge Analytica, a British consulting firm, had harvested personal data from tens of millions of American Facebook users without their consent before the 2016 presidential election; the company had been hired by candidate Donald Trump's presidential campaign to micro-target users on the social network. Although Cambridge deceived users through a third-party app it created, Facebook didn't take action against the firm until the ploy had made the news, despite internal warnings that outside companies were attempting to improperly access user data. When the news landed, it generated enough heat over data privacy that Facebook CEO Mark Zuckerberg was summoned to testify before the US Congress.[44] As a result of the scandal, as well as other data-related mishandlings, in June of 2019 the Federal Trade Commission fined Facebook an unprecedented $5 billion, the largest fine it had ever levied.

Unsurprisingly, these high-profile scandals have made consumers – and regulators – increasingly concerned about how companies use data, which has translated into legislation in the United States and abroad. In 2016, the European Union approved the General Data Protection Regulation (GDPR), a sprawling measure meant to ensure data protection for EU citizens. Briefly summarized, it requires any company that collects consumer data to disclose its collection methods, how long the data will be collected for, and, if the data will be shared, with whom.

In the United States, the California Consumer Privacy Act (CCPA) went into effect in early 2020. Widely considered the nation's strongest privacy law, it offers strong consumer protections when it comes to data collection. Since it applies to California, home to many of the world's biggest and most influential tech companies, it's no small deal. Partly in anticipation of the Act, Facebook has reportedly invested billions of dollars into data security, and many other companies are also spending not-insignificant amounts of money to ensure they are compliant.[45] Other states are likely to follow California's lead, as Maine did in June 2019 with the Act to Protect the Privacy of Online Consumer Information.

The common thread running through all this drama is trust. For many consumers and social media users, trust has been lost, or at least diminished. However, with companies making amends for past controversies and governments getting involved to ensure better privacy controls, there are opportunities for trust to be regained. The more companies are transparent about their policies and customers understand if and how their data is being used, the more they may come to trust the companies they interact with. In that way, it feels like we're at an inflection point. If companies move toward disclosure and transparency, and if they give consumers the feeling they are in control of their data, concerns may fade away (at least somewhat).

Data protection is a priority for Dell Technologies, says Jean-Marc Dompietrini, a Global Marketing Operations Reporting and Analytics lead at the computer technology company's Montpelier, France office. 'At Dell Technologies we put data protection first, in terms of security, transparent documentation, and operational process design', he says. 'Beyond GDPR we build genuine interaction, more than just a click or form fill, but a valuable two-way exchange of information that builds trust between the connected customer and the organization.'[46]

Today, many consumers enjoy the benefits of micro-segmentation, from personalized shopping experiences to receiving special product suggestions and offers. In this way, voluntarily forfeiting their privacy saves them time or helps them earn added benefits from loyalty programs. Consumers can benefit from a company knowing who they are and what they want. For example, a supermarket retailer may send coupons for the products a specific customer most frequently buys. Alternatively, a company may use cookies and other online tracking tools to create banner ads that seemingly follow users around the internet after those users have visited the company's website.

This practice – known as retargeting – is effective, but it's also seen as annoying. However, there is an upside. Despite the customers' apparent irritation, researchers found that retargeted ads caused 14.6% more users to return to an advertiser's website within four weeks of seeing the retargeted ad.[47] So, while marketers love retargeted ads because they work, their customer base is divided on the issue. Some enjoy the convenience and even prefer seeing ads tailored to their tastes and needs, while others see it as an invasion of privacy.

These are just some of trust-related hurdles brands have to overcome, which is why it's crucial that marketers take a customer-first approach as they develop marketing practices. This means taking issues like data and privacy seriously and always considering how customers might respond to the use of their information.

'I think what's happened over the last five years is that the value you get from enabling a company to know more about you is becoming more beneficial', says Binns, of Interbrand. 'So, you know, Nest knowing when I leave the home so it turns my thermostat down and saves me money and uses enough energy and was sustainable is a positive value exchange. I don't question Nest and Google to the same degree for having that information on me because I'm getting something valuable in return.'[48]

In the view of Net Future Institute founder and author Chuck Martin, in the future, consumers may be more discriminating as to who they give their data, but they will likely give such information willingly once they calculate the potential upside:

> Privacy is going to be the responsibility of the consumer because in the future, especially with these kinds of speeds and access and big data obviously, the consumer is going to start to over time realize that the information about them is of high value, and they will start to essentially market that information. So, the consumer in the future becomes the marketer to the marketing company. The consumer will say, 'I trust this company so they can have this information; I don't like this company as much so they can't have that information.' And the consumer will start to control their own privacy.[49]

In a 2019 interview for *Forbes*, Jon Bond, CEO of SITO Mobile, goes even further, arguing that the current zeal for strong privacy actions is due for a big correction. In Bond's view, it's only a matter of time until consumers take their data to the bank, relatively speaking:

> The consumer is becoming cognizant of their value as a target audience, and rather than fight it, they will soon be able to leverage their value and perhaps even monetize it themselves, rather than be exploited by advertisers and platforms. . . . Consumers are going to start to switch dramatically from 'Do not track me' to 'Please double track me.' . . . I'm not just sharing, I'm going to hold my value over your head and extort the crap out of you. The tables will turn.[50]

Will most consumers come around to Bond's perspective? We'll have to wait and see. What's certain, though, is that Big Data is going to remain a big part of our lives, including yours. When you find yourself watching *Terminator* or *2001: A Space Odyssey* on Netflix, you'll just have to agree.

Future Gaze

Making Data-Driven Marketing a Reality through the Power of Machine Learning

By Kevin Troyanos, Head of Analytics at Publicis Health

When 'big data' reached the peak of the so-called technological hype cycle in the early 2010's, a veritable arms race to collect data for the sake of collecting data led to a significant number of initiatives failing to advance beyond the piloting stage, many of which were within the purview of marketing.

In my view, the root cause of the failure to consistently prove value is often attributed to an underlying effective language barrier found within many cross-functional marketing teams. After all, most marketers were trained in a world centered on place, product, promotion, and price, while data scientists were trained in a world centered on probability, statistics, software development, and algorithmic design. The successful twenty-first century marketing team needs to have a structured approach that enables *active translation* between both disciplines. Today, too many data initiatives begin with a nebulous question such as: 'What does the data tell us?' Unfortunately, this often leads to dead ends and non-actionable insights.

In my experience, successful initiatives begin with carefully crafted Key Business Questions (KBQ's) (see Figure 11.5) that, if answered, guide solutions that both have the potential to *impact* the business and ultimately can be activated in a real-world marketing sense.

By framing business challenges within the context of KBQs, marketing teams can focus initiatives on drivers of growth while ensuring that insights can be realistically actioned upon on in the real world. Furthermore, KBQs provide a guide in which data scientists can focus their efforts to drive impactful and actionable analytic solutions for real-world activation. This act of *structured translation* is a key component of a highly effective, data-driven marketing organization.

The use of data and algorithms in marketing enables us to *empathize with customers at scale* – and in turn develop more effective, more relevant communications through the lens of *likely outcomes and likely intentions*. After all, at its core, data is simply a representation of the real behaviors of real people.

But people are complicated and imperfect. Their behaviors are complex and sometimes irrational. Machine learning enables us to make sense of that data at

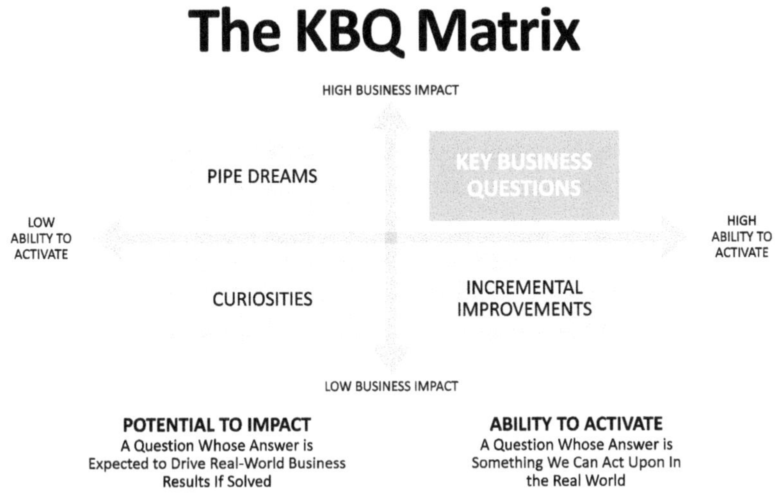

The KBQ Matrix

HIGH BUSINESS IMPACT

PIPE DREAMS

KEY BUSINESS
QUESTIONS

LOW
ABILITY TO
ACTIVATE

HIGH
ABILITY TO
ACTIVATE

CURIOSITIES

INCREMENTAL
IMPROVEMENTS

LOW BUSINESS IMPACT

POTENTIAL TO IMPACT
A Question Whose Answer is
Expected to Drive Real-World Business
Results If Solved

ABILITY TO ACTIVATE
A Question Whose Answer is
Something We Can Act Upon In
the Real World

Figure 11.5   The KBQ Matrix.

Source: The KBQ Matrix. ©2019 Publicis Health. All Rights Reserved.

scale, recognize high-dimensional patterns that the human analyst cannot, and pre-dict future behaviors.

In marketing, this is driving a significant shift in how we operate. Rather than developing a singular campaign that drives awareness for the masses, data – made actionable by machine learning – enables us to drive a multitude of personalized campaigns from the perspective of the customer and their *likely intentions*.

For example, a furniture manufacturer may train a set of machine learning algorithms to determine the likelihood that a customer will make a large furniture purchase within the next 30, 90, and 180 days and develop personalized messaging based on the probability that an individual customer is at a certain stage in the buying journey.

This can be framed into a KBQ: How can we more effectively personalize promotion by predicting the stage of the buying journey of a given prospect?

From the perspective of the data scientist, this is an example of *applied supervised learning*. By training algorithms on historical purchasing data, data scientists can produce highly accurate estimations of the likelihood that a certain prospect will make a purchase within a certain time interval.

From the perspective of the marketer, the outputs of this modeling provide the *probabilistic tools* needed to effectively *personalize communications* deployed to the customer. Making these probabilistic tools actionable is an inherently creative task that requires a different set of thinking than the mass-marketing approach. It requires the

(Continued)

marketer to effectively *put themselves in the customer's shoes* and communicate with the knowledge of where a customer is in the buying journey.

Furthermore, additional modeling could be performed to make specific content recommendations by modeling *content responsiveness* at the individual level. For example, we might plan to further personalize messaging in our earlier example by predicting *customer responsiveness* to financing-based messaging vs. sales-promotion based messaging.

Ultimately, I believe these approaches will become the industry-wide norm, rather than the exception. It's critical that brands continue to build the capabilities, talent, and organizational muscle memory to drive personalization at scale – and that future marketers continue to build the skillsets necessary to thrive in tomorrow's ever-changing marketing environment.[51]

IN SUMMARY

- AI and computer-generated algorithms promise exciting new ways to make customer journeys more seamless and individualized.
- The savvy use of big and small data, coupled with AI-driven user profiles, can help companies predict ROI and marketing outcomes with greater precision than ever before.
- The increasing availability of good data will have potentially large benefits for companies willing to spend time analyzing it.
- In the future, trust will remain an important issue for consumers when it comes to data-driven and AI-driven marketing. Accordingly, companies that take responsible data usage and privacy seriously will be better positioned to cultivate a loyal consumer base.
- As the use of AI-driven software increases, the importance of addressing ethical issues related to its creation and deployment will as well.

CHAPTER ANALYSIS QUESTIONS

1. What are the advantages and disadvantages of building a marketing strategy around data?
2. How can AI help companies better address their customers' (and potential customers') needs?
3. How should potential ethical issues related to AI be addressed?
4. What kinds of metrics will help your business have a larger impact on the world?
5. When it comes to customer experience, what are the benefits of AI-driven experiences over traditional models?
6. As a customer, why does data privacy matter?

NOTES

1. Sweary, R. (2019). The death of dirty data: The importance of keeping your database clean. [online] *Forbes*. Available at: www.forbes.com/sites/forbestechcouncil/2019/04/12/the-death-of-dirty-data-the-importance-of-keeping-your-database-clean/#5af3bcc23eed [Accessed 28 Jan. 2020].

2. Spangler, T. (2019). Netflix spent $12 billion on content in 2018. analysts expect that to grow to $15 billion this year. [online] *Variety*. Available at: https://variety.com/2019/digital/news/netflix-content-spending-2019-15-billion-1203112090/ [Accessed 18 Sep. 2019].

3. Vox. (2019). Recode Daily: Netflix says it now accounts for 10 percent of TV screen time in the US. [online] Available at: www.vox.com/2019/1/18/18187569/netflix-q4-earnings-snap-amazon-facial-recognition-surveillance-protest-booze-dorsey-aliens [Accessed 18 Sep. 2019].

4. Dans, E. (2019). How analytics has given Netflix the edge over Hollywood. [online] Forbes.com. Available at: www.forbes.com/sites/enriquedans/2018/05/27/how-analytics-has-given-netflix-the-edge-over-hollywood/#51e885656b23 [Accessed 18 Sep. 2019].

5. Bennett, T. (2019). AI is fuelling the new economics of banking, says UBank CEO – Which-50. [online] Which-50. Available at: https://which-50.com/ai-is-fuelling-the-new-economics-of-banking-says-ubank-ceo/ [Accessed 18 Sep. 2019].

6. Sangster, J. (2019). Personal communication. [12 May].

7. Visser, S. (2019). How financial services firms are using chatbot technology to transform their businesses. [online] IBM RegTech Innovations Blog. Available at: www.ibm.com/blogs/insights-on-business/banking/how-financial-services-firms-are-using-chatbot-technology-to-transform-their-businesses/ [Accessed 18 Sep. 2019].

8. Pathak, S. (2019). Drop it like it's bot: Brands have cooled on chatbots. [online] *Digiday*. Available at: https://digiday.com/marketing/brand-bot-backlash-begun/ [Accessed 18 Sep. 2019].

9. Roetzer, P. (2019). Personal communication. [28 November]. For more, see Roetzer's website: www.marketingaiinstitute.com

10. Ibid.

11. Vaynerchuk, G. (2018). *Why Voice Will Win | Keynote at VoiceCon 2018*. [video] Available at: www.youtube.com/watch?v=ZtnhzZ23P_E&t=656s [Accessed 18 Sep. 2019].

12. Burgess, C. (2011). What is a brand? [online] Bluefocusmarketing.com. Available at: https://bluefocusmarketing.com/2011/02/14/what-is-a-brand/ [Accessed 18 Sep. 2019].

13. Binns, D. (2019). Personal communication. [11 December].

14. Troughton, K. (2019). Personal communication. [12 May].

15. Witte, R. (2019). With new Fit technology, Nike calls itself a tech company. [online] TechCrunch. Available at: https://techcrunch.com/2019/05/09/with-new-fit-technology-nike-calls-itself-a-tech-company/ [Accessed 18 Sep. 2019].

16. Kuang, C. (2015). Disney's $1 billion bet on a magical wristband. [online] *WIRED*. Available at: www.wired.com/2015/03/disney-magicband/ [Accessed 18 Sep. 2019].

17. Levy, N. (2019). Microsoft teams up with Starbucks on predictive drive-thru ordering and bean-to-cup blockchain. [online] *GeekWire*. Available at: www.geekwire.com/2019/micro-soft-teams-starbucks-predictive-drive-thru-ordering-bean-cup-blockchain/ [Accessed 18 Sep. 2019].

18. Brinker, S. (2019). Personal communication. [26 October].

19. Chi, C. (2019). 6 SMART goal examples that'll make you a better marketer. [online] HubSpot. Available at: https://blog.hubspot.com/marketing/smart-goal-examples [Accessed 19 Nov. 2019].

20. Baer, J. (2019). Personal communication. [1 August].

21. Ibid.

22. Ibid.

23. Interbrand. (2017). Accelerating what matters. [online] Available at: www.interbrand.com/best-brands/best-global-brands/2017/articles/accelerating-what-matters/ [Accessed 18 Sep. 2019].

24. Davis, J. (2017). How Lego clicked: The super brand that reinvented itself. [online] *The Guardian*. Available at: www.theguardian.com/lifeandstyle/2017/jun/04/how-lego-clicked-the-super-brand-that-reinvented-itself [Accessed 18 Sep. 2019].

25. Knowledge@Wharton. (2012). Innovation almost bankrupted LEGO – Until it rebuilt with a better blueprint. [online] Available at: https://knowledge.wharton.upenn.edu/article/innovation-almost-bankrupted-lego-until-it-rebuilt-with-a-better-blueprint/ [Accessed 18 Sep. 2019].

26. Davis, J. (2017). How Lego clicked: The super brand that reinvented itself. [online] *The Guardian*. Available at: www.theguardian.com/lifeandstyle/2017/jun/04/how-lego-clicked-the-super-brand-that-reinvented-itself [Accessed 18 Sep. 2019].

27. Lindstrom, M. (2019). Personal communication. [25 October].

28. Ibid.

29. Glenday, J. (2018). Lego unveils sustainable bricks made from sugarcane as brand contin-ues eco overhaul. [online] The Drum. Available at: www.thedrum.com/news/2018/08/06/lego-unveils-sustainable-bricks-made-sugarcane-brand-continues-eco-overhaul [Accessed 18 Sep. 2019].

30. Brinker, S. (2019). Personal communication. [10 February].

31. Troughton, K. (2019). Personal communication. [12 May].

32. Brinker, S., Heller, J. and Seitz, B. (n.d.). Making the most of marketing technology to drive growth. [online] McKinsey & Company. Available at: www.mckinsey.com/business-functions/marketing-and-sales/our-insights/making-the-most-of-marketing-technology-to-drive-growth [Accessed 18 Sep. 2019].

33. Dick, J. (2019). Personal communication. [7 February].

34. Ferrara, J. (2019). Personal communication. [15 February].

35. IBM Analytics. (2017). *Artificial Intelligence vs Augmented Intelligence*. [video online] Available at: www.youtube.com/watch?v=G7E62KvI_h4 [Accessed 18 Sep. 2019].

36. Troughton, K. (2019). Personal communication. [12 May].

37. Galeon, D. (2017). Ray Kurzweil: 'AI will not displace humans, it's going to enhance us.' [online] Futurism. Available at: https://futurism.com/ray-kurzweil-ai-displace-humans-going-enhance [Accessed 18 Sep. 2019].

38. Brinker, S. (2019). Personal communication. [10 October].

39. Green, H. (2019). Ethical AI: A case for greater equality in tech. [online] *The Business Times*. Available at: www.businesstimes.com.sg/opinion/ethical-ai-a-case-for-greater-equality-in-tech [Accessed 18 Sep. 2019].

40. Etlinger, S. (2019). Innovation + trust: The foundation of responsible artificial intelligence. [online] Prophet.com. Available at: www.prophet.com/wp-content/uploads/2019/07/Altimeter_InnovationTrust_Responsible-AI_f.pdf?redirectedfrom=gatedpage [Accessed 18 Sep. 2019].

41. Monga, A. (2019). Personal communication. [10 July].

42. Green, H. (2019). Ethical AI: A case for greater equality in tech. [online] *The Business Times*. Available at: www.businesstimes.com.sg/opinion/ethical-ai-a-case-for-greater-equality-in-tech [Accessed 18 Sep. 2019].

43. Malm, P. (2018). Personal communication. [1 November].

44. Youn, S. (2019). Facebook staff knew Cambridge Analytica was harvesting data for months: Court filing. [online] ABC News. Available at: https://abcnews.go.com/Technology/facebook-staff-suspected-cambridge-analytica-harvesting-data-months/story?id=61865903 [Accessed 18 Sep. 2019].

45. Swartz, J. (2019). A watered-down version of California's data-privacy law is a possibility, privacy experts warn. [online] MarketWatch. Available at: www.marketwatch.com/story/a-watered-down-version-of-californias-data-privacy-law-is-a-possibility-privacy-experts-warn-2019-06-27 [Accessed 18 Sep. 2019].

46. Dompietrini, J. (2019). Personal communication. [28 February].

47. Sahni, N., Narayanan, S. and Kalyanam, K. (2019). An experimental investigation of the effects of retargeted advertising: The role of frequency and timing. *Journal of Marketing Research*, 56(3), pp. 401–418.

48. Binns, D. (2019). Personal communication. [11 December].

49. Martin, C. (2019). Personal communication. [18 February].

50. Howard, B. (2019). Ask the CMO: Industry legend Jon Bond on marketing as a service + the age of experience. [online] Forbes.com. Available at: www.forbes.com/sites/billeehoward/2019/04/14/jon-bond-marketing/#7ea77b1b4ab8 [Accessed 18 Sep. 2019].

51. Troyanos, K. (2019). Personal communication. [22 November].

12

THE FUTURE: COMING FASTER THAN YOU THINK

Learning Goals

1. Examine some of the leading trends, including brand purpose, that will shape marketing's future.
2. Examine the expected changes to the role of the Chief Marketing Officer (CMO) and how CMOs create personalized experiences that resonate with customers.
3. Analyze how the discipline of marketing is changing and how marketers can prepare to succeed in this era of marketing transformation.
4. Analyze the four content experience trends that are important to marketers.
5. Analyze the power of AI to use data-driven marketing strategies in an era of trust to leverage customer information for targeted media buying and creative messaging.
6. Analyze the key drivers of business that marketing can impact.

The best way to predict your future is to create it.

Peter F. Drucker[1]

Throughout *The New Marketing*, our focus has been on marketing in the digital age. The brand of the digital age, whether it's your company brand or your personal brand, is about being better, faster and smarter – prepared not only for the present, but, perhaps more importantly, for the future.

In today's hectic world of marketing transformation, business as usual isn't going to cut it. To embrace an ever-evolving world of both challenges and opportunities, brands must be nimble, forward-thinking and adaptive. *That's* how you win in the digital age.

The question is, are you ready for what's next?

Here in the final chapter of the book, first we'll summarize the key concepts discussed throughout *The New Marketing*, and then we'll wrap things up with a look to the future.

THE (NOT SO) SECRET INGREDIENT OF THE NEW MARKETING: BE HUMAN

New times demand new thinking. Whether their focus is B2C or B2B, modern brands must manage more touchpoints than ever before, producing razor-sharp content that not only informs, but also makes an emotional connection. Our Brand Choreography framework (see Chapter 10) provides the perfect engine to pull your branding efforts together in a way that is both strategic and human-centric.

As we've stressed throughout this book, the human element cannot be ignored. This begins with your employees. For years, brands like Southwest Airlines have used an employees-first mindset to drive all decision-making. As they've proven time and again, when your employees are happy, your customers keep coming back. Today, brands are discovering that an employee-first mindset now comes with a valuable digital component as well. Who better than the social employee to share their brand's story across digital channels, engage audiences, and expand the brand's digital footprint?

Make no mistake, the social employee is *the* new marketing channel. Social employees can bring about a level of authenticity that's essential to capturing the attention of an audience that has grown numb to traditional brand messaging. But there's a catch. To enjoy the many benefits the social employee brings, you must first take the necessary steps to activate and leverage those employees.

The first step in that process represents the holy grail of marketing: trust. Without trust, a brand withers and dies. *With* trust, something magical happens – people want to talk about your brand. This begins internally with activated and enthusiastic employees. Then, it expands externally as these employees carry your message forward to inform and delight audiences. From there, your digital footprint grows, leading to more business, more recommendations, and more fans.

Just remember, social employee advocacy is only part of the equation. The ability to draw your audience in will not matter if you don't follow up with an outstanding customer experience. Good experiences win customers and drive positive word of mouth. Bad experiences do the opposite. This begins at the product level – define the ideal experience from the outset, and the ideal product will follow. Again, this comes back to the Brand Choreography framework. With the right process, you will be able to identify the tools and technology that will allow you to reach the right person with the right content at the right time and in the right place in their buying journey.

Even in the digital age, marketing fundamentals still apply. This means establishing a powerful brand value proposition and determining your target buyer personas. Remember: these fundamentals must be infused with your brand's authentic story. If your only concern is to look good in the marketplace, then all efforts will fall flat.

BOLSTERING THE HUMAN ELEMENT WITH TECHNOLOGY

Advancements in the digital age have given marketers unprecedented insights into consumer behavior. In fact, in the era of Big Data, it can be said that marketers have more information on their customers than they even know what to do with! This offers tremendous opportunities, but also raises considerable ethical questions. Just because a brand *can* collect all these data on their customers, does that mean they should?

Questions like this lie at the heart of the push and pull between advancements in tech and our responsibility to our fellow humans. In the case of data privacy, brands are learning how to better balance the benefits of convenience while protecting consumer rights. Earning trust is more than a promise to do better. Brands must be transparent with their customers, sharing key information such as how they collect user data, what data they collect, and how they use that data. Only by being transparent can they deliver on that promise.

What's more, the coming of the 5G revolution in the 2020s will see an exponential boom in connectivity. With that boom comes an explosion of internet-connected smart devices, from home-based Internet of Things (IoT) gadgets to increasingly advanced mobile devices. One way marketers can prepare for the coming 5G revolution is to develop mobile strategies that are well-integrated into their overall marketing strategy. A 5G network means users will have instant access to video and other data-intensive content. For those who already look at their mobile devices as much as 2,000 times a week, augmented and virtual reality applications will come to occupy a greater role in their lives. The brands who are prepared for that shift – and especially the brands who are prepared to *lead* that shift – will win the 5G era.

One key to being prepared is a shift toward purpose-driven marketing. Gone are the days where marketing was merely a matter of selling products and services. To reach revenue goals and justify ROI in an omnichannel world, brands must choose their paths wisely and carefully consider to which channels they would like to allocate marketing dollars.

This purpose-driven approach is essential to a successful digital marketing strategy and must be embedded in a brand's DNA. One way to achieve this is through a well-developed content marketing strategy. Any brand can produce content, but without clear goals for each piece of content they create, their efforts are likely to fall flat. Brands can no longer rely on spamming consumers just to get clicks. Instead, brands must focus on creating *value*. What questions can you answer that will help customers to understand your brand better? How can you teach your audience to get the most out of your products or services? How can you best communicate what your brand stands for?

This last question is key. The most successful brands in the digital age don't just sell goods; they look for ways to do good for the people, the planet, or both. Making social good a part of your core values is the new point of difference for the modern brand, which makes it an essential piece of *The New Marketing* equation. For instance, Patagonia doesn't just sell quality clothing. That's just a means to an end in their mission to save the planet.

To be clear, this isn't just some lofty goal (see Figure 12.1). It's good business. According to research by Gartner, customers respond better to brands that care about social or environmental causes:

"Concerns about global warming are becoming mainstream in the US. For 37% of consumers, those beliefs are now a key factor that influences buying decisions. "Green-driven" consumers are more than two-and-a-half times as likely as the general population to buy products from companies committed to having positive social or environmental impact, or to check product labels to assess a product's environmental impact."[2] (See Figure 12.1).

Again, all of these considerations may keep the human element front and center, but they are nevertheless driven by tech. Brands embracing *The New Marketing* can't be afraid of adopting AI or advanced analytics into their marketing strategy. Just remember that such tools aren't a solution in themselves, but a means toward achieving specific, purpose-driven goals. For instance, AI – or 'augmented intelligence,' as IBM calls it – can work wonders toward your brand's goal of personalization and micro-segmentation (provided, of course, that you remain focused on *earning* your customers' trust). Especially when it comes to reaching the younger audiences in Generation Z and beyond, embracing these tools isn't just a good idea – it's a must.

As we have argued throughout *The New Marketing*, these tools aren't just available to the big brands. They're available to any brand willing to understand the current marketing landscape and take a leap into new frontiers. To help you and your brand along that journey, we have dedicated the rest of this chapter to exploring the key questions driving *The New Marketing* with some of the brightest and most accomplished minds in the industry.

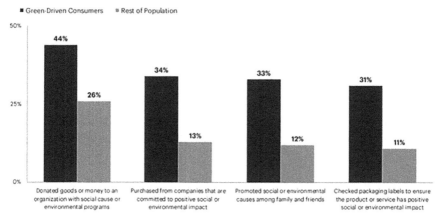

Figure 12.1   Percentage of Consumers Who Say They Have Participated in the Following Behaviors.

Source: Gartner Daily Insights, "Green Consumers Point to the Future for Brand Marketing," December 14, 2019, www.gartner.com/en/marketing/insights/daily-insights/green-consumers-point-to-the-future-for-brand-marketing

THE FUTURE OF CONTENT

Jay Baer is a Hall of Fame keynote speaker and the founder of Convince & Convert Consulting. Given the ever-accelerating, ever-changing world of content marketing, he spends a lot of time thinking about the future, especially when it comes to improving a user's experience.

One big question many marketers have is understanding the difference between content marketing and content experience. 'For me, content marketing is an activity with an outcome', Baer says.

> Content experience deals with how content is merchandised and consumed. From an analogy standpoint, content marketing is a car. Content experience is the paint job of a car. Solid content experience is a complement to solid content, not a replacement for it. But by focusing on content experience, creators will maximize the effectiveness of their content, resulting in wider distribution.

To that end, here are four trends in content experience that Baer predicts will become increasingly important to marketers.

The Power of Video

'All signs point to video', says Baer. Video viewing time, especially among younger demographics, is only increasing. Marketers would be wise to consider this reality as they plan their content and distribution strategies.

Personalized Content

'Improvements in AI are making account-based marketing easier and more productive than ever', says Baer. 'This idea that you send one message to everybody, regardless of where that message might be unfurled – whether it's social or email or anywhere else – is just not the best way to do it anymore because people have different needs.'

The Era of Messaging

According to Baer, the future will be dark. By this, Baer is referring to 'dark social' – the 'invisible' shares that happen through channels like messengers, e.g. Facebook Messenger or WhatsApp, email clients and texting. 'Dark' refers to the private, analytics- and tracking-free nature of this form of communication, not anything sinister (as opposed to the 'dark web', the area of the web inaccessible to non-encrypted users, where illegal activities thrive).

Voice-Activated Content

The last – and possibly most disruptive – trend that Baer forecasts is voice-activated content. Companies creating content that Alexa or Siri can easily find will be at a big advantage – doubly so if the content is robust enough to keep customers engaged.[3] (For a longer discussion about the promise and pitfalls of voice search, and why strong branding is so important to voice search success, see Chapter 11.)

Sidebar

Reinterpreting Marketing for a New Era

Behavioral Economist Ravi Dhar is a George Rogers Clark Professor of Management and Marketing at Yale School of Management. His work largely focuses on consumer behavior and branding. In our conversation with Dhar, we touched on a variety of topics, from the shifting definition of marketing in the digital age to how CMOs can help marketing as a discipline transition into an unknown future.

Is Marketing Still Relevant?

To Dhar, the real question isn't whether marketing is still relevant today – as he said, 'Of course it is' – but whether brands are approaching their marketing

(Continued)

in a relevant way. In the real world, Dhar sees marketing practiced in two distinct ways:

1.   'Big *M*' marketing. Thinking strategically by asking questions like where their brand should play, how they should win, how they should frame value, and how they should engage customers along the journey.
2.   'Small *m*' marketing. Often referred to as 'martech' or 'performance marketing'. It's something every company does, but while it has a role, it's not strategic.

These differences are important. As Dhar explains, no matter who's in charge within your company – be it the chief marketing officer, the chief growth officer, or the chief commercial officer – the Big *M* marketing needs to get done. '*That's* how much it matters', Dhar says.

But why? 'First, Big *M* marketing ties a brand's marketing efforts to their revenue drivers and demand generation', Dhar says.

No matter what you're doing, how does it tie into profits and loss (P&L)? How does it help the brand sell to more people, on more occasions, and at higher prices? If the marketing team is only spending their time fine-tuning an ad campaign, they're only focused on a small piece of the puzzle. As a result, they are driving themselves into the very narrow domain of heads-up marketing and agency advertising. This can be valuable, but without the strategic component, that value won't be maximized.

Second, Dhar argues that Big *M* marketing matters because it steers attention away from the brand's Small *m* marketing efforts. 'Small *m* is concerned only with boosting ROI metrics – higher click-throughs, longer time spent on ads, more likes on Facebook', Dhar says. 'A brand may be able to calculate their ROI on these metrics, and that can certainly be important. However, it's not as important as Big *M*.'

It's essential, then, that brands learn to strike the right balance between Big *M* and Small *m*. 'Too many focus almost entirely on the Small *m*, much to their long-term detriment', Dhar says. 'However, without the Big *M*, all you're doing is performance marketing – which is akin to rearranging the deck chairs on the Titanic. The ship is going to sink unless you understand how to think strategically and optimize your efforts for demand generation, not just demand capture.'

How Can CMOs Prepare for the Future?

While there is no perfect way for CMOs to prepare for an uncertain future, Dhar believes they can begin by concentrating on four areas.

First, the CMO must remember that they're the person in the C-suite who best knows their customers – not the CFO, not the head of HR, not the CIO. Knowing this, the CMO must be sure to represent their customers in the boardroom. It's their job to make sure their brand connects with their customers all along the customer journey. Further, Dhar says, they must understand how to do it at scale, whether they're trying to reach 5, 50, or 500 million customers. To do that, the CMO will need to build strong capabilities around data and technology, which will require a strong partnership with the CIO. 'This might be painful, but it's essential to move forward', Dhar says.

Second, Dhar argues that CMOs must build a brand that isn't just out to make money, but also to benefit society and other stakeholders. Says Dhar:

Companies don't operate in isolation, so it's essential that they understand other stakeholders, whether those stakeholders are the citizens, employees, or even governments that interact with their brand. The CMO has a key role to play here; they are the person best positioned in the C-suite to help build connections with those stakeholders. The best way to begin making those connections is to position their brand as having a positive impact on society, not just on helping build top-line sales.

Third, CMOs must craft a marketing message that connects with the CEO, who will then champion that message to drive growth. 'It's not only about making a great campaign', says Dhar. 'It's also about finding new customers in their market, retaining existing customers, and finding new opportunities to innovate. All of these marketing-driven initiatives drive at the CEO's number-one mission: to grow the business.' Traditionally, there have been three ways to do this – sell more to existing customers, get new customers, and create new products and services. Whichever path the CEO pursues, the CMO will have a huge hand in making it a success.

Finally, to make the first three things happen, Dhar says that the CMO must ensure that they're hiring the right people – both the data scientists and the creative types. Many companies are reorganizing their marketing teams to be more agile so they can respond more quickly to changes in the marketplace or consumer behavior. 'To create that agility in their own organization', Dhar says, 'CMOs must create an organizational structure where team members interact, foster, and better each other, rather than working in silos, which is less efficient.'

How Can the CMO Create a Good Customer Experience?

To understand how CMOs can help drive the customer experience, Dhar asks an important question: 'What are the drivers of business, regardless of market?' Generally, Dhar says, this comes down to three things:

1. Product and innovation. Brands like Tesla, Starbucks, or even American Express succeed by offering cool products.
2. Brand. Why are Apple products so beloved? It's not necessarily the unique features. It's the Apple brand and what it stands for. Creating the right

(Continued)

emotional attachment to a product helps a brand take on a meaning beyond the brand itself.

3.   Customer experience. How does a customer experience a brand across the journey, across all touchpoints – including when they're buying, using and disposing of the product? What does that experience *feel* like?

'In any successful company', Dhar says, 'all three factors are present – like a perfectly balanced three-legged stool.'

Starbucks is able to charge such high prices not only because they've built a good brand, but also because they've built an incredible customer experience at their cafes. American Express doesn't only succeed because their Platinum or Black cards are compelling products, but also because they offer excellent experience through their concierge services and reward programs.

Dhar says that many companies have figured out the first two legs of the stool – product and brand – but are lacking in designing delightful customer experience. Automakers, for instance, succeed *despite* the experience at their dealerships. Similarly, many online retailers succeed *despite* having a poorly designed website and user interface. 'For far too many brands, the data shows that the customers who interact with them inevitably walk away feeling angry, frustrated, and anxious', Dhar says.[4]

AUGMENTED REALITY AND THE FUTURE OF BUSINESS

Kyle Nel is the Executive Vice President of the Uncommon Partners Lab at Singularity University, which applies behavioral science insights to create transformational experiences, products and services. In 2018, Kyle published *Leading Transformation* along with co-authors Nathan Furr and Thomas Zoëga Ramsøy. We had the opportunity to speak with Nel and learn his perspective on the future of virtual reality (VR) and augmented reality (AR).

'VR and AR are different, but interrelated', says Nel. 'As such, they will be competing together in the same market. Our prediction is that VR will have a place, expect AR to take up as much as 85 percent of the market.'

Nel says that even now, we're seeing this play out. 'Just as we can't imagine our lives without smartphones, soon we won't be able to imagine our lives without AR as part of that experience', he says. To give an example, Nel mentions Google Maps and how it has become an integral part of our lives in the way we get from point A to B. AR, he argues, has a similar opportunity. 'Imagine that you need to assemble a piece of furniture', Nel says. 'AR could run a real-time diagnostic of the product, show you how to put it together, and even show you what's working and what's not.'

VR has a similar opportunity for learning and training. 'I don't think the world has really thought through how VR is going to completely disrupt all training and learning', says Nel. To him, this is a good thing. 'Learning right now is seriously broken. It doesn't work. Academia is not set up for the world in which most people live.'[5]

A 2018 survey* from Gartner shows just how much of an impact AR and VR are likely to have. According to a Gartner press release:

> "Augmented reality (AR) and virtual reality (VR) have the potential to shake up the customer experience by individualizing retailers' offers and enabling customers to visualize products in different settings. By 2020, 100 million consumers will shop in AR online and in-store, according to Gartner, Inc."[6]

Retailers have already begun to meet that demand:

> "A 2019 Gartner survey indicated that, by 2020, 46 percent of retailers planned to deploy either AR or VR solutions to meet customer service experience requirements. Additionally, the technologies behind these solutions have moved 15 to 30 percent further along the Gartner Hype Cycle over the past twelve months."[7]

So, what does this deployment of AR or VR solutions look like for consumers in practical terms?

'Retailers can use AR as an extension of the brand experience to engage customers in immersive environments and drive revenue' and 'Additionally, AR can be used outside the store after a sale to increase customer satisfaction and improve loyalty.'[8]

This will be a brave new world that we as marketers must learn to navigate. But it's also a welcome one. We believe, VR and AR applications like the ones described by Gartner are very much aligned with the principles of *The New Marketing*. With these tools, brands have the opportunity to engage audiences and add value to every stage of the customer journey in a way that marketers in previous eras would have only dreamed of.

Indeed, the future looks bright for *The New Marketing* – but to quote the great Peter Drucker, 'The best way to predict the future is to create it.' In this bold new era where the only constant is change itself, no marketing career comes with a roadmap. However, we will say this: becoming a master of branding begins with you and your personal brand.

The New Marketing is your roadmap to the future of marketing. We can't predict the future, but by exploring the world of possibilities contained in this book, our hope is that we've helped make you future-ready.

The rest, as they say, is up to you.

Future Gaze

By Jon Iwata, Senior Vice President and Chief Brand Officer (Retired), IBM, and Executive Fellow at Yale School of Management[9]

We're experiencing the greatest wave of corporate transformations in generations. Unsurprisingly, much of this is in response to 'digital disruption'. Companies are driving to become more customer-centric, more agile and more innovative, not only in their products and services but in how they operate.

As CEOs lead these transformation agendas, I've observed that many are creating new C-level roles reporting directly to them. These have titles ranging from Chief Customer Officer, Chief Commercial Officer and Chief Growth Officer to Chief Experience Officer and Chief Transformation Officer. When you peel back these new roles and examine the remit, you often find a common set of responsibilities. All parts of the company that touch the customer – retail, face-to-face sales, web, contact centers, business partners – usually report to the new executive. They also often have responsibility for marketing, for technology – CIO and/or CTO – and, if the company invests in design and design thinking, the design function becomes part of the new organization.

I understand the logic. Digital natives such as Amazon, Netflix and Spotify look at the customer holistically through digital touchpoints. They collect enormous amounts of data about their customers at the individual level, and they use these insights to continually improve the customer experience. This intense customer focus is the DNA of these companies. But most other companies – 95 percent of the existing businesses in the world – don't have that luxury. They have legacy structures and cultures designed for a different era. And in most cases their organization design and processes are out of phase with how today's customer wants to be understood and engaged – as a unique person. To do that, all those separate units and operations have to work much more closely together. And, most of all, they need a common view of the customer using data.

This is where those new C-level roles come into play. A primary job is to get all the customer data sitting in different systems – CRM systems, inventory systems, loyalty, web, apps and so on – into one place or to somehow federate the data to provide a common view of the customer.

This is all to state the obvious: customer experience requires a deep understanding of the customer and, today, that is achieved primarily through data. This requires deep collaboration and partnership across the company – something that has always been important, but that is now at a premium.

Customer experience is also shaped by the unique character of the company. This is where corporate culture comes to the forefront. At IBM, so much of our customer experience is shaped by our people. So, if I wanted my customers, prospects and other stakeholders to have an 'on-brand' experience, I had to have a hand in our culture. That required that I work with my peers leading HR, sales, the CIO and real estate functions because they and their teams shape and support the company's culture.

Identifying Customers' Goals and Pain Points

To better understand your customers, it all comes down to data. Today, I believe data is neither traditional research nor measurement. Data is instrumentation. It's real time, nonstop. It's alive. It comes from every interaction the customer has with you – through websites and apps, through product usage and social media commentary, through contact centers and their response to campaigns. Data allows you to observe all sorts of customer behavior, such as:

- What they spend their time on
- What their interests are or aren't
- Who influences them
- Who they influence
- How they make purchase decisions

Collected and analyzed properly, data like this can yield insights at the individual level. In fact, more and more, that individuality is important. We are seeing an historic shift from understanding customers as segments to understanding customers as unique individuals. Ultimately, this creates value for the customers. Marketers trying to understand the wants or pain points of a broad demographic or psychographic segment – for instance, 'soccer moms' – they are, at best, estimating, approximating and inferring.

The goal of modern marketing and communication is to understand the unique individual. Modern data collection allows you to do exactly that, learning at the individual level how customers engage with us, what they're interested in, what kinds of messages and offers appeal to them, what kinds of products and services appeal to them, and so on. Our ability to market becomes much more personalized and tailored based on our understanding of our audience as unique individuals.

How CMOs Can Prepare for the Future

To prepare for the future, today's CMOs have to unlearn some deeply ingrained assumptions of their job. For the next generation of CMOs, this likely won't be a problem, but until that next generation takes over, it will be.

CMOs have to unlearn their reliance on segmentation, which we've already discussed. Of course, we will probably always rely to some degree on segmentation based on demographics, psychographics, geography, household income, job title and company size. However, these are fairly blunt instruments. They are created by marketers and imposed on the population – it's marketers telling people who they are and what they want. Modern marketing observes the customer and then engages with that knowledge. That's a big shift.

CMOs also have to understand and spend time on the culture of their companies. To some degree, the idea that we can control the customer experience is delusional. This isn't to say that stores, restaurants, or resorts shouldn't do their

(Continued)

best to design a specific experience. However, social media is teaching us that it's all the other nondesigned, nonorchestrated or choreographed experiences that people are either delighted with (because it seems serendipitous or authentic) or disappointed with. In either outcome, customers are happy to tell the world about that experience.

While we can't design every aspect of the experience, we *can* work to define and support our cultures and influence our company's collective behavior.

The final component that CMOs have to rethink is brand stewardship. CMOs who have responsibility for their corporate brand mostly think of the customer. But people expect different things of corporations today, and that has to be reflected in how the brand is stewarded. Employees increasingly expect their companies to speak out on a wide range of societal issues. Investors expect companies to create societal value, not just shareholder value. Customers increasingly care about how the company affects the environment, how it treats its employees and suppliers, how diverse and inclusive its culture is. The corporate brand must be emblematic of the company's position and actions in all these dimensions. CMOs rarely have a formal role in identifying, developing and debating these issues for their companies. Yet I think this is what modern corporate brand stewardship requires.

Using AI to Gain Strategic Advantage

From a B2B or enterprise perspective, the ultimate value of AI may be your ability to out-learn your competition. The core revolution in AI isn't voice or facial recognition. It's the ability for systems to learn by themselves.

While we sleep, the AI systems deployed in our companies continue to ingest data, learn from data and learn continuously from interaction. AI applications, whether they're customer- or employee-facing, in your supply chain, cyber-security operations or elsewhere in your company, will always be learning. They will literally make your company smarter. And, because they're always learning, the faster you deploy AI systems, the better. Brands that wait are going to be at a fundamental disadvantage. They'll face a learning gap that will grow deeper and wider.

What Is the Future of Marketing?

By 2025, marketing won't look radically different from how it does in 2020. One change that may happen is a shift away from content marketing, which is heavily focused on lead generation and customer acquisition, to a more insights-based approach that influences what the company actually develops and takes to market.

That's always been the role of marketing for Consumer Package Goods (CPG) companies like Procter and Gamble, Unilever and PepsiCo. But for businesses in other industries, this will certainly mark a shift. The more the CMO is seen as having the means to collect and analyze customer data, the more their insights are going to become incredibly valuable and influential within their companies.

CHAPTER ANALYSIS QUESTIONS

1. What are some of the core tenets of *The New Marketing*?
2. Why is it so important that brands focus on humanizing their marketing efforts?
3. What role will VR and AR play in future marketing efforts?
4. How can CMOs best prepare for the future?

NOTES

1. Goodreads.com. (n.d.). A quote by Peter F. Drucker. [online] Available at: www.goodreads. com/quotes/16406-the-best-way-to-predict-your-future-is-to-create [Accessed 31 Jan. 2020].

2. Kolls, R. (2019). *Green Consumers Point to the Future for Brand Marketing*. [online] Gartner. Available at: www.gartner.com/en/marketing/insights/daily-insights/green-consumers-point-to-the-future-for-brand-marketing [Accessed 19 Dec. 2019].

3. Baer, J. (2019). Personal communication. [1 Aug.].

4. Dhar, R. (2019). Personal communication. [30 Aug.].

5. Nel, K. (2018). Personal communication. [8 Nov.].

6. Omale, G. (2019). Gartner Press Release *"Gartner* says 100 million consumers will shop in augmented reality online and in-store by 2020". [online] Gartner. Available at: www. gartner.com/en/newsroom/press-releases/2019-04-01-gartner-says-100-million-con-sumers-will-shop-in-augme [Accessed 19 Dec. 2019]. (*Gartner's Unified Retail Retailer Survey was conducted online and via computer-assisted telephone interviewing (CATI) from July 2018 through August 2018, with 97 respondents in Europe (including the U.K.), the U.S., Canada and China.)

7. Ibid.

8. Ibid.

9. Iwata, J. (2019). Personal communication (10 Oct.).

The New Marketing is here and future-ready. In their tour de force work, Cheryl Burgess and Mark Burgess disrupt the status quo of the already outdated marketing textbook by giving students and marketing professionals a sorely needed perspective and tools to confidently operate in a field that is transforming at warp speed. Reading this book, which is inspired by the authors' journey deep into and across the disciplines of marketing, I'm struck by *five forces* that powerfully signal how marketing is changing and where it's heading.

FORCE 1: CMO SHIFT

Nothing says more about the transformation of marketing than the role of the CMO. The job is at once evolving, shrinking, disappearing, growing, ascending, or shifting, depending on the view and company. McDonald's, Uber and Johnson & Johnson have eliminated the title – not because the function is irrelevant, but because the portfolio around communications, technology and customers is now too big for one executive to handle.

Their reorganizations underscore a 'change or die' operating mantra. Focusing on customer acquisition and brand storytelling is no longer enough for the CMO. Leveraging data-driven insights and martech tools, led by brand, is critical. Marketing leaders have a role to play in designing and optimizing the customer experience to help them meet revenue goals they increasingly answer for. Modern CMOs must also influence the employee experience, to better align with the customer experience, by collaborating with HR and talent executives to define and measure how employees operationalize the brand.

Successful marketing chiefs are working side by side with chief experience officers, chief growth officers, chief brand officers, chief people officers, chief digital officers, chief information officers and/or chief revenue officers, reporting to them or having them as reports. From there, the key is execution. As former IBM chief brand officer Jon Iwata notes in Chapter 12:

When you peel back these new roles and examine the remit, you often find a common set of responsibilities. All parts of the company that touch the customer – retail, face-to-face sales, web, contact centers, business partners – usually report to the new executive. They also often have responsibility for marketing, for technology – CIO and/or CTO – and, if the company invests in design and design thinking, the design function becomes part of the new organization.

Of course, the answer isn't only about effective data and systems. As behavioral economist and Yale Professor Ravi Dhar also points out in Chapter 12, CMOs must demonstrate that their brand does more than just create profits:

Companies don't operate in isolation, so it's essential that they understand other stakeholders, whether those stakeholders are the citizens, employees, or even governments that interact with their brand. The CMO has a key role to play here, they are the person best positioned in the C-suite to help build connections with those stakeholders. The best way to begin making those connections is to position their brand as having a positive impact on society, not just on helping build top-line sales.

It can be a difficult balance to strike, but one that requires fusing the human element into a highly systematic approach. However, when approached correctly, organizations will see their customer experience and brand value grow by leaps and bounds.

FORCE 2: EMPLOYEE EXPERIENCE

Old-world marketing was all about 'one to many' – one brand to many (albeit one mass of consumers). Today, the rise of the internet, Big Data, and now AI allows marketers to build one-to-one customer relationships by managing and personalizing complex consumer or business journeys, which are elegantly depicted in the book.

Mark and Cheryl Burgess's previous work, *The Social Employee*, was trailblazing in revealing the untapped power of 'many to many' (employees to market). This emergent channel is all of the brand's employee ambassadors, not just front-line, marketing and sales associates. Social employees embody and endow their brand with a human face, authenticity, passion, mass and energy.

Management thinker Tom Peters loves the book's metaphor capturing this employee power as a 'bag of marbles' (diverse, mass-energy of employees) vs. a baseball (monolithic, static marketing department); the former maximizes surface area and connectivity. Big social media platforms, as well as internal networks, help amplify employee voices, and build trusted connections.

Purpose-driven Millennials make up the majority of employee and customer bases, so marketers have an opportunity to align and harmonize audiences around shared brand goals and better experiences. Just as customer experience (CX) is getting attention and resources from the CMO, so too is the employee experience (EX). Employees are now clients or targets of the marketing department. EX is part of retention and recruiting plans and a critical key performance indicator (KPI) for both HR and marketing.

FORCE 3: BRAND AS ECOSYSTEM

The strongest, most valuable brands operate holistically not only internally, but also externally. Brand leaders no longer think or act as B2C or B2B but as a brand-to-the-world or a brand-to-people, a brand as an ecosystem. While marketing technology has enabled one-to-one personalization, our social digital world now requires brands to think bigger and show how they profit society, as Dhar says. Using data and transparency, business brands must demonstrate how they create value for consumers and the planet, while consumer brands need to prove goodness in their sources, labor practices, and supply chains.

The parent of many billion-dollar consumer brands, Procter & Gamble, now has a face as a brand that is making the world greener, not just cleaner and clean-shaven. The circular economy imperative means business and industrial end-products being produced and consumed responsibly and reused to benefit society. *The New Marketing* cites Larry Fink, CEO of BlackRock, the largest investment management company in the world with $6.84 trillion in assets, on the importance of brand purpose. Says Fink:

> Profits are in no way inconsistent with purpose – in fact, profits and purpose are inextricably linked. Profits are essential if a company is to effectively serve all of its stakeholders over time – not only shareholders, but also employees, customers, and communities. Similarly, when a company truly understands and expresses its purpose, it functions with the focus and strategic discipline that drive long-term profitability.[1]

Many other prominent business leaders agree. For instance, in 2019, the Business Roundtable (a who's who of the top companies and CEOs, from Amazon's Jeff Bezos to JPMorgan Chase's Jamie Dimon) overturned the long-sacred principle of 'shareholder value' that guides a corporation, in favor of value to society and employees.

FORCE 4: CHINESE REVOLUTION

Marketers today play in a digital world that is being shaped by Chinese innovation. The Middle Kingdom, in fact, may now be ahead of the West in aspects of brand-building. The authors show a new strategic model being deployed by brands based on China's unique market characteristics. For instance, Chinese brand marketers are highly evolved in using technology to predict and perfect customer experience.

China's consumers, essentially denied self-expression and brand culture pre-Tiananmen, now express their identities and enjoy a middle-class lifestyle enabled by socialized brand experiences and digital technology. Chinese brands like Xiaomi and Vivo are skillfully creating 'online to offline', or the other way – 'offline-to-online' (O2O) – journeys to deliver better, fuller consumer experiences; collect richer data; and build greater customer affinity and trust. The BAT economy (Baidu, Alibaba, Tencent – which runs WeChat) in which users can social share, search and shop in one place gives marketers an unprecedented consumer view and data set for personalization; by contrast, the picture of the Western user's journey is more problematic given 'walled garden' platforms specializing in limited touchpoints, such as Facebook (social), Google (search), Amazon (e-commerce) and Apple (mobile device).

Western consumers and authorities worry about Facebook's loose policies and protection of personal data. Still, Beijing's ultimate oversight over BAT and China's big brands should give *all* marketers and consumers some pause about the promise of this Chinese revolution. As the Burgesses discuss in Chapter 4, the role and value of brands for Chinese marketers (and consumers alike) have come a long way – from a time in the not-too-distant past where branding was all but nonexistent, to the adoption of today's META (Maintain, Evolve, Transform, Approach) model. By focusing on hyper-relevance to consumer values (for example, the model shows how brands can broadly position while adapting themselves to local needs), META gives brands a framework for establishing their *why* in a way that applies to all audiences.

FORCE 5: MAN–MACHINE CONVERGENCE

The New Marketing deftly explores the intersection of marketers, technology and customers. Innovations, from AI to IoT, AR to 5G, create opportunities for brands and consumers to realize better and more valuable experiences. Machines, assistants like Alexa and Siri, and IoT devices can improve a customer's experience by intelligently analyzing and responding to their physical environment, auditory language and electronic activation.

Companies and brands developing and applying these technologies are only now starting to incorporate the aspect of human emotion, empathy and perception into their software and hardware. As they do, marketers and customers can benefit even more. *The New Marketing* 'gazes' into 'Emotion AI' products that read and respond to human faces, eyes, voices and emotions (some technologies activate from brain activity).

Reliability is one challenge for Emotion AI technologies. But Elon Musk famously worries about another issue – AI being harnessed for evil purposes or by bad actors. Innovators like Affectiva, whose products help improve automobile safety (in addition to cabin comfort and convenience) by detecting driver fatigue through facial expressions, go out of their way to show how AI can be used not only to enhance brand experiences but also to make the world better.

What's next? Machines merging with man? Chips implanted into our brains? That's what Musk's Neuralink venture seeks to do.

How these five forces ultimately shape marketing over the next decade or two is unclear. What is certain is that to be successful, the next generation of marketers will need to create an ecosystem that is adaptable, engaged, intelligent and purposeful. In *The New Marketing*, authors Cheryl Burgess and Mark Burgess have laid out a blueprint for success that will make this book an essential guide for years to come.

Kevin Randall, brand strategist and
contributing writer for *The New York Times*.

NOTE

1.   Fink, L. (2019). Larry Fink's Letter to CEOs. BlackRock. Available at: www.blackrock.com/americas-offshore/2019-larry-fink-ceo-letter [Accessed 27 December 2019].

APPENDIX A

AD AGENCY COMPETITIVE ANALYSIS TEMPLATE

Name: Date:

Advertiser name:

Product:

Elements (indicate): TV AD _____ Print Ad _____YouTube Video _____

Other _____

The Objectives
What are the advertising objectives of this ad?

Selling Proposition
What is the core message of this ad?

Support for Selling Proposition
What are the supporting facts that the selling proposition is based on?

The Target Audience
Who is the message targeted to – demographics, psychographics, etc.?

Metrics
How do you think the advertiser will measure the success of this ad?

PERSONAL BRANDING WORKBOOK TEMPLATE

Step 1: Scan my environment	Actions I need to take:

To take stock of the competitive environment, ask yourself these questions:

> What's out there I need to be aware of?
> What are the major trends in the market?
> What skills will be highly valued in the future – and do I have them?
> How do I compare to my competition?

Step 2: Create my brand value proposition (BVP)	Actions I need to take:

To start defining your BVP, ask the following questions:

> Who are you?
> What do you stand for?
> What are your beliefs and values?
> What are your personal traits?
> What makes you unique?
> What is your passion?

Step 3: Position brand YOU	Actions I need to take:

First, tie your BVP to your environment scan above.

> How do you want people/employers/recruiters to think about you?
> What space in their minds can you own?
> What makes you stand out from your competition?

Then, complete this personal positioning framework:

For [target market], the [brand] provides [point-of-difference] because [reason to believe].

Step 4: Figure out your brand story	Actions I need to take:

People remember stories. Be authentic. Ask yourself:

> What's your purpose?
> How can your purpose become part of your personal brand story?
> Why should an employer or recruiter choose you over your competitor?

Step 5: Develop a content strategy

Actions I need to take:

It's time to share your authentic story with your target audience! To focus on getting high-quality content out into the marketplace, ask yourself these questions:

> Where are my customers? How do I reach them?
> What type of content is best-suited for my product (ME) and my audience (i.e. articles, blogs, newsletters, videos, etc.)?
> What content topics will generate a positive enthusiastic response from my audience?

Step 6: Develop a content distribution strategy (a.k.a. as media plan)

Actions I need to take:

To tell your personal branding story across relevant social media channels, start by asking yourself what channels will go the furthest in telling your story to your audience:

> Your LinkedIn profile? A LinkedIn blog?
> A Facebook page?
> An Instagram, Facebook, or Periscope video?
> Guest blogging on established blogs?
> Twitter?

Step 7: Measure results

Actions I need to take

The last step is to measure the results of your media plan. Set some aspirational but realistic goals.

> Are you set up to win by measuring and tracking everything you should be?
> How can you tweak your positioning, purpose, or BVP to improve results?
> Are you incorporating other feedback to continue improving your brand?
> Are you celebrating the small victories without losing sight of the big picture?

INDEX

www.ingramcontent.com/pod-product-compliance
Ingram Content Group UK Ltd.
Pitfield, Milton Keynes, MK11 3LW, UK
UKHW050040131224
452429UK00003B/44